Noir Anxiety

Kelly Oliver
Benigno Trigo

University of Minnesota Press
Minneapolis • London

Published by the University of Minnesota Press
111 Third Avenue South, Suite 290
Minneapolis, MN 55401-2520
http://www.upress.umn.edu

Printed in the United States of America on acid-free paper

The University of Minnesota is an equal-opportunity educator and employer.

Library of Congress Cataloging-in-Publication Data

Oliver, Kelly, 1958–
    Noir anxiety / Kelly Oliver and Benigno Trigo.
      p. cm.
Includes bibliographical references and index.
Filmography:
    ISBN 0-8166-4109-9 (hard : alk. paper) — ISBN 0-8166-4110-2
(pbk. : alk. paper)
    1. Film noir—United States—History and criticism.
I. Trigo, Benigno. II. Title
    PN1995.9.F54 O44 2002
    791.43'655—dc21
                                        2002007575

12 11 10 09 08 07 06 05 04 03   10 9 8 7 6 5 4 3 2 1

To Kit and Forest and Sunday Brunch

It is simply that, when the mother is disseminated into remembrances and words, when the women that are loved are forgotten-deserted-invented, the very memory that guarantees our identity is shown to be an ongoing metamorphosis, a polymorphy.

—Julia Kristeva, *Strangers to Ourselves*

Contents

Acknowledgments

We would especially like to thank Doug Armato for his encouragement and keen suggestions. Thanks to Juliet Flower MacCannell for her insightful comments that helped us improve the book. Ann Kaplan gave fruitful suggestions in the early stages of the project, for which we are grateful. We would like to thank Katy Vernon for bibliographic suggestions for the chapter on *The Lady from Shanghai*. For productive conversations along the way, we thank Harvey Cormier, Temma Kaplan, Ruthy McGillic, Bennett Sims, and Luis Trigo. Thanks to Sobeira La Torre, Jiahui Li, Elena Machado, Jennifer Matey, Shannon Hoff, and Julia Sushytska for research assistance. Finally, we would like to thank the Museum of Modern Art in New York City for the film stills reproduced in this book.

Dropping the Bombshell

> Someday fate, or some mysterious force, can put the
> finger on you or me for no reason at all.
>
> —*Detour* (1946)

The "Free-Floating" Anxiety of Noir

Given that the film noir genre was born at the end of World War II, critics often attribute its anxieties and fatalism to the turmoil of the postwar era.[1] Some critics point to changes in the social structure that opened the door for more public participation by women and African Americans in various social institutions:[2] while men were away fighting in Europe, women were needed in the factories to manufacture the war machines;[3] African American men who were drafted to fight in World War II insisted that having fought for freedom, this country was theirs, too; with the GI Bill, African American men had new opportunities and new expectations. These critics argue that upon returning home from the war, men, particularly white men, discovered that in their absence their authority in the home, in the factory, and in the city was being challenged on all sides, that their fear was that "their" women had left them for jobs or other men, their families and children were no longer theirs to control,[4] that the family breadwinner and head of household had been displaced, and that although patriarchal and racist values kept white men in positions of power, the confluence of various historical factors was starting to chip away at their authority. In general, these critics identify this breakdown of patriarchal authority as the source of the anxieties and fatalism of noir. They interpret the sense of fate or doom in film noir as a response to white men's sense of a loss of control and authority, especially control and authority over women.

Other critics maintain that film noir represents a type of free-floating existential anxiety that is seen either as being part of the human condition or as related to the moral ambiguity of the times.[5] At the opposite extreme from those who argue that noir is a response to specific changes in social institutions, and more in line with the existentialist philosophy of the postwar period, these critics find in noir an existential angst and anxiety over fate inherent in the human condition. These critics reject the historicism of theorists who link noir to specific changes in social institutions of the postwar era, including women moving into the workforce and African American men advancing socially with the GI Bill. Whether they find this existential anxiety in the narratives or the style of noir, or both, these critics invoke the "nihilistic worldview" of film noir.[6] Like the protagonist of *Detour*, they conclude that fate can put the finger on us for no reason at all.

In *Noir Anxiety*, we interpret what some critics call the "remarkable style" of noir along with "the terse elliptical dialogue, insoluble plots, and nihilistic mood" as various condensations and displacements of symptoms of concrete anxieties over race, sex, maternity, and national origin that threaten the very possibility of identity by undermining its boundaries.[7] The existential angst, moral ambiguity, and style of noir produce a sense of free-floating anxiety that we anchor to a complex constellation of concrete anxieties over race, sex, and maternity often displaced onto an abstract angst over the fickle finger of fate or a nihilistic human condition. Anxieties over racial, sexual, and national identities work together in film noir to create a sense of free-floating anxiety or existential angst and a nihilist worldview. Behind the free-floating anxiety of noir is a primal anxiety over borders and boundaries that manifests itself in specific fears and phobias of race, sex, maternity, and national origin. To interpret the anxieties of noir either as a mere reflection of postwar changes in social institutions or as a mere example of a nihilistic worldview and existential angst is too simple.

In *Noir Anxiety*, we complicate both the historicist and the existentialist interpretations of noir by locating the anxiety of noir at the heart of identity formation itself. With its distinctive style and investigative narrative structure, film noir displays unconscious anxieties over the borders of identity. By interpreting film noir as a type of Freudian dream-work marked by condensations and displacements of unconscious desires and fears, we begin to see some of the ways in which anxieties over borders operate both as the return of the repressed and as defense mechanisms in the service of identity. Condensations and displacements between various concrete anxieties over race, sex, maternity, and national identity constitute complex interactions between unconscious desires and fears as they become manifest in film noir. For this reason, it becomes difficult to identify one cause or origin of film noir; it becomes difficult to categorize the essential elements of noir. Indeed, the anxiety over categorizing and defining film noir in the early noir criticism resonates with the anxiety over ambiguous borders and border crossings displayed within film noir itself. Just as film noir can be interpreted as a manifestation of anxieties over the arbitrary and blurred borders of race, sex, and nationality, so noir criticism with its debates over definitions and origins displays a similar anxiety over the breakdown of the borders of genre and national origins. Questions of whether film noir is truly an American genre echo anxieties over national origin manifest in the films themselves.[8]

Not only is the free-floating existential anxiety of film noir a screen for concrete anxieties over arbitrary and blurred boundaries of racial, sexual, and national identity, but the confluence of these concrete anxieties produces the sense of a free-floating anxiety. Because these anxieties come together in curious and complicated ways, their significance is not always obvious. Again, like the Freudian dream-work, the most significant and telling aspects of film noir often appear as insignificant details or marginal figures. As in the dream-work, *condensations* and *displacements* of various anxieties over race, sex, and origin work to camouflage the centrality of race and racism, sex and sexism, and nationality and nationalism to film noir, sometimes behind the screen of an amorphous and free-floating existential anxiety over fate or the human condition in general. In *Noir Anxiety* we diagnose some of the condensations and displacements that at once hide and reveal central anxieties over race, sex, and origin.

Condensation and Displacement in Film Noir

Sigmund Freud suggests that the psyche gives shape to all forms of creative endeavor through its constitutive processes. He lists sublimation and repression among these processes (others are reaction-formation, aim-inhibition, and idealization), but he calls artistic creation a sublimated type of human activity. Sublimation is a dynamic process that redirects sexual energy to a new nonsexual aim such as sublime artistic production. Repression, on the other hand, is an operation of the psyche that does not so much divert as it repels sexual energy, confining it to the unconscious, which it helps create together with thoughts, images, and memories.

Freud locates condensation and displacement in the unconscious. For Freud, these are processes responsible for the creation of psychological phenomena different from creative endeavor. These include jokes, slips of the tongue, and, most importantly, dreams. Though Freud clearly has much invested in the distinction between repression and sublimation, his discussion of works of art is always tentative. He will sometimes describe art in terms of condensation and displacement, which are closer to the unconscious, to psychological symptoms, and are of a seemingly different order from sublimation. For example, in his famous discussion of Leonardo da Vinci's *St. Anne with Two Others*, Freud writes, "By his combining this fact about childhood with the one mentioned above (the presence of his mother and grandmother) and by his condensing them into a composite unity, the design of 'St. Anne with Two Others' took shape for him" (1989, 470). The statement echoes the rest of the essay's complication of a strict distinction between sublimation and repression, and between art and the unconscious. Freud suggests that both the content of da Vinci's paintings and the form of his compositions are preceded and overdetermined by the repression of an infantile sexual desire for the mother.

In *Noir Anxiety* we follow Freud's insight into the complex relation between repression and sublimation manifest in paintings like da Vinci's. Judging from that work, Freud's commentary on creative endeavor cannot be reduced to psychological processes like sublimation and should be extended to the unconscious and its processes. Indeed, our readings of film noir suggest that its primary forces are the main operations of the dream-work and of the unconscious: condensation and displacement.

Freud first introduced the notion of condensation along with the notion of displacement, which he had developed earlier (1895), in *The Interpretation of Dreams* (1900). Although he identifies condensation and displacement with the dream-work, he makes it clear throughout his writing that both processes occur in waking experience as well. For Freud, condensation and displacement are two of the primary processes of psychic life. They are both means by which unconscious desires make their way into consciousness without being detected by conscious censorship. Condensation and displacement are unconscious techniques used to disguise repressed wishes so that they can pass into consciousness unrecognized. This disguising operation is also what makes it difficult to interpret condensed and displaced desires or fears. Freud describes condensation as an operation by which one idea or image represents several ideas with which it is associated. This way several repressed desires or fears can make their way into consciousness disguised as one figure, idea, or image. Condensation can operate in different ways: one idea can show up repeatedly in the figure or image of different persons, things, or ideas; various elements of different ideas or desires can be combined into one figure or composite image; or the condensation of several ideas or images may result in one image that retains only those traits that the repressed ideas or desires have in common.[9] Freud describes displacement as the operation by which an idea's or desire's intensity is detached from it and attached to other ideas or images that otherwise were of little intensity but are related to the repressed idea by some sort of association. On this analysis, minor details and marginal figures or scenes become central to interpreting the meaning of a dream, or, in the context of our project, the meaning of a film.

As in dreams, in film repressed desires or fears, and unconscious wishes or terrors, can make their way into consciousness through the operations of condensation and displacement. For example, we can interpret the recurrence of the femme fatale character in various forms throughout film noir as a condensation of an anxiety over female sexuality. Often in the films that we analyze here, sexual, racial, and ethnic difference appears in condensed composite figures through which anxious relations to race and sex are brought together in one figure. For example, Elsa in *The Lady from Shanghai* (1948) has a mysterious past marked by both dangerous ethnicity and sexuality; Carlotta in *Vertigo* (1958) is both ethnically marked and sexually questionable; Tanya in *Touch of Evil* (1958) is marked as both ethnically and sexually questionable; Mrs. Mulwray in *Chinatown* (1974) is marked by a mysterious combination of incestuous sex and her connection to Chinatown; Daphne in *Devil in a Blue Dress* (1995) is marked by a questionable racial origin and a mysterious sexual force. In our analysis of most of these films, we describe some of the ways in which fears of racial difference are displaced onto fears of sexual difference and maternal sexuality, and vice versa. In general, we are concerned with the ways in which various phobias, fears, and anxieties over race, sex, and origin are displaced and condensed to create a sense of free-floating existential angst in film noir. Indeed, in important ways these condensations and displacements of race and sex create the suspense and logic of noir. Throughout *Noir Anxiety* we describe how both the narrative and the style of noir are motivated by anxieties over race and sex.

In these films the representation of nationality and place can also be interpreted as a type of condensation of several images or ideas into an idea that retains only the repressed unconscious fears or desires that they have in common while blurring those traits that they do not share. For example, Chinatown and Asia are condensed into figures of exotic mystery and danger in films such as *The Maltese Falcon* (1941), *Murder, My Sweet* (1944), *The Lady from Shanghai*, *The Crimson Kimono* (1959), and *Chinatown*; or Mexico and Latin America are condensed into figures of unrepressed criminality and sexuality in *Notorious* (1946), *Ride the Pink*

Horse (1947), *Out of the Past* (1947), *The Secret beyond the Door* (1948), *Where Danger Lives* (1950), *His Kind of Woman* (1951), and *Touch of Evil*; and Harlem is condensed into figures of self-imposed segregation and separatism in *Odds against Tomorrow* (1959) and *Devil in a Blue Dress*.

Along with the notion of condensation, with the theory of displacement, elements that seem marginal or insignificant can become the key to interpreting the unconscious fears and desires of film noir. In subsequent chapters, for example, we analyze the significance of what seems to be a marginal scene in a bar with an Asian theme in *Murder, My Sweet*, or what seems to be an ordinary Irish accent in *The Lady from Shanghai*, or a seemingly insignificant reference to Sleeping Beauty in *The Secret beyond the Door*, or the use of the color red in *Vertigo*, or what seems to be a marginal scene with a pigeon's egg in *Touch of Evil*, or the passing mention of a Creole mother in *Devil in a Blue Dress*, or the innocent repetition of the phrase "make it real" in *Bound* (1996). All of these seemingly insignificant details become significant in analyzing films when they are interpreted as the sites of displaced anxiety or desire. Anxieties and fears about sexual, racial, or national differences or borders can be displaced onto minor elements in a film: a jade necklace in *Murder, My Sweet*, a fun house mirror in *The Lady from Shanghai*, a bouquet of flowers in *Vertigo*, or some hot chili in *Touch of Evil*. As the striking style of film noir suggests, a shadow, a light, a sound, or a camera angle can also become the repository of displaced desire or fear.

Analysis of these films is complicated by the fact that condensation and displacement of desires and fears trade on each other. The primary processes that both hide and reveal unconscious desires and fears through condensation and displacement do so by combining and displacing desires and fears onto each other. The fear of, or desire for, racial difference can be displaced onto a fear of, or desire for, sexual difference. The fear of maternal sexuality can be displaced onto or condensed into the threat of racial difference. The fear of, or desire for, sexual difference can be condensed into fear of, and desire for, the maternal, which in turn becomes fear of, and desire for, nuclear destruction. Condensation and displacement allow almost any possible associations.

In *Kiss Me Deadly* (1955), for example, fear of women and sexual difference trades on fear of nuclear destruction and vice versa. After the woman he rescues from the highway is murdered, private detective Mike Hammer (Ralph Meeker) follows mysterious clues, hoping to make a lot of money, only to find a hot box full of glowing, hissing radioactive material. Tricked by the villain's girlfriend, Gabrielle (Gaby Rodgers), Hammer loses the box and ends up dying (or almost dying, depending on the version of the film) because, in spite of warnings to the contrary, Gabrielle opens the box and ignites a giant explosion. Dr. Soberin (Albert Dekker), Gabrielle's villain boyfriend, warns her that the box contains "Medusa's head" and that if she opens it, like Pandora and her box, Gabrielle will loose all evil on the world; he reminds her of Lot's wife, who disobeys and is turned into a pillar of salt. In spite of his warnings, or maybe because of them, Gabrielle's curiosity and greed for what is in the box lead her to shoot him and open the box. Here man's desire to control the world is displaced onto woman's desire to know, which like Pandora's curiosity and Lot's wife's disobedience is made responsible for evil and destruction, even nuclear destruction.[10]

Nuclear destruction, in turn, is compared to the destructive power of woman herself, represented by the figure of Medusa's head. Like Medusa's head, the glowing box has the power to turn men to stone. Freud interprets Medusa's head as the spectacle of the exposed female genitals (1922). He maintains that Medusa's head elicits in man the fear of castration; decapitation stands in for castration. When the male child sees his mother's pubis, he sees the spot of a missing penis surrounded by hair. In Freud's reading, Medusa's snakelike hair becomes a throng of penis substitutes that both evoke and protect against castration. Medusa's hair becomes a fetish—it both acknowledges and denies castration by setting up penis substitutes. In light of Freud's interpretation, the connection between the fear of nuclear destruction and female sexuality becomes more apparent in Dr. Soberin's comparison between Medusa and the nuclear box. For man, nuclear power, like female sexuality, both elicits and protects against castration fears. The threat of nuclear destruction makes man potent but also threatens him with something beyond his control and ultimately with death itself. The association between nuclear destruction and female sexuality in *Kiss Me Deadly* also suggests that women are connected to death.

At the end of *Kiss Me Deadly*, Gabrielle shoots Hammer, saying, "Kiss me Mike, I want you to kiss me—the liar's kiss that says I love you but means something else; you are good at giving such kisses ..." A woman's man, pegged right away by the woman whom he rescues on

Gabrielle (Gaby Rodgers) opens the "great whatsit" in *Kiss Me Deadly*.

the highway as a self-indulgent man who thinks only about himself, Hammer kisses most of the women in the film. *Kiss Me Deadly*, however, suggests that a woman is more dangerous than the most vicious criminal, and that Hammer is a brave man. His secretary and sometimes girlfriend Velda (Maxine Cooper) tries to warn him to stay away from the window because someone might "blow him a kiss." A woman's kiss is associated with death and ultimately with nuclear destruction, just as the "bomb" that destroys everything in sight at the end of the film is compared to a woman, Medusa. In the words of film critic Lucia Bozzola, "with macho 'bedroom dick' Hammer using any violence necessary, this darkest of 1950's noir films sends him on a search for the 'Great Whatsit,' an ominously incandescent box encompassing America's nuclear nightmares, as well as man's deepest fears about unpredictably explosive female potency."[11] Female potency and women's power to create life become displaced onto the association between woman and death. Her power to give life becomes the deadly power to take life. The deadly force of nuclear destruction, disguised as female sexuality, and vice versa, has the power to destroy Mother Nature herself. In *Kiss Me Deadly*, the power of female sexuality threatens even the power of Nature.

Hollywood bombshells or film noir femmes fatales, fatal women, are manifestations of the condensation of women and danger, sex and death, and the ultimate threat of maternal sexuality, in particular. The bomb becomes a symbol of female sexuality, and female sexuality becomes a symbol of nuclear destruction: the sexy woman as "bombshell." Film noir is full of "bombshell" femmes fatales. One of the most popular of the Hollywood bombshells was Rita Hayworth (*The Lady from Shanghai, Gilda* [1946]), whose picture was painted on the atom bomb by scientists during World War II. Mass destruction took the shape of a woman, the ultimate femme fatale or fatal woman.

Female sexuality is explicitly linked to deadly force in what is known as "nose art" from World War II. Pinup bombshells decorated the noses of U.S. fighter planes and bombers. Nose art is populated by sexualized, naked, or scantily clothed women in provocative poses often riding bombs.[12] For example, "Two Beauts" displays a naked woman reclining on a bomb. Her sister images include "Temptress," "Iza Vailable" and "Iza Vailable Too," "Luscious Lady," "Daddy's Delight," "Pistol Packin' Mama," "Vicious Virgin," "Miss Bea Haven," and "Bad Penny." The uncanny doublet woman-bomb is echoed in the names of these bombers. These puns signal a double and ambiguous meaning, which serves as an anxious screen for the association between female sexuality, maternity, and danger. Given theses associations, it is not surprising that the plane that delivered the atom bomb that ended World War II was named after the pilot's mother.[13]

This danger is intensified when it is inflected by race in other nose art images such as "Miss Manooki," "Shangri-La Lil," "Belle of San Joaquin," "Shoo Shoo Baby," "Miss Umbriago," "Aloha," "Miss Quachita," "The Old Squaw," and "Poque Ma Hone." While many of these images are modeled after Milton Caniff's "Orientalized" comic strip characters Dragon Lady, Madame Shoo Shoo, and Burma, others reflect a more generalized fear of racial difference, here conflated with a fear of female sexuality. In World War II nose art, anxieties about racial difference appear through the iconography of the sexualized bombshell. Racial difference takes the form of a "sexy" naked woman, and in the imaginary of the United States, race intensifies her threat.

Unmoored female sexuality, repressed racial identity, and phallic killing power eerily converged in 1946 when Margarita Carmen Cansino's, aka Rita Hayworth's, picture was painted on an atom bomb that scientists and soldiers called "Gilda," after Hayworth's most famous femme fatale character (*New York Times*, 30 June 1946). Significantly, on the day that the bomb was dropped, the *Washington Post* described the radioactive cloud from Gilda as "beautiful but deadly" (1 July 1946); and the *New York Times* described it both as a "cosmic flower" and as "cosmic fire" (1 July 1946). The *New York Times* also described Gilda as "the world's most powerful weapon" (30 June 1946).

At various moments in his work, Freud addresses the anxious connection between women, maternity, and death. In his essay on "the uncanny," he concludes that the ultimate source of the uncanny is the most *unheimlich* place of all, the former home *(Heim)*, the most unfamiliar and familiar of places, the mother's genitals, because they recall our first home and foreshadow our final resting place; both birth and death are displaced onto the mother's sex (1919, 245). As Freud describes it, the anxiety over the female genitals is also related to castration anxiety. Castration anxiety and anxiety over death coalesce in the fear stimulated by the female genitals, most particularly the mother's sex, through which reunification with the maternal womb signifies both becoming part of an emasculated female body (castration) and becoming one with the womb of Nature (death).[14]

Freud's association between the female or maternal sex and the castration threat is useful to interpret the bombs ridden by pinups painted onto bombers as fetish substitutes for the missing maternal penis. The bomb is a perfect fetish insofar as, like Freud's classic fetish, it both protects against and evokes castration. The bomb replaces the missing feminine/maternal penis and thereby reassures man that he won't be castrated, and yet this image of potent female sexuality is also a deadly image. The bomb with its deadly force is designed to protect, and yet it necessarily also kills. In light of Freud's theory of fetishism and castration, it is especially telling that fighter pilots would name their bombers after their mothers.

Freud's connection between women, maternity, and death, however, may be more symptomatic than diagnostic. For Freud, the life-giving power of the mother is the uncanny double of her death threat. Significantly, Freud's analysis of one of his own dreams in *The Interpretation of Dreams* makes this connection. In his dream of the "Three Fates," after going to bed tired and hungry, Freud dreams of three women in a kitchen. One of them is making dumplings and tells him that he will have to wait; he is impatient and tries to put on his overcoat to leave, but the coat is too long, its fur trim and embroidery suspicious, and seems to belong to another man. In his analysis of the dream, Freud identifies the woman making dumplings with his mother. His dream appears to him as the wish fulfillment of the basic needs for food and love, which he claims come together in the mother's breast. In his analysis, however, no sooner is the maternal figure in his dream associated with love and nourishment than she becomes a messenger of death. Freud associates the dumpling-making hand motion with an experience from his childhood when his mother convinced him that everyone dies and returns to the earth by rubbing her hands together as if making dumplings to show him the "blackish scales of *epidermis* produced by the friction as a proof that we are made of earth" (1900, 238). For Freud, the mother is the symbol of life-giving nourishment (dumplings), but also of the inevitability of death and returning to the earth.

The three women in Freud's dream might usefully be interpreted using another one of his works, "The Theme of the Three Caskets," in which Freud diagnoses the reappearance of three beautiful women connected to choice and death in literature and myth as three faces of woman—birth, sex, and death—that ultimately belong to the mother: "We might argue that what is represented here are the three inevitable relations that a man has with a woman—the woman who bears him, the woman who is his mate and the woman who destroys him; or that they are the three forms taken by the figure of the mother in the course of a man's life—the mother herself, the beloved one who is chosen after her pattern, and lastly the Mother Earth who receives him once more. But it is in vain that an old man yearns for the love of woman as he had it first from his mother; the third of the Fates alone, the silent Goddess of Death, will take him into her arms" (1913a, 522). For Freud, birth, sex, and death are condensed into the figure of the mother as a triple and ultimate threat. In this theory, then, Freud naturalizes a threat that is itself a symptom of a psychic process that calls for further diagnosis.

Ambivalent Mothers in Noir

There has been considerable work on representations of women in film noir and the figure of the femme fatale in film in particular;[15] much feminist criticism of noir shows how film noir exhibits an ambivalence toward women.[16] And though there has been significant work in feminist film criticism on representations of maternity in film, particularly melodrama, there has been little work on the place of the maternal in film noir because the mother rarely appears in noir.[17] While the femme fatale, with her good-girl alter ego, can be read as an explicit symptom of the psychic ambivalence toward women, the ambivalence toward the maternal is rarely so explicit in film noir. The maternal is one of the most repressed elements of film noir, and yet, or perhaps therefore, it returns repeatedly at the margins of these films, displaced onto seemingly minor characters, places, and things. Often like a ghost in the shadows, the mother haunts film noir. She is mentioned but never seen, yet she leaves her traces throughout film noir. Paralleling the dichotomy of the bad omnipresent or bad absent mother, in film noir the mother is everywhere and nowhere.[18]

One notable exception is the noir/melodrama *Mildred Pierce* (1945), in which the noir protagonist is not only a woman but also a mother who obsessively devotes herself to her daughter.[19] This film noir is exceptional not only because there is substantial commentary on the figure of the mother but also because it is one of the only noir films that features a maternal protagonist. The film opens with Monte Beragon (Zachary Scott) saying "Mildred" with his last breath as he is shot to death. Mildred Pierce (Joan Crawford) confesses to the murder and, in traditional noir style, tells her story in voice-over accompanied by flashback. We see Mildred go through various men and jobs for the sake of her daughters. Her daughters are the primary objects of her attention, and when the youngest daughter, Kay (Jo Ann Marlowe), dies, Mildred devotes herself to the oldest, Veda (Ann Blyth). Mildred's love for Veda becomes a controlling obsession, and Veda reciprocates with cruelty and insults, to the point of having an affair with her stepfather, Mildred's husband Monte Beragon. In the end, we find out that Veda killed Monte, and Mildred again sacrifices herself to protect Veda. The moral of the film seems to be that Mildred is a "bad" mother because she loves too much; her "smother-love" results in her evil daughter. Film critic Lucia Bozzola says that "Crawford's glamorously fur-clad Mildred initially appears to be a femme fatale as she walks down a dark, rain-slicked pier after a murdered man dies uttering her name. Evenly lit flashbacks, however, reveal Mildred as an upwardly mobile working mother ... trying to make a good life for her daughters."[20] This tension between femme fatale and concerned mother reappears at the margins of other noir films. The sexual mother is either impossible or the ultimate corruption and evil. Perhaps she is both, impossible and therefore the ultimate corruption and evil.

There are three other notable mothers in classic noir films: Helen in *The Blue Dahlia* (1946), Katie in *The Big Heat* (1953), and Mrs. Harper in *The Reckless Moment* (1949). In *The Blue Dahlia*, we find out that party girl and unfaithful wife Helen (Doris Dowling) is a mother only when she confesses to killing her son in a drunken car wreck. Helen is a bad mother because she has desires and acts on them; she likes to drink and to have sex. Unfaithful wife, bad mother, and blackmailer, Helen looks and acts like a classic femme fatale, and she is killed for her sins just after the film opens; the threat of the sexual mother must be extinguished. Even the good mother, Katie Bannion (Jocelyn Brando), in *The Big Heat* is killed when she is the victim of a bomb meant for her police detective husband, Dave Bannion (Glenn Ford). With the good mom and superego out of the way, Bannion struggles with his own sadistic violent and sexual urges throughout the rest of the film as he tries to maintain his saintly image of his wife while avenging her death. In *The Reckless Moment*, Joan Bennett plays Lucia Harper, a devoted mother, who tries to stop the older man with whom her daughter, Beatrice (Geraldine Brooks), has been having an affair from making public Beatrice's love letters to him. A struggle with the man ends in his accidental death, but he doesn't have the letters. Martin Donnelly (James Mason) appears, claiming to have the letters, and tries to blackmail Mrs. Harper. Donnelly falls in love with Mrs. Harper, particularly with the ways that she reminds him of his own mother, and finally he sacrifices himself to save the family. Yet precisely because she is a good mother, Mrs. Harper cannot actualize her own sexual desire.[21] It is this tension between sexuality and maternity that dominates the unconscious of much of film noir. As we suggest in the chapters that follow, the ambivalence toward maternal sexuality is both concealed and revealed by processes of condensation and displacement at the margins of noir.

Certainly, 1940s films are full of representations of ambivalent relationships to the mother in particular and to women in general. Freud describes the Oedipus complex as a "conflict of ambivalence" that includes both "a well grounded love and a no less justifiable hatred towards one and the same person" (1927, 102).[22] Freud's analysis of fetishism is helpful in understanding (male) ambivalence toward the mother. Freud maintains that when the boy sees that his mother has no penis, he becomes aware of the possibility of his own castration (1927). The maternal sex is a threat to the male because it evokes in him the fear of castration. As a defense against the threat of castration, he substitutes a fetish for the missing maternal phallus and thereby both denies that his mother is "castrated" and protects himself from castration. The fetish object both recalls the castration threat and protects against it. The fetishist will alternate between tender and hostile treatment of the fetish object as a result of his dual denial-recognition of the possibility of castration.

We could say that the femme fatale in film noir is a fetish object that both protects against castration and threatens it at the same time. With her powerful will, cigarettes, and guns, like the pinups riding bombs, the femme fatale is phallic and thereby helps the male deny the possibility of his castration by denying what Freud would call the "reality" of her castration. In addition, her sex appeal reassures the male of his own phallic desire and thereby shores up his masculinity. This same phallic power and sexual power over him, however, threatens to render him powerless and castrated. It is as if by endowing the woman with a phallus, man gives her the power to castrate him and take his place. The dual provocation of the castration threat and protection against it explains why the male protagonist (and viewer) feels such ambivalence toward the femme fatale. She, like the fetish, is treated with tenderness and hostility.

The ambivalence toward the mother can also be explained as Oedipal jealousy. The Oedipal attachment of the child (both girls and boys) to the mother makes the child jealous of others. The child wants to be the sole object of the mother's affection. The child is especially jealous of maternal desire for someone else, particularly sexual desire.

Given its immature development, the child is no match for the mother's adult sexual partner. Whatever gratification the child can provide for the mother, it cannot provide sexual gratification. In this regard, the child cannot compete for the mother's love. Sexual desire in the mother, then, threatens to take the mother away from the child. This threat is even more devastating than the castration threat; indeed, the separation from the mother and her desire is how Jacques Lacan refigures Freud's concept of castration. Fear of separation from the mother is another form of the castration threat. This fear causes ambivalent feelings toward the mother. The child loves the mother when she devotes herself to it, but hates the mother when she goes out with someone else (this is the root of Mark Lamphere's "evil" in *The Secret beyond the Door*).

Taken as a whole, however, throughout his work, reiterating rather than diagnosing the threat of the mother, Freud has little to say about maternity or the role of the mother in psychoanalysis or the psyche. For Freud, the mother is reduced to the first object or the first, short-lived instance of phallic authority. Although his hypothesis about the relation between maternal sex and castration anxiety is intriguing, it is plagued with masculinist notions of psychic and sexual identity that make the theory problematic for any attempt to think through the relationship between woman, the feminine, and the maternal, or to diagnose the threat of maternity, outside of what always returns to the simple explanation that men are afraid of women/castration. In our attempt to think through the anxiety and power of maternal sexuality, Melanie Klein's theory of ambivalence and Julia Kristeva's theory of abjection are useful supplements to Freud's conjectures on the connection between the mother and death.

Abjection and the Lost Boundaries of Noir

Coincident with the heyday of film noir, in the 1940s and 1950s in Britain, Melanie Klein was developing her theory of ambivalence, which is primarily directed toward the mother: "For her, the instinct is ambivalent from the start: 'love' for the object is inseparable from its destruction, so that ambivalence becomes a quality of the object itself. As such an ambivalent object, perfectly benevolent and fundamentally hostile at one and the same time, would be intolerable," so "the subject struggles against his predicament by splitting it into a 'good' and a 'bad' object" (1973, 27). "The qualities 'good' and 'bad' are attributed to these objects not only in consequence of their gratifying or frustrating nature but also because of the subject's projection of his libidinal or destructive instincts on to them" (188). The mother is the primary object of such ambivalence and the prototype for all others: "The good breast—external and internal—becomes the prototype of all helpful and gratifying objects, the bad breast the prototype of all external and internal persecutory objects" (Klein 1952, 200). The "good" nurturing breast and "bad" withholding breast eventually become the "good" nurturing mother and "bad" punishing mother. The split into the "good" and the "bad" mother is a defense against the anxiety caused by her ambiguity within the child's imaginary.

Klein's thesis that ambivalence, and the subsequent splitting of the mother into good and bad, is a defense against ambiguity is suggestive in terms of our analysis of film noir. In *Noir Anxiety*, we show how the threat of lost boundaries and blurred borders between races, sexes, and origins results in the anxiety manifest in film noir. One defense against this anxiety is ambivalence or the polarization of the ambiguity into extremes that can easily be located and can help reestablish lost boundaries: black or white, masculine or feminine, familiar or foreign. These extremes, symptoms of the anxiety over ambiguity, overcompensate for lost boundaries with artificially fixed borders constantly threatening to collapse not only as a result of their sheer arbitrariness but also as a result of the return of the repressed ambiguities that haunt them.

With her theory of the abject and abjection, Julia Kristeva develops Klein's thesis that ambivalence is a defense against ambiguity. Relying on the work of Mary Douglas in *Purity and Danger* (1969), Kristeva defines a notion of abjection with which she diagnoses separation and identification in both individuals and nations or societies.[23] Kristeva suggests that the abject is not, as we might ordinarily think, what is grotesque or unclean; rather, it is what calls into question borders and threatens identity. The abject is on the borderline, and as such it is both fascinating and terrifying. Ultimately, the abject is identified with the maternal body, since the uncertain boundary between maternal body and infant provides the primary experience of both horror and fascination.[24] The maternal body is the most powerful location of abjection because it poses the greatest threat to the borders of every individual who was once part of the maternal body and born out of it.

In *Powers of Horror*, Kristeva describes the maternal body as the source of the most primordial ambiguity (1982). The infant struggles against the ambiguity of its own borders in relation to the maternal body in order to gain its identity as an individual. To do so, however, the infant tries to project outward toward an other everything that it finds abject and threatening in itself, and thereby seeks to establish an identity of self versus other. In Kristeva's analysis, the male child can eroticize the abject maternal body in order to love a woman by splitting the disgusting abject body from the fascinating abject body. The female child, on the other hand, too closely identifies with the maternal female body to split the object and instead splits herself by identifying with the abject maternal body.[25]

As Kristeva describes it, through the process of abjection, the infant finds the maternal body disgusting, if still fascinating, and is able to leave it behind. It is only by leaving the maternal body that the infant can enter the realm of signification through which s/he can subsequently take the mother as an object. Still within the phase of abjection, before the distinction between subject and object, the infant struggles with separation. Abjection is the process through which the infant overcomes its identification with the mother.

Kristeva describes how both individual and social identity are formed through a process of abjection aimed primarily and most fundamentally at the maternal body: prohibitions against unity with the maternal body found both social rituals and the boundaries of the individual psyche. The return of the repressed maternal body in literature, culture, and the individual psyche threatens the borders of the always precarious status quo and thereby opens up the possibility of transformation, even revolution.

Unlike Freud, who attributes socialization to the paternal function and castration threats and ignores the function of the mother as anything other than the primary (phallic) object, Kristeva emphasizes the importance of the maternal function in social development. With her theory of abjection, Kristeva resists Freud's identification of the maternal body as the infant's first object. She insists that there is a process of identification and separation that complicates the infant's relation with the maternal body. The maternal body is not simply an object, or the first object, or even a partial object, for the infant. Before the mother or the maternal body becomes an object for the infant, it is an abject; it is neither object nor nonobject, but something in between. Out of this in-between, subject and object are born. But they are maintained always and only precariously through the repression of this in-between, ambiguous place, which gives them life but also threatens their dissolution. In-betweenness and ambiguity are repressed to form proper stable, if always precarious, identity. Attempts to fix the borders and boundaries of this proper identity are always threatened by the return of repressed ambiguity.

On both the individual and societal level, the defensive operations of identity formation make the abject appear as an external threat. As Kristeva argues, however, the power of the abject and its true threat is that it is internal.[26] It threatens from within. The real threat of the abject is that it is part of the clean and proper, that it is integral to the borders of that clean and proper, and that those clean and proper borders are merely arbitrary attempts to categorize what is inherently ambiguous. Clean and proper identity, then, is itself a defense against the ambiguity inherent in its own construction. The threat of the return of the repressed abject is always the threat to proper borders posed by ambiguity.

Kristeva also challenges Freud's analysis in *Moses and Monotheism*, where he maintains that the social is set up against the murder of the father. She argues that the social is defined by repressing maternal authority; matriarchy becomes patriarchy with the shift from polytheism to monotheism. She extends her analysis of the way in which an individual identity is constructed against the exclusion of the abject maternal body to the way in which a cultural or national identity is constructed against the exclusion of maternity and the feminine. Kristeva argues that collective identity formation is analogous to individual identity formation. She claims that abjection is coextensive in both individual identity and collective identity, which operate according to the same logic of abjection. Whereas an individual marks his difference from the maternal body through a process of abjection, society marks off its difference from animals through a process of abjection. In her analysis, however, the animal realm has been associated with the maternal, which ultimately represents the realm of nature from which human culture must separate to assert its humanity.

Kristeva's analysis of the process of abjection from the maternal inherent in social formation supplements Freud's thesis that the social is founded on the murder of the father and the incest taboo. Kristeva's provocative reading of the incest taboo as the operations of abjection through which we attempt to guarantee the separation of culture from nature is useful to cultural theorists interested in the dynamics of marginalization and exclusion, especially insofar as Kristeva continually elaborates various ways that the repressed abject returns. The process of abjection is never completed. Rather, like everything repressed, it is bound to return. Although language and culture set up separations and order by repressing maternal authority, this repressed maternal authority returns, especially in literature and art, where imagination frees up unconscious fears and desires in a way similar to dream-work.

The repetition of marginal mothers and mother figures in film noir demonstrates the force of the anxiety over ambiguity experienced most intensely as an anxiety over maternal sexuality and maternal borders. Although maternal characters are rarely central figures in noir, the anxiety over the mother shows up repeatedly in various forms. From a maternal femme fatale like Mildred in *Mildred Pierce* to racialized mother figures like Carlotta in *Vertigo* or Bessie in *Lady from Shanghai*, from off-screen mothers like Mrs. Lamphere in *Secret beyond the Door*, Susie's mother in *Touch of Evil*, and Ruby Hanks in *Devil in a Blue Dress* to perverse mothers like Mrs. Mulwray in *Chinatown*, from maternal voices that speak through the directors of noir (Hitchcock, Welles, and Polanski) to absent or missing mothers in *Murder, My Sweet* and *Bound*, anxieties over maternity haunt film noir.

If as Freud suggests, anxieties over maternity are fastened to the maternal sex, then the marginal mothers of noir prove themselves all the more anxiety producing by evoking sex in one way or another. For Freud, maternal sex is the central locus for anxieties over birth, sex, and death. This is why, for Freud, maternal sex and maternal sexuality remain the uncanniest of the uncanny. This is also why maternal sex and sexuality would be the most repressed of the repressed. The addition of Kristeva's notion of abjection to Freud's speculations about the connection between the mother and death allows us to explain the threat of the maternal sex insofar as it evokes fears of birth, longings for return to the womb, threats of castration, or foreshadowings of death as the anxiety over blurred borders and ambiguous boundaries. This abject threat and fascination explains the power of incestuous fantasies and prohibitions. The return of the repressed mother, especially the sexual mother or maternal sex, threatens to blur the boundaries of the very identity of self or subject; it threatens to break down all borders between subject and object, between inside and outside, between man and woman, male and female, masculine and feminine. Any stable desire or identity—who we want and who we are—is challenged by the return of the repressed primary processes displaced onto the maternal sex, the processes of abjection.

Applying the theory of abjection to film noir, we can interpret condensed and displaced figures of race, sex, and origin as the return of repressed abjection, which is to say the return of repressed ambiguity and blurred boundaries. The sites of condensation and displacement that we analyze in subsequent chapters mark the return of continuous and fluid races, sexes, sexualities, and relations with the maternal body before defensive ambivalence and dualistic notions of self and other, us and them, circumscribe the "proper" boundaries of identity. These sites of the return of repressed abjection challenge any stable racial, sexual, or national identity by bringing racial and sexual ambiguity back into the construction, and process, of identity.

By analyzing the ambivalence of film noir as a screen for repressed ambiguity, we can open spaces for that ambiguity and difference to reappear on the margins of these films. Interpretation makes visible the traces of possibilities that are repressed and excluded so that race, sex, and national identity defend their "proper" borders—black/white, masculine/feminine, familiar/foreigner. In the process of interpretation, identity itself is transformed and again made fluid. Moreover, by interpreting the sites of condensation and displacement of race, sex, and origin, we begin to expose the paradoxical processes through which racial, sexual, and national identities are formed and stablized at the same time that they are deformed and destablized. After all, these are sites that both reveal and conceal ambiguities inherent in the process of identity formation. These marginal figures and elements of noir are at the same time defenses against repressed ambiguity in the attempt to stabilize identity and the very return of that repressed ambiguity, which constantly threatens the borders of any stable or proper identity. By exposing these paradoxical processes of identity formation in film noir, we hope to reveal some of the fears and desires concealed within its stunning styles and hypnotically convoluted narratives.

CHAPTER 1

Noir in Black and White

Most critics agree that there is a particular "dark" style and mood associated with film noir, hence the name *noir*. But just as *femme fatale* is not translated into English as *fatal woman* in popular discourse or film theory, neither is *film noir* translated into *black film*.[1] It is as if the French phrases camouflage sex and race and make them less threatening, as if translating these phrases into English would produce too much anxiety. Although the stories of noir films are those of white men and women on the borders of morality, often crossing borders into Mexico or Chinatown, the style of noir films makes these white characters visually black. The "dark" style of noir puts both protagonists and villains into the shadows, so much so that they appear visually black on the screen. Whereas some of the most popular films of the period, the "Negro problem" films of the 1940s and 1950s, explicitly address blacks passing as visually white, film noir presents whites who look visually black.[2]

In this chapter, we argue that the "Negro problem" films and film noir manifest the same anxieties over racial ambiguity. By analyzing the "Negro problem" films together with film noir, we can highlight the various ways in which anxiety over racial ambiguity is manifested in these films. Many of the "problem" films, such as *Intruder in the Dust* (1949) and *Home of the Brave* (1949), deliver a moral message about race and race relations through the mouth of a white authority figure. We interpret this white superego as a defense against racial difference and racial ambiguity, a defense that shows up more obliquely in the condensations and displacements of film noir. If self-righteous lawyers, doctors, and judges police the boundaries of racial identity in the problem films, noir detectives, themselves on the outs with the law, nevertheless continue to navigate the borders of race in ways that manifest an anxiety over lost boundaries and racial ambiguity. Like Uncle John's lectures on proper race relations in *Intruder in the Dust*, Marlowe's hard-boiled banter about Chinese jade in *Murder, My Sweet* also circumscribes race relations. In a significant way, both the doctor's prescription that blacks are the same as whites in *Home of the Brave* and the layers of repressed ethnicity condensed into the visually whiter-than-white character of Elsa in *The Lady from Shanghai* betray anxiety over racial difference and ambiguity. And detective Mike Vargas in *Touch of Evil* occupies a similarly paradoxical position policing the borders of race as the black mothers, Dicey Johnson, Delilah, and Annie, in *Pinky* (1949) and both versions of *Imitation of Life*.

While the threat of racial ambiguity is the explicit theme of some "problem" films like *Lost Boundaries*, *Pinky*, and *Imitation of Life*, anxieties over racial ambiguity are also conjured in the style of film noir. Whereas Dr. Carter and his family pass for the quintessential all-American white suburban family in *Lost Boundaries*, noir protagonists and detectives occupy a space on the other side of the clean white suburbs; their lost boundaries are evidenced not only by their travels across class, racial, and national borders but also by their visual blackness in the shadows of noir. Whereas in *Pinky*, Pinky Johnson stands out against the dark background of the film as visually whiter than white, sometimes almost glowing (several white characters in the film comment on the extreme of Pinky's whiteness), shadows cast the Swede in *The Killers* as black faced, Black Irish Michael O'Hara becomes visually black in *The Lady from Shanghai*, Helen Grayle becomes visually blacker than black in the shadows of *Murder, My Sweet*, Madeleine Elster becomes a black silhouette in *Vertigo*, and Celia fades into the shadows in *The Secret beyond the Door*.

The visual blackness of noir femmes fatales is so striking that critic Michele Wallace describes how she found a place for herself as a black female spectator by identifying with the blackness of these women: "It was always said among Black women that Joan Crawford was part Black, and as I watch these films again today, looking at Rita Hayworth in *Gilda* or Lana Turner in *The Postman Always Rings Twice*, I keep thinking 'she's so beautiful, she looks black' . . . there was a way in which these

Pinky Johnson (Jeanne Crain) in *Pinky*.

films were possessed by Black female viewers. The process may have been about problematizing and expanding one's racial identity instead of abandoning it" (1993, 264).[3] Wallace suggests that the visual blackness of these powerful femmes fatales opens up a spectator position, albeit complicated, for black women.

Although the issue of race, particularly black-white relations, is rarely the explicit theme of film noir, visually the dark style of film noir, with its sharp black-and-white contrasts, conjures the specter of race like no other cinematic style. Implicitly, then, film noir is always and everywhere about race. In his innovative essay "The Whiteness of Film Noir," Eric Lott argues that film noir's obsession with the "dark" side of white American life covers over both the racism of the association between darkness and evil and the racism of corrupt white society as it is displaced onto visually black (white) characters. Analyzing the racialized association between "violence, obsession, and guilt" and blackness, both visual blackness and the "dark side" of the white self, Lott shows how this double-sided racism (visual and moral blackness) works in several classic noir films, including *Double Indemnity* (1944), *A Double Life* (1948), *The Reckless Moment*, *In a Lonely Place* (1950), and *Kiss Me Deadly*. Lott concludes that "the troping of white darkness in noir has a racial source that is all the more insistent for seeming off to the side. Film noir is replete with characters of color who populate and signify the shadows of white American life in the 1940's. Noir may have pioneered Hollywood's merciless exposure of white pathology, but by relying on race to convey that pathology, it in effect erected a cordon sanitaire around the circle of corruption it sought to penetrate. Film noir rescues with racial idioms the whites whose moral and social boundaries seem in doubt. 'Black film' is the refuge of whiteness" (1997, 85). Lott argues that the style of film noir not only associates darkness with evil but also displaces white corruption onto visibly black figures and thereby absolves whites of the responsibility for evil and moral ambiguity.

Although Lott acknowledges that film noir invokes racial ambiguity, he concludes by reducing the issue of race to black and white. For Lott, racial ambiguity itself becomes associated with blackness, darkness, and evil. Racial undecidability becomes black, and black becomes bad and thereby absolves whiteness so that it can continue to be good. Lott's analysis is provocative, but it oversimplifies the anxiety over blackness in noir. It is not simply that film noir absolves whites of their moral ambiguity by making them black. Rather, the moral ambiguity of the narrative of noir covers over a source of even greater ambiguity that is displaced onto the style of noir: racial ambiguity. Racial ambiguity, not the fear of blackness, is the real anxiety of noir. The anxiety over racial ambiguity manifest in noir cannot be reduced to a simple association between blackness and evil. Rather, the "evil" or threat in these films is a complicated fear of racial ambiguity, the fear of not being able to tell the difference between blackness and whiteness. If moral ambiguity causes anxiety, racial ambiguity may be its source. Indeed, as we argue throughout *Noir Anxiety*, the moral ambiguity of the narrative of noir is a screen for concrete anxieties over race, sex, and (national/maternal) origin.

Racial ambiguity in these films provokes what Kristeva calls *the abject*, the in-between, the undecidable, the borderline, "lost boundaries" (1982). The ambiguity of the abject both fascinates and terrifies at the same time. Recall that according to Kristeva's theory, the ultimate excitement and the ultimate anxiety are caused by not knowing how to classify someone or something. Applying Kristeva's theory of abjection to the anxiety over race, we can diagnose the anxiety caused by racial ambiguity as a fear of the loss of boundaries between races. If abjection is not what is evil or unclean but rather what calls into question proper borders, then racial ambiguity threatens the boundaries of proper identity. The process of identity formation excludes to its margins racial difference and racial ambiguity in order to defend the borders of the proper self. Racial otherness and racial ambiguity are abjected so that the proper self-identity can be formed. Yet in Kristeva's theory what is abjected, like everything repressed, continually returns. Racial difference and racial ambiguity are repressed so that proper identity, especially white identity, can be formed, but they always return to threaten that identity. Moreover, because proper identity is formed by arbitrary, overdetermined, and artificially fixed boundaries, repressed ambiguity is all the more powerful because it recalls the arbitrariness of the process of identification. Indeed, it reminds that ambiguity and abjection are necessary elements of all clean and proper identity.

In this way, the return of repressed lost boundaries provokes both an opening onto difference and a retreat into sameness. Ambiguity can open new ways of seeing the world, of seeing black and white, but it can also lead to a reactionary need to reclassify the world into neat black-and-white categories. The "problem" films open up the possibility of seeing race differently even while they harbor fears of blacks passing for white or whites (like young Howard and Shelly Carter in *Lost Boundaries*) discovering that they are really black. Film noir, with its visibly black characters, opens up the possibility of challenging the racial purity of whiteness even if, as Lott argues, it perpetuates the racist association between darkness and evil. The racial ambiguity of film noir both reflects a concrete anxiety about racial difference and implicitly challenges any black-and-white notions of race. Despite their ambivalence toward race—or maybe because of it—the 1940s and 1950s "problem" films and film noir redefine race by undoing its "natural" links to skin color or to blood (for example, the little girls in Sirk's *Imitation of Life* who cut themselves to discover no difference between their blood). The racial ambiguity of these films begins to open the door for a more complex cultural and less biological (or perceptual) conception of race at the same time that it signals fears of miscegenation.[4]

Race in Noir

A significant number of classic noir films have ethnic or racialized characters (usually minor characters), but few of these films make ethnicity or race an explicit theme. Although the height and heyday of film noir coincides with the Hollywood postwar "racial tolerance" films or "Negro problem" films, there are virtually no noir films in which race or racism is an explicit plot theme, which might also explain why so little film criticism has analyzed the role of race and place in film noir.[5] Yet the "dark" style of noir presents us with scores of visually black characters whose racial ambiguity is not limited to their appearance in the shadows. As we show throughout *Noir Anxiety*, film noir is full of condensations and displacements of race that show up on the margins of these films. Indeed, it is significant that so many noir films include marginal ethnic and racialized characters, and the populations of various Chinatowns or cities in Mexico, along with individual characters such as Carlotta in *Vertigo*, Tanja or Mike in *Touch of Evil*, and Elsa in *The Lady from Shanghai*.

Only one classic film noir deals explicitly with racism, *Crossfire* (1947), which tells the story of a group of servicemen, one of whom is a violent anti-Semite who murders a Jew. In *Crossfire* four World War II vets meet a couple in a bar one night and end up back at their apartment. One of the soldiers, Monty Montgomery (Robert Ryan), is a violent anti-Semite who kills his host, Joseph Samuels (Sam Levene), because he is Jewish. At one point in the film, the investigating detective (Robert Young) gives a soapbox-style speech condemning anti-Semitism; here again we have the white authority figure acting as the superego of the film, lecturing on the evils of racism. In the wake of controversy over this film, director Edward Dmytryk was denounced by the House of Representatives' Un-American Activities Committee during the McCarthy investigations of the 1950s. In the same year, 1947, another important film about anti-Semitism was released, *Gentleman's Agreement*, starring Gregory Peck as a newspaper reporter who passes as Jewish in order to write a story.[6] It is noteworthy that the presumption of this film is that ethnicity is a performative utterance, that the protagonist can know what it is like to be Jewish just by saying that he is Jewish. He doesn't engage in any specifically Jewish practices, and still he passes as Jewish among Jews and Gentiles alike with the simple proclamation "I am Jewish."

In 1959, just one year after what is considered by many to be the last film noir, *Touch of Evil*, two other noir films were released that made racism a plot theme, *Odds against Tomorrow* and *The Crimson Kimono*, which is about two army buddies, one Caucasian and one Asian, whose friendship is threatened by jealousy and racism. In *The Crimson Kimono*, Korean War army buddies (Glenn Corbett and James Shigeta) are working for the Los Angeles homicide squad when a stripper (Gloria Pall) is murdered. During their investigation, they meet and both fall for a woman (Victoria Shaw) implicated in the murder. Their friendship is threatened by their competition and jealousy. Shigeta believes that Corbett's jealousy is the result of racism. In the end, they catch the murderer and reconcile their friendship in L.A.'s Little Tokyo during the Japanese New Year celebration. Although issues of race and racism become explicit in Samuel Fuller's *The Crimson Kimono*, the film trades on stereotypes of race and race relations. For example, a Japanese fan dance performed by a white stripper is what critic David Cochran calls "a symbol of interracial understanding" and the exoticization of Little Tokyo (Cochran 2000, 148).

Odds against Tomorrow is the only one of these three noir films to take up the theme of black and white racism. The film stars Harry Belafonte (who also produced the film) as Johnny Ingram, a jazz musician who has debts that make him desperate. His gambling at the track has put him in debt to mobster Bacco (Will Kuluva), who threatens Johnny's life if he doesn't pay up. In addition, he has child support to pay to his ex-wife Ruth (Kim Hamilton) for his young daughter Eadie (Lois Thorne). Johnny is suspicious of white-dominated culture, and he warns his wife that pandering to the white PTA members or white society in general is not the way to get ahead; he says, "Drink enough tea with them and stay out of the watermelon patch and maybe our little girl will grow up to be Miss America, is that it? Wise up Ruth, it's their world, and we're just living in it." Against his better judgment, Johnny is forced to team up with racist Earl Slater (Robert Ryan) and their old friend Dave Burke (Ed Begley Sr.), an ex-cop who masterminds the ill-fated bank heist.

Earl Slater is a bitter war vet who can't get a job and begrudgingly lives off of his girlfriend's (Shelley Winters) income. His masculinity is obviously threatened by his girlfriend Lorry's success, and he feels like a failure. His insecurity about his masculine potency not only makes him desperate to support himself financially but also leads him to make a pass at a neighbor woman while Lorry is at work. Although Lorry begs him not to get involved in the scheme and implores him to be careful because she loves him and is totally devoted to him, Earl brushes her off because her demands for love only remind him of her threat to his masculinity. Earl Slater is the quintessential white World War II veteran threatened by changing gender and race relations. He is threatened by Lorry's career because it makes him feel that he is less of a man if he doesn't have control of the money, and it makes her more dangerous and controlling. He is threatened by the fact that Johnny not only has a job but also is of a higher social class. Just before they attempt the heist, Earl says to Johnny, "You're just another black spot on main street." When Dave tries to calm him down, Earl replies, "I know how to handle him. I've been handling 'em all my life. He's no different because he's got a twenty-dollar pair of shoes." Under the surface of his racism is the fear that this black man, like his career woman girlfriend, renders him (socially and economically) impotent. Earl's desperation and inability to adjust to life after the war is in part due to the fact that he can't accept that women and African Americans are gaining power. In his paranoid and oppositional attitude, he sees their gains as his losses. His defensive reaction to both racial and sexual difference can be interpreted as a fear of the return of the repressed racial and sexual ambiguity out of which his sense of himself as a white man is produced. That which he abjected to erect proper boundaries returns to threaten those boundaries.

In the end, Earl's racism and Johnny's response to it get them both killed. Because Earl won't trust Johnny with the car keys, they can't make a quick getaway, and Dave is shot trying to carry the money to the car. The last chase scene has Earl and Johnny more concerned with chasing and killing each other than escaping from the pursuing police. The final shoot-out between Earl and Johnny takes place on the top of a giant, towering oil tank where they shoot each other and ignite the tanks in the process. The ensuing explosion leaves their bodies charred and indistinguishable to the police investigators. Racial hatred is the true danger that ignites the deadly explosion. Yet in the end, the film equates Earl's racism with Johnny's anger in the face of it. The film does not distinguish between violent racism and violent resistance to racism, even as a form of self-defense. The film does not open a space from which we can understand Johnny's violent reaction to racism as anything but another form of race hatred. In this way, rather than allow for resistance to racism as a means for achieving equality, let alone a justifiable reaction, *Odds against Tomorrow* equates the victim of racism with the racist; in the end, they are literally indistinguishable charred black bodies. The moral of the film is that race hatred, no matter its source, is a dead end. The film makes this plain when in the penultimate shot we see a sign hanging from the fence of the oil refinery that says, "Stop, Dead End." And the explosion at the end of the film evokes a nuclear explosion followed by the apocalyptic final scene in which everything is charred and dead.

In the decade between the neo-noir *Odds against Tomorrow* and the "problem" films of 1949, we see the disappearance of the white authority figure who acts as the superego in the "problem" films: the lawyer Uncle John in *Intruder in the Dust*, the doctor in *Home of the Brave*, the detective in *Crossfire*, the policeman in *Lost Boundaries*, the judge in *Pinky*. We also see more complex race relations that can involve working through racism in order to form friendships. Academy Award winner *The Defiant Ones* (1958) is a prime example of complex white and black characters working through their race hatred to become friends. Tony Curtis and Sidney Poitier play escaped convicts chained together on the lam. To survive, they have to overcome their racial hatred and suspicions. In the end, they become friends, each willing to sacrifice himself for the other. The problem films just a decade before don't have anything like this type of complex relationship between black and white characters. Indeed, some of the problem films present what we might call hardboiled race relations that insist on race segregation as a defense against anxieties about miscegenation and racial ambiguity.

Racial Ambiguity in the "Problem" Films

The anxiety over racial ambiguity manifest in the style of film noir comes into stark relief in the context of the "Negro problem" films released during the same period. Indeed, it may seem curious that for the most part, race and ethnicity remain implicit in film noir even as they enter the popular consciousness in big box office hits like the 1949 trio *Pinky, Home of the Brave, and Lost Boundaries,* or *Intruder in the Dust,*[7] and later in the Academy Award–winning *The Defiant Ones* (1958) or Douglas Sirk's popular remake of *Imitation of Life* (1959), which appeared in the same year as the race-conscious neo-noir *Odds against Tomorrow.* The "Negro problem" films of 1949 were the highest-grossing films of the year for their studios.[8] Racial tension sold tickets. *Intruder in the Dust* was not as popular at the box office as the other three but is considered by some critics to be the best of the 1949 "problem" films. Based on a novel by William Faulkner, the film takes place in his hometown, Oxford, Mississippi. The film tells the story of a black landowner, Lucas Beauchamp (Juano Hernández), who is wrongfully accused of murdering a white man. The dead man's brother and murderer, Crawford Gowrie (Charles Kemper), tries to instigate a lynch mob to kill Lucas before he comes to trial. Ultimately, justice is served, and Lucas is released.

While in the narrative Lucas is portrayed as a strong, knowing, sympathetic character, visually he looms over other characters, and in one scene he looks like a monstrous Cyclops desperately glaring through the jail cell bars. The only other black character in the film with an important supporting role is Aleck (Elzie Emanuel), the stereotyped slow-witted, wide-eyed step-and-fetch-it son of the white Mallison family's black maid. Only a young white boy, Chick Mallison (Claude Jarman Jr.), and an elderly white matron, Miss Habersham (Elizabeth Patterson)—who fends off the lynch mob with her knitting needles— believe in Lucas. The rest of the town presumes that he is guilty. Chick's uncle John (David Brian) is the lawyer whom Lucas requests to defend him. And although Uncle John doesn't believe Lucas any more than the rest of the town, he agrees to defend him. Uncle John spends most of the film lecturing young Chick on the ways of the world, but his ser- mons are filled with both racist presumptions and condemnations of racism. In the end, it is Uncle John who delivers the moral of the film when he criticizes his own racist presumptions and those of others and proclaims Lucas to be his "conscience."

In this final scene, Lucas comes to Uncle John's office to pay him for his services, but Uncle John is embarrassed to see him because of his past racist presumptions; still, he tells Chick that he isn't worried about a confrontation because Lucas is too decent and polite to mention it. If anything, Lucas is Uncle John's *guilty* conscience. In this scene, Uncle John's guilt and shame appear as anger directed at Lucas. And yet Uncle John is the voice of the white superego in the film, constantly lecturing Chick and the audience about justice and racial tolerance. He claims to know more about black experience than the black characters in the film.

Box office hit *Home of the Brave* also has a white superego explaining away the effects of racism and diagnosing a black man's response to racism as pathological. Whereas in *Intruder in the Dust* the black man's ignoring white racism is considered polite and decent behavior, in *Home of the Brave* the black man's not ignoring white racism is considered pathological. In *Home of the Brave* the black soldier—the only black character in the film—Peter Moss (James Edwards) becomes paralyzed in the war when the only white friend he has ever had, Finch (Lloyd Bridges), gets killed by a sniper just after he almost calls Moss a "yellow-bellied nigger." Because Finch is the only white man who has ever treated Moss with respect, he feels betrayed by Finch's racial slur. Later, back at the hospital, the doctor (Jeff Corey)—the film's white superego—tells Moss that he can't walk because he feels guilty for his friend's death, not because of the racial slurs but because everyone wants the person next to him to die in battle instead of him.

Completely discounting the reality of racism or the possibility that racism could be debilitating, the doctor repeatedly tells Moss that his problem has nothing to do with being a Negro and that he is just like everyone else. For the doctor, race and racism are just displaced war trauma that Moss suffers. Trading on the reality and significance of war trauma, the trauma of racism becomes a form of hysteria—"it's all in your head." The doctor eventually "cures" Moss by yelling racial slurs that make Moss so angry that he walks toward the doctor and collapses in his arms. At the same time that the doctor denies the effects of racism on Moss and insists that he is too sensitive—indeed, that his sensitivity is pathological—he uses the powerful effect of racism to incite Moss to walk.

In spite of the doctor's mixed messages, the film ends with Moss internalizing the words of this white superego, repeating, "I am just like anyone else" in the face of more racial slurs from T.J. (Steve Brodie), another soldier who has been insulting Moss throughout the film. Mingo (Frank Lovejoy), a third soldier who accompanied the group on the fateful mission, insists that T.J.'s racial slurs are no different than any of the other mean or insulting things that T.J. says to white people, including himself. At the end of the film, then, racism is reduced to individual temperament or meanness, and any reaction to racism is not only a sign of individual weakness but also a sign of individual pathology. The lesson of the film is that there is no such thing as institutional or cultural racism; rather, it is just a few white bullies needling a few oversensitive head cases.

These films are full of hard-boiled racial hatreds that jar modern sensibilities. But more curious than the harsh racism of the "bad guys" are the hard-boiled attitudes of the moral authority figures. The hard-boiled characters in these films are the authority figures—lawyers, doctors, judges, policemen—who deliver the moral messages. These white superegos function to circumscribe racial boundaries and racial difference to contain racial ambiguity. The strength of the superego is in direct correlation to the power of the abject and its threat to proper boundaries.

Again recall that the abject is what is on the border, what does not respect borders. It is "ambiguous," "in-between," "composite" (Kristeva 1982, 4). Kristeva describes the in-between as "a terror that dissembles, a hatred that smiles, a passion that uses the body for barter instead of inflaming it, a debtor who sells you up, a friend who stabs you" (4). The abject is not what it seems; it is neither one nor the other; it is undecidable. The abject, then, is not a "quality in itself." Rather, it is a relationship to a boundary and represents what has been "jettisoned out of that boundary, its other side, a margin" (69). The abject is what threatens identity. It is neither good nor evil, subject nor object, ego nor unconscious, but something that threatens the distinctions themselves. It is not an object that corresponds to an ego; rather, it is what is excluded by the superego: "To each ego its object, to each superego its abject" (2). Society is founded on the abject, which is to say, on constructing boundaries and jettisoning the "antisocial." The abject threatens the unity and identity of both society and the subject by calling into question the boundaries on which they are constructed. The abject is the return of the repressed ambiguity out of which proper identity is formed.

Even jettisoned, the abject still threatens the social order. Social order is the result of constructing and maintaining borders, and the abject points to the fragility of those borders. Society is parceled into sexes, races, classes, castes, and so forth, and ambiguity is what is repressed so that these neat and proper categories might exist. Both social and individual identity are formed through defensive operations that artificially and arbitrarily fix and bind the ambiguity inherent in the process of identification. Ambiguity, then, is what has been excluded by the superego for the sake of identity.

If we apply this theory to race and race relations, it is not blackness that threatens proper white identity; rather, racial ambiguity is the real threat to the proper boundaries of white (and black) identity. In the problem films, the white authority figures' heavy-handed speeches about racial tolerance that erase racial difference and silence the black characters function to police the borders of identity. Racial difference threatens the proper boundaries of identity by recalling racial ambiguity. Both the position that there is no difference between black and white (*Home of the Brave*'s "You are just like everyone else") and the position that we need to maintain a radical separation between black and white (the message of *Pinky* and *Imitation of Life*) are defenses against racial ambiguity. The extremes of sameness and difference have in common the force with which they deny racial ambiguity. Even while these films present us with a strong superego that acts as a defense against abjection and ambiguity, they are full of both narrative and visual contradictions and ambivalence that reveal that repressed racial ambiguity.

The superego of film noir, often manifest in the detective character's voice-over, is also haunted by the return of the repressed ambiguity that shows up in both its narrative and visual style.

Two other "problem" films of 1949 display an anxiety over racial ambiguity that brings the anxiety over racial ambiguity in film noir into even greater relief. The explicit theme of both *Lost Boundaries* and *Pinky* is racial ambiguity and passing. The explicit threat in these "problem" films where black characters are visibly white, and the implicit threat in noir films where white characters are visibly black, is not a fear of blackness but rather a fear of the inability to distinguish between black and white, a fear of "lost boundaries" between races. Racial ambiguity is the real threat that lies behind both these "problem" films and film noir. Concern over racial ambiguity that motivates the narrative of films such as *Pinky* and *Lost Boundaries* is manifested in the style of noir.

In *Lost Boundaries*, a black doctor, Scott Carter (white actor Mel Ferrer), passes for white in a small New Hampshire town. During World War II he joins the navy until his "true" race is discovered and he is expelled from the navy and is forced to tell his children that they are black. The film opens with Carter graduating from medical school and marrying Marcia (white actress Beatrice Pearson). Dr. Charles Howard (Emory Richardson), a distinguished African American doctor receiving an honorary degree, offers Carter an internship in a black hospital in Georgia. When he arrives, Carter is denied the internship because his skin is too light and the board of directors has decided to give preference to "Southern" applicants. Because he "looks" white but "is" black, Carter doesn't belong among whites or blacks.

Marcia's father, a light-skinned African American who is living as white, suggests that the young couple do the same. He objects to their association with blacks and recommends that like him they distance themselves from the black community. "I won't have my daughter seen in the company of Negroes," he says. But Carter insists that he make his applications as a Negro doctor; as a result, he gets rejection after rejection. Tired of his job making shoes, Carter eventually accepts an internship in Portsmouth, New Hampshire, where no one asks about his race. When war breaks out, both Carter and his son Howard (Richard Hylton) join the navy. Carter is dismissed when they discover that he is black. Now he has to tell his children, whom he and Marcia have raised as white, that they are black. When he tells his son, Howard runs off to Harlem to see what it is like to be black. There he wanders the streets to the strains of jazz music and stays in a run-down boardinghouse and dreams of his family and even his white girlfriend, whom we see turning black in images over his head.

In response to Howard's depression and confusion, a friendly black police officer (Canada Lee) gives a passionate speech about race and racism in which, like most of the black characters in the film, he tells Howard why his father didn't want him to be black and concludes that if you could be white, then you would never want to be black. Although the superego of this film is a black authority figure, the policeman, rather than a white authority figure, his law is "It's better to be white if you can." The film ends happily with the family reunited and accepted by the community at a church sermon in which the minister is preaching racial tolerance. Although the film tries to address the problem of racial discrimination, it ends up presenting an argument for passing as the answer to racism: if all blacks were whites, then we could have community and racial tolerance.

If the moral of *Lost Boundaries* is "Pass if you can," *Pinky* makes passing a sin against God, mother, community, and self. *Pinky* opens with Pinky returning to her grandmother's house after attending nursing school "up north" in Boston. We find out that her grandmother, Dicey Johnson (Ethel Waters), has worked washing clothes for the townspeople and waiting on Miss Em in order to send Pinky to school. We also find out that Pinky has come home to run away from the man she loves because she can't tell him that she is black. Pinky's grandmother knows that Pinky has been passing as white and tells her that it is a sin against God and a shame and makes her get down on her knees to ask forgiveness. Pinky's grandmother enforces the law of racial segregation. Upon her return, Pinky is subjected to brutal racist discrimination made all the more striking by the fact that she is treated with respect because she looks white but she is treated with abuse when the same people find out she is black. After this abuse, Pinky starts to pack her bag to leave, but her grandmother insists that she stay and nurse Miss Em, who is on her deathbed. When Miss Em dies and wills her estate to Pinky, her nearest relatives take her to court. After a moving speech about the evils of racism and the true wishes of Miss Em by Pinky's lawyer, Judge Walker (Basil Ruysdael), Pinky wins the case and gets the estate. As in *Home of the Brave* and *Intruder in the Dust*, the white authority figure, Judge Walker, appears as the superego in *Pinky*. He not only lectures Pinky on race and racism but also explains the workings of both the white and black minds.

Pinky's boyfriend Tom (William Lundigan) still wants to marry her after he finds out that she is black, but he wants to keep it a secret and move to Denver, where no one will know that she is black; he says that after they are married there will be no more Pinky Johnson, just Mrs. Adams. In the end, Pinky decides that she must be true to herself because, as she says, "You can't live without pride." Yet Pinky's decision is heavily influenced by the last words and will of Miss Em, who told her to be true to herself and left the estate to her because she had confidence that Pinky would put it to good use. The central part of the agony of her decision is trying to decipher Miss Em's last wishes; Pinky repeatedly asks what Miss Em wanted from her and what she meant. Although Pinky decides that she doesn't want to keep her race a secret like some kind of past shame, in the end, her decision is made out of an obligation to Miss Em. The white plantation owner as benefactor commands Pinky from beyond the grave to do her bidding, benevolent as it seems when Pinky starts a clinic and nursery school for the children in her black neighborhood.

The protagonists in both *Pinky* and *Lost Boundaries* overcome class and race boundaries through the benevolence of whites. At the same time that they are portrayed as exceptional individuals who leave behind the rest of their race—shown as the questionable black neighbors in *Pinky* and the black masses in Harlem in *Lost Boundaries*—they are dependent upon the kindness of their white benefactors. In *Crossing the*

Line, Gayle Wald insightfully diagnoses this paradox in the liberal discourse of individualism: "By disseminating the image of the 'exceptional Negro' as an argument for a limited and provisional racial equality, *Pinky* and *Lost Boundaries* embrace both sides of this paradox of liberal discourse, framing the representation of black citizenship within the context of a symbolic conversation between 'white' benevolence and generosity and 'black' self-discipline and gratitude. As a result, neither film is capable of representing its black protagonists as capable of meaningful collective association with other black people" (2000, 114–15).

Wald argues that class mobility is substituted for race mobility in these films. The protagonists are allowed to move up in class only so long as they accept race boundaries. The American Dream of class mobility is dependent upon the reinscription of a black-white racial binary. Wald's analysis suggests that these films display a displacement of race mobility onto class precisely to stabilize the categories of race. As Wald points out, in the end Pinky is successful in moving up in class because she accepts her true race and returns to gendered domestic work, only now as a landowner (106). And the Carters are accepted back into the community after their true race is revealed only because Scott Carter is a doctor and has already moved up in class; his class status protects him against his race, but only insofar as the Carters accept the position of penitents confessing their sins in church to the white community (112). In both films, whites are continually reinscribed in positions of power to determine the fate of the black characters, a fate that always remains just out of their control in spite of their discipline and gratitude.

Both *Lost Boundaries* and *Pinky* manifest an anxiety over racial ambiguity. *Lost Boundaries* conjures the fear that any white could really be black. This possibility evokes not only the anxiety that we can't tell the difference between black and white but also the anxieties that whites may discover that they are black and that any white neighbor may really be black. The *Twilight Zone*–type revelation to Carter's children that although they have known themselves to be white all of their lives, they are really black, signals an anxiety over racial origin and blood. Any white person could wake up black one day. In addition, any community could discover that its beloved white doctor, neighbor, and friend is black. *Pinky* too conjures the anxiety that any white girlfriend or boyfriend could turn out to be black and that we can't tell white from black. Throughout the film, various characters comment on how white Pinky is. Her name highlights her lightness. And as if that is not enough to conjure anxieties over racial ambiguity, visually the film presents Pinky as whiter than the white characters. In some scenes, especially in her white nurse's uniform, she is almost glowing, as if she has a white aura. As Elaine Gisnberg says in her introducton to *Passing and the Fictions of Identity*, "when 'race' is no longer visible, it is no longer intelligible: if 'white' can be 'black,' what is white?" (1996, 8). Insofar as race passing conjures an invisible blackness in these films, it is a symptom of cultural anxiety over the security of white identity.

Maternal Origins as the Site of Race

In *Pinky*, unlike *Lost Boundaries*, blackness is associated solely with the maternal. Pinky's dark maternal origin haunts her throughout her life. Even though she passes for white at school, she cannot escape the blackness of her maternal legacy. Her hidden dark maternal origin returns just as she is compelled to return to it. Behind her whiter-than-white exterior lies the darkness of the racial mother who determines her fate. Pinky has to choose between being true to her (grand)mother and herself or succeeding in the white world. Her (grand)mother is on one side of the racial divide, and her success is on another. Her mother is not only the repressed maternal force that nurtures and gives life to the white family but also the repressed maternal force that makes it possible for her daughter to pass. Behind every white success there is a repressed black mammy. Miss Em and her family and her wealth are possible only by virtue of Dicey Johnson. And Pinky's whiteness in relation to the white plantation conjures the specter of repressed racial violence and rape through which white plantation owners maintained their slaves. Even more repressed than Pinky's dark maternal past is an absent, unspoken, guilty paternal legacy suggested by the fact that Pinky is the heir to the estate.

The dark maternal origin both threatens the proper "white" identity of the daughter, of all children, with racial ambiguity at the same time that it guarantees racial identity. Appearances may be deceiving, and white may not be white, but as long as there is a black maternal origin, racial identity can be determined to be black or white. *Pinky, Lost Boundaries*, and *Imitation of Life* do not address the question of how blacks come to appear white. Instead they create an opposition between appearance and reality that finds at its center the undeniably black mother. If maternity is the source of blackness and therefore associated with a contaminating force, it is also a screen for condensed anxieties over ambiguities in racial, sexual, and individual identity.

As in *Pinky*, maternity is the origin of racialization in Fannie Hurst's novel *Imitation of Life*, and the two film versions of the novel, Douglas Sirk's in 1959 and John M. Stahl's in 1934.[9] In Stahl's version, Beatrice "Bea" Pullman (Claudette Colbert), a poor white widow and single mother trying to make ends meet selling door-to-door, meets Delilah Johnson (Louise Beavers), a poor black widow and single mother who comes to work for Bea. Although segregation is never questioned in the film, and Delilah never stops being Bea's maid, Bea and Delilah become friends. They also become business partners when Bea decides to market Delilah's special pancake recipe. Delilah cooks the pancakes, and Bea sells them as "Aunt Delilah's" pancake mix. They both become rich. In spite of her savings, Delilah insists on continuing to serve Bea and her daughter Jessie (Baby Jane Holzer/Rochelle Hudson); as the man (Paul Porcasi) who suggests boxing the pancake mix says, "Once a pancake, always a pancake." As the film progresses and Bea moves from lower class to upper class, in spite of their partnership, the boundary between Bea and Delilah is more clearly marked by their separate spaces in the large house. And, Delilah becomes more and more a mammy figure, both in her appearance and in her character. Her picture as "Aunt Delilah," a precursor to Aunt Jemimah, is on the pancake box.

Delilah's light-skinned daughter Paola (Dorothy Black/Fredi Washington) insists that she should have the same privileges as Jessie and repeatedly and successfully passes as white until her mother shows up and blows her cover. Paola runs away to pass and returns to her mother's funeral blaming herself for her mother's death. Like Pinky, Paola is forced to choose between loyalty to her mother and succeeding in the white world where she can pass. Unlike Pinky, Paola's dark maternal past haunts her throughout the film when her mother repeatedly follows her and exposes her racial origins and sabotages her attempts to pass. Both Bea and Delilah lecture Paola on the evils of passing for what she is not. Both emphasize that by passing, Paola is betraying her mother. For Paola, race cannot be separated from maternity. Her struggle with her mother is a struggle with race and racism.

Throughout Stahl's *Imitation of Life*, it is clear that whiteness is better than blackness, but Paola is repeatedly scolded for trying to pass; the film does not acknowledge that racism and discrimination make it more desirable to be treated as white than as black. At the same time that the film privileges whiteness, it denies the difference that race makes when Bea and other characters continually tell the children that it doesn't matter if you are black or white. In the end, Stahl's *Imitation of Life* presents itself as the story of two mothers who sacrifice themselves for their daughters. Bea and her daughter Jessie fall in love with the same man, Steve (Warren William), whom Bea gives up for Jessie's sake; the film implies that Bea must give up her sexual desires to be a good mother. But Delilah cannot give up her race and therefore is by nature a bad mother. Even as she is condemned for being black, Delilah enforces the law of racial boundaries with her daughter. Yet Bea and Delilah are presented as occupying the same position, the position of the sacrificing mother, which reduces the life-and-death struggle between black mother and daughter to the tensions between white mother and daughter and reduces race and racism to the tensions inherent in any mother-daughter relationship, something that Sirk's later version does not do.

In Sirk's 1959 film, Lana Turner plays Lora Meredith, an aspiring actress and white single mother who meets black single mother Annie Johnson (Juanita Moore) on the beach one afternoon after Lora loses her daughter Susie (Terry Burnham/Sandra Dee).[10] Annie implores Lora to take her in as her maid, and though at first Lora refuses because she can't pay, Annie ends up taking care of the house, the cooking, the kids, and Lora. As Lora's acting career takes off, Annie bears more of the burden of raising the kids, keeping a large house, and catering parties because she refuses to accept hired help. Lora doesn't insist that Annie stop working or accept help; in fact, as the film progresses, Annie complains of being tired and gets sicker and sicker, but Lora continues to ask her to host parties and take care of her and her famous guests. Like Delilah in Dahl's version, Annie becomes more segregated as Lora becomes more successful; she is clearly part of Lora's glamorous new upper-class world only as the maid in uniform serving the guests. At one point, her daughter Sara Jane (Susan Kohner) mimics the stereotypical black servant when Annie asks her to serve hors d'oeuvres. In another scene, after Annie finds Sara Jane working in a nightclub and passing for white, a coworker asks if Annie is her mammy and Sara Jane tells her that she has had a mammy all her life.

Sara Jane is light skinned and, to the consternation of her mother, wants nothing more than to pass as white. As Sara Jane repeatedly passes as white and then is exposed by her black mother, both her mother and "Miss Lora" continually tell her not to lie about what she is or she will be hurt. The discrimination that Sara Jane suffers as she is exposed as black is never attributed to racism but rather to her own deception and misplaced ambition. Sara Jane is the only critical voice in the film. She insists that she is as white as Susie and that she should not have to sleep in the back room or enter through back doors, that she should not have to date the sons of servants and chauffeurs, that she wants more for her life. Her mother also wants more for her daughter but reminds Sara Jane that she was born for pain and that she must accept her fate because "God made her black for a reason." The film sends the clear message that there are natural divisions between blacks and whites that must be maintained, and fighting the racial hierarchy can only lead to pain and self-imposed suffering.

Repeating the implicit message of *Pinky*, *Imitation of Life* teaches us that the difference between blacks and whites is not skin color, since visually white women are really black; rather, the difference between blacks and whites is something more natural, something ordained by

God, that it is painful to fight, something natural that is associated with a dark maternal legacy. Indeed, it seems that race has nothing to do with one's skin color but rather is a result of one's maternal origin. The natural racialized, and therefore bad, mother stands on the other side of the boundary of proper white society. The mother has been abjected for the sake of proper identity. She is the repressed that threatens to return, bringing with her all of the ambiguities of sexual, racial, and individual identity. By refusing to identify with the abjected mother, the daughter is betraying her maternal genealogy for the sake of her own success.

Although these films suggest that betraying the mother is necessary for success, at the same time they insist that the law of nature or God requires that daughters be identified with, or by, their mothers. These black mothers—Dicey Johnson, Delilah, Annie—sacrifice themselves for their daughters, but they also sacrifice their daughters to the law of racial segregation. These mothers enforce the "natural law" of racial segregation. Daughters are caught between the rock of racialized maternity and the hard place of racist culture.

Unlike the white authority figures in other problem films, men such as Uncle John in *Intruder in the Dust* or the doctor in *Home of the Brave*, these black mothers present a more complicated and problematic superego enforcing the laws of race and race relations. The position as superego or authority figure is paradoxical in these black mothers. They insist that their daughters respect the civil, social, and psychic laws of racial segregation and by so doing bring their daughters down. By insisting that their daughters identify with their own abjection, these mothers sacrifice their daughters to a law of pain. Their attempts to pull their daughters back into their proper place in society signify the mothers' own resignation as to their proper place as second-class citizens. Yet at the same time that they insist their daughters respect the boundaries of black and white and stay in their proper place, they also want more for their daughters. Anything more, however, requires matricide on the part of the daughters.

Policing the borders of the racial divide, these mothers are also policing themselves. Whereas the white male authority figures of the other "problem" films invest in the extremes of racial difference or racial sameness to contain the threat of abjection and ambiguity and expel it from their own identity, these black mothers represent the abject at the same time that they police the boundaries of clean and proper identity that their own existence threatens. These black mothers in particular, those who give birth to whiteness, threaten proper boundaries between black and white.

Even more than their white male counterparts, then, the mothers' authority to enforce the laws of race and race relations is compromised. They enforce the law of racial segregation, and yet as blacks, women, and mothers, they do not have the authority to enforce the law. More-over, enforcing the law, a law based on the abjection of blacks, women, and mothers, enforces their own abjection and exclusion from the social order. In this way, they are bound to enforce their own matricide: either their daughters identify with them and thereby identify with what is abject and excluded, or their daughters refuse to identify with them and thereby abject and exclude them. These mothers' compromised and paradoxical position puts their daughters in a bind: either identify with the abject mother and suffer death yourself, or resort to matricide.

Taking this presumption to its limit, *Imitation of Life* suggests that Sara Jane's refusal to accept her fate causes her mother's death. At her funeral, the distraught Sara Jane throws herself at her mother's coffin, crying, "I killed my mother." Sara Jane's ambitions to change her sta-tion in life are presented as the cause of her own pain as well as her mother's death. Lora Meredith, on the other hand, also wants to change her station in life. She is ambitious and eventually succeeds. Whereas Lora's ambition pays off, Sara Jane's ambition is deadly. Like Lora, Sara Jane aspires to the stage, but unlike Lora (and Susie), always dressed in light colors and portrayed as morally pure, Sara Jane dresses in bright colors, especially orange, and revealing outfits. Whereas Lora is glam-orous, Sara Jane is sexual. Whereas Lora starts in the theater and refuses to sleep her way to the top, Sara Jane starts dancing in a bar and a chorus line where she flaunts her sexuality. Unlike the childlike and pure Susie, Sara Jane represents voluptuous femininity made more danger-ous by her racial ambiguity.[11]

More glamorous than sexual, Lora can be ambitious and have it all thanks to the hard work of her black maid Annie, who takes care of Lora and her family as she climbs to stardom.[12] Still, she is portrayed as a bad mother because of her devotion to her career and her ambition. From her deathbed, Annie tells Lora that Susie doesn't confide in her because she is never around. Susie laments that she has everything except her mother's love. And Lora admits that she is ambitious and this is what made her a bad mother. Annie tries to console Lora by telling her that they both tried to be good mothers but in spite of their efforts they have failed—Lora because she has a career, and Annie simply because she is black. Underlying this sentiment is the presumption that, in itself, being black makes a woman a bad mother. Racialized maternity produces the greatest anxiety in films like *Pinky* or *Imitation of Life*, where maternal genealogy is not only the origin but also the mark of racial difference that at once guarantees and threatens proper racial identity.

Film noir also presents us with racialized maternity and racialized feminine sexuality that make for the powerful and anxious origin of the dark, mysterious mood of noir. As we show in the chapters that follow, condensations and displacements of race, sex, and maternity are often the motor behind the compelling style and investigative narrative structure of noir. For example, in our interpretation of *The Lady from Shanghai* we develop the connection between voice, race, and sex to reveal the film's ambivalence about the sexual power of the racialized femme fatale Elsa Bannister. Or in our analysis of *Murder, My Sweet*, we argue that the most powerful representative of evil in the film is actually the absent maternal sex associated with the missing jade necklace. The connection between maternal sex and Chinese jade allows the already dangerous maternal sex to take on more mystery and fascination and becomes more threatening through the film's Orientalism.

The association between maternity and race takes a strange turn in *The Secret beyond the Door*. We argue that ultimately the secret beyond the door is the secret of uncanny maternal sexuality and maternal desire outside the purview of the male gaze. In this film, desire and instinct become associated with Mexico as the uncanny double of a more civilized yet inhibited New York. Here again the mixture of ethnicity and maternal sexuality make for a deadly brew. In our reading of Hitchcock's *Vertigo*, we interpret the role of femininity and maternal sexuality in terms of melancholy. The latent threat of the abject mother in film noir becomes the explicit threat of an identification with a depressed and mad mother, Carlotta. The return of the repressed mother, and Scottie, the detective's (and audience's) identification with her, throws the spectator into the position of the melancholic unable to mourn or lose this maternal sex that threatens madness. Here again the threat of maternal sexuality is associated with Carlotta's dangerous ethnicity.

Our analysis of Welles's *Touch of Evil* describes how the maternal body is sacrificed for the purposes of creating a place of racial equality. This purported equality entails not only a matricide but also the creation of a borderland that covers over the fear of "lost boundaries" and racial and sexual ambiguities. Ultimately, however, the ambivalent spirit of this racially inflected matricide opens surprising and uncanny spaces of resistance in the film. We also find the matricidal impulse in neo-noir *Devil in a Blue Dress*, where Daphne, like Pinky, Paola, or Sara Jane, is forced to choose between her racial maternal origin or passing and succeeding in the white world.

In various ways at the margins of film noir, race, sex, and maternity appear in condensed and displaced forms. Often the most telling elements of noir threaten from the margins and are associated with maternity, mothers, or an absent mother. Significantly, many of these threatening mothers are inflected with race in a way that makes them anxious origins. The evil of our femmes fatales can be traced back to their suspicious maternal origins, origins that represent the source of both their moral ambiguity and their racial ambiguity. Both their moral "darkness" and their repressed racial blackness are associated with a questionable maternal origin. Given Kristeva's hypothesis that maternity is the most threatening and repressed site of ambiguity and therefore of abjection, it is not surprising that the lost boundaries of racial identities would be displaced onto maternal figures (and vice versa) who threaten from the margins of noir.

CHAPTER 2

Poisonous Jewels in
Murder, My Sweet

Wily powers, "baleful schemers" from whom rightful beneficiaries
must protect themselves.... an asymmetrical, irrational, wily,
uncontrollable power ... the feminine, becomes synonymous with
a radical evil that is to be suppressed.

—Julia Kristeva, *Powers of Horror*

Femininity and Evil

Director Edward Dmytryk's *Murder, My Sweet* (1944) gives us a classic
femme fatale, Mrs. Helen Grayle, aka Velma Valento (Claire Trevor),
who represents pure evil. As her stepdaughter Ann Grayle (Anne
Shirley) proclaims after her father fatally shoots Helen, "She is evil,
all evil. What difference can it possibly make who killed her?" Detective Philip Marlowe compares Helen to a spreading cancer. The role of
femininity in the film is complicated by the fact that the most prominent "bad guys" are feminized, and in a strange twist of Chandler's novel
on which the film is based, the femme fatale is not only a classic bombshell spider woman but also an evil stepmother. In this film, the good-
girl/bad-girl split typical of film noir is a screen for a sexual power even
more deadly than the femme fatale, the *mère fatale*. Behind the good-
girl/bad-girl split (Ann/Helen) there is a femininity more dangerous,
since it belongs to men, and there is a sexuality more dangerous, since
it evokes the maternal sex.

   Murder, My Sweet opens with a shot from the ceiling down a light
cord to a table where a blindfolded Philip Marlowe (Dick Powell) is
being questioned by a group of detectives. As Marlowe begins to tell
the story of his involvement with several murders, the camera takes
us out the window to the city, while Marlowe's voice-over explains a

flashback to his office late one night. Marlowe is trying to cook up a date with a woman over the phone when Moose Malloy (Mike Mazurki) appears and asks him to find his missing girlfriend, Velma Valento. Marlowe agrees to the job because he needs the money. Shortly after his initial investigations into the whereabouts of the missing girlfriend, Marlowe gets a visit from Lindsay Marriott (Douglas Walton), who wants to hire Marlowe to help him retrieve some stolen jewels. In the attempt to buy back the jewels, Marriott is killed, and Marlowe is knocked unconscious. The next day, Marlowe gets a visit from Ann Grayle posing as a newspaper reporter inquiring into the murder of Marriott and the missing jade. On to Miss Grayle's ruse, Marlowe forces her to take him home to meet her father and his wife, Helen. There Marlowe finds out that Helen Grayle had a very expensive jade necklace stolen and that Marriott was hired to get it back. Helen hires Marlowe to find her necklace.

Mrs. Grayle's therapist, Jules Amthor (Otto Kruger), also wants the necklace and kidnaps and drugs Marlowe to find out its whereabouts. In the course of his investigation, Helen tries to enlist Marlowe in a plan to kill Amthor because he is blackmailing her to get the necklace. Marlowe goes along with the plan because he has a plan of his own. On the night that he is to kill Amthor at Mrs. Grayle's beach house, Marlowe brings Moose Malloy along with him. Ann and her father, Mr. Grayle, also show up at the beach house. Mr. Grayle shoots Helen for being unfaithful to him. Moose, who has been waiting outside for Marlowe's signal, enters the beach house when he hears shots to discover that Marlowe has found his girlfriend Velma and that she has been shot. At this point, we find out that Helen Grayle is Velma Valento. To avenge her death, Moose shoots Mr. Grayle. Marlowe gets caught in the cross fire, and his eyes are burned by gunpowder. In the final scene, the film returns to the police station where Marlowe is being interrogated. Satisfied with his story, the police chief lets him go. Ann Grayle, who has been at the station all along listening to his story, follows him into a taxi, and the film ends with them kissing in the cab.

Murder, My Sweet presents us with a classic film noir femme fatale and a version of the good-girl/bad-girl split typical of the genre. Helen Grayle is sexually powerful and therefore all evil, whereas her step-daughter Ann Grayle appears to be the desexualized good girl and the detective's real love object. Helen is manipulative and self-serving and will do anything for money and class standing. She is not emotionally attached to any of the other characters. She is sexually powerful and uses sex to seduce men and get what she wants. She is the object of obsessive desire: Moose Malloy will do anything to get her back; he is so obsessed with her that he ogles her and calls her "cute as lace pants" even after she is dead; Mr. Grayle is willing to shoot her rather than lose her; and Ann Grayle is as obsessive about Helen's affairs as her father is. Helen has a questionable, hidden past that involves committing a crime and manipulating Moose to take the rap. She has killed at least one man, Lindsay Marriott, and she continually lies to the detective and attempts to seduce him in order to use him in her scheme.

On closer examination, Ann Grayle, like the femme fatale, is also a morally ambiguous character. Although she is desexualized in the narrative when various characters call her a "kid" and a "strange child," she is sexualized visually when she is shown wearing fitted suits, and high heels, and painted nails. She is sexualized in the narrative by Marlowe when he repeatedly refers to her "cute figure," which the camera also repeatedly shows us. Moreover, Ann is not all good. She is deceptive, a snoop and an eavesdropper. She doesn't always tell the truth, and like Helen, she isn't always what she seems. When the detective Marlowe (and the audience) first meets her, she is pretending to be a newspaper reporter. She wants to protect her father—she tells Marlowe that she is "fond of her father, more than fond," but he wouldn't understand that because it doesn't have anything to do with money—and yet she too has an obsessive relation to Helen. She hates any man that comes near Helen. She is jealous of Helen, not just of Helen's relation to men but of their relation to Helen. And in the end, after her father has been killed, she doesn't mourn him, suggesting her ambivalence toward him; instead she tries to deceive Marlowe by taking the place of the police-man escorting him home.

What is more interesting than the film's representation of femininity in its women characters is the feminization of the male characters throughout the film. The feminization of the evil characters or "bad guys" suggests that the feminine itself is evil and threatening, especially when it appears where it does not belong. This is an example of what Kristeva calls the "asymmetrical, irrational, wily, uncontrollable power" of femininity, which disturbs the proper patriarchal order of authority; it is a power that appears where it does not belong. But even more threatening is feminine power in men because it challenges the very boundary between men and women, masculine and feminine, that supports patriarchal authority. The appearance of femininity in men calls into question the borders of identity and recalls repressed abjection and ambiguity out of which identity is born. The extraordinary threat from the feminine men of *Murder, My Sweet* is the result of their ambiguous gender. With these characters, the difference between feminine and masculine threatens to collapse. The boundaries between feminine and masculine, between women and men, become lost. And, these lost boundaries conjure the threat of abjection that comes with primal ambiguity.[1]

The Threat of Femininity in Men

The two main villains in *Murder, My Sweet*, Lindsay Marriott and his boss Jules Amthor, are both feminized characters. First, both Lynn and Jules have feminine names. They are both described as "pretty boys" and are both associated with flowers. Lynn is often identified by the smell of his rosewater perfume, and Jules always wears a carnation. Unlike the macho police detectives, Lynn and Jules do not sport hats and plain dark suits. Rather, Lynn wears a light-colored coat and a scarf that he constantly adjusts, and Jules wears a fitted striped suit. Unlike the macho police who smoke filterless cigarettes out of crumbled packs, Jules Amthor smokes his cigarette in a long cigarette holder more typically used by women in early Hollywood films. Jules's apartment is full of fancy, frilly decorations. And Marlowe comments on the way that Lynn's interest in clothes and jewels comes easy, but he isn't "the whole works."

In *Farewell, My Lovely*, the Raymond Chandler novel on which the

film is based, Marlowe describes Amthor in loving terms, the most en-
dearing in the book. Even his "sweet" remarks about Ann Riordan
are usually tinged with sarcasm. But the description of Amthor is full of
awe and appreciation. He calls Amthor's hands "the most beautiful
hands I have ever seen" (Chandler 1976, 125). He compares his hair to
"silk gauze" (125), his face to "an angel's wing" (126), and says that his
skin is "fresh as a rose petal" (125). Even when Amthor's thugs are beating him, Marlowe remarks on the beauty of Amthor's smile (131) and
calls him a "thin beautiful devil" (132). Marlowe is powerless against
Amthor's beauty.

Significantly, in *Murder, My Sweet*, whereas Marlowe isn't seduced
by the femme fatale, he is duped by the villains because they seem as
harmless as women and yet their femininity is more powerful because
they aren't women. The blindfolded Marlowe is blind to the threat
and power of these feminine men. Marlowe claims that he doesn't feel
threatened by Lynn or Jules. When Lindsay Marriott threatens to punch
Marlowe on the nose, parodying Marriott's aristocratic tone, Marlowe
responds, "I tremble at the thought of such violence." And when he first
meets Jules Amthor, Marlowe remarks, "You look harmless to me." Yet
both times that Marlowe is knocked unconscious, it is because of these
supposedly harmless feminine men. In the film's attempt to do away
with the threat of feminine evil, like the femme fatale, these feminine
men end up dead.

In the 1975 film version of *Farewell, My Lovely*, and remake of
Murder, My Sweet, the character of Amthor is transformed from the
beautiful, effeminate Jules of Chandler's novel and *Murder* into a mean,
butch madame who runs the local cathouse. Inverted, Amthor (Kate
Murtagh) becomes a masculine woman instead of a feminine man and is
even more abusive to Marlowe. This complex, if short-lived, character
is at once a matronly mother figure for the prostitutes in her care and
a strong, threatening lesbian figure. Full of maternal protectiveness and
some deeper jealousy, she goes ballistic when she catches her favorite
childlike prostitute (Noelle North) with her boyfriend Jonnie (Sylvester
Stallone). Jonnie shoots Amthor to defend his girl when Amthor attacks

her in a jealous rage. Like the feminine men in the novel and *Murder*, the masculine mother in the 1975 film calls into question the borders of sexual and individual identity. She threatens the borders of proper gender identification. In the end, like the threatening feminine man, the threatening masculine mother/woman is killed.

In *Murder, My Sweet*, Marlowe himself is identified with feminine characters and is thereby made morally ambiguous. For example, in the final scene, wearing a detective-style trench coat, Helen identifies herself with Marlowe. She says that they are both just a couple of mugs with fancy names. On the surface, it seems that they both will do anything for money—police chief Randall calls Marlowe a slot machine. In the end, however, they both want more than money; Helen wants social standing, and Marlowe wants to solve his case and get the girl. Unlike Helen, however, Marlowe, is "blind" to what is really going on and plows ahead anyway, accepting his fate. Helen, on the other hand, tries to escape her fate by manipulating others from behind the scenes; she wants to overcome her past and her station in life to become a rich aristocrat with "the name of a Duchess." Paradoxically, Marlowe resigns himself to his castrated fate—repeatedly insisting that he doesn't know, that he isn't smart—while Helen tries to wield a phallic power (and a gun) that isn't rightfully hers. We could say that if man is emasculated, then woman is to blame for trying to usurp his phallic power. In addition, while Helen insists on upward mobility, in spite of his professed ambitions, Marlowe seems to resign himself to being poor. In the end, Helen is punished for class passing.

Marlowe is also identified with Ann in that both are doing detective work to find out the truth about Helen. Unlike Marlowe, however, Ann is a spy, not a hard-boiled detective. She sneaks around in the shadows and listens behind doors, whereas Marlowe (as he tells Amthor), is used to coming in the front door "big as life." She tries to disguise herself, whereas Marlowe is up front in his search for truth. She uses her ears, whereas Marlowe uses his nose and his stomach. Like a bloodhound, he sniffs out the truth. He is a blindfolded private eye—a private eye that can't see but instead smells the truth. In the film, he is constantly shown sniffing the air or smelling a cigarette. When he is driving the car for Marriott, he tells us in voice-over that he knows they are being watched because he feels it in his stomach. As he admits to police chief Randall, "sometimes I'm not smart, but it's all I know." The hard-boiled detective uses his gut instincts and not his reason to "solve the case." If Marlowe is the hard-boiled detective, a "tough guy," as he says, then Ann is a wily feminine spy who resorts to subterfuge and deception to "solve the case."

Marlowe is not only identified with the two women in the film but also identified with both the criminals and the police. He tells Helen that he once worked at the district attorney's office but was fired for "talking back." Like Moose, Marlowe has spent some time in "the caboose." And he warns Marriott that the people he is supposed to meet to buy back the jewels might not like him showing up as "twins." Like most other hard-boiled film noir detectives, *Murder*'s Marlowe is an ambiguous character caught between the law and crime, between good and evil, and in this case between masculine law and feminine evil and deception. When Marlowe shows up at Ann's apartment after he has been kidnapped and drugged by Amthor, she tells him, "You don't even know what side you're on," and he replies, "I don't even know who's playing."

In the context of discussing the threat of femininity posed by both the male and female characters in *Murder, My Sweet*, it is interesting to note that until his role as Marlowe in *Murder*, Dick Powell was known as a crooner in musicals. Powell desperately wanted to escape from the feminine roles that he played in musicals to play a tough-guy role. He lobbied unsuccessfully to get the leading role in *Double Indemnity*. Powell was chosen for *Murder* only because he insisted that he would not star in another musical until the studio gave him a tough-guy role. *Murder*'s director Edward Dmytryk says that studio executives were worried that Powell was too feminine for the part of Marlowe until they saw that Powell was taller and "more masculine" than he appeared in the feminine makeup and costumes of his musical roles. For fear that audiences would associate Chandler's original title *Farewell, My Lovely* with a musical because it starred Powell, they changed the name of the film to *Murder, My Sweet*. To suggest his transformation from effeminate crooner to tough guy, the movie posters read "Meet the New Dick Powell." Because the popularity of musicals was dying out, Powell's perceived femininity was a real threat to his career. And after *Murder*, he never starred in another musical.

With the bisexual Marlowe moving between femininity and masculinity, and the feminine villains, *Murder, My Sweet* challenges stereotypical notions of masculinity. On the one hand, positive images of masculinity like Marlowe or Moose Malloy are compromised by femininity, homoeroticism, and excessive violence. On the other hand, the film presents images of men who are "feminine and deviant" and challenge stereotypes of normal masculinity.[2] In his study of representations of masculinity in film noir, Frank Krutnik suggests that "male masochism can be seen as manifesting a desire to escape from the regimentation of masculine (cultural) identity effected through the Oedipus complex. The masochist seeks to overthrow the authority of paternal law and the determinacy of castration.... Indeed, the 'tough' thrillers continually institute a discrepancy between, on the one hand, the licit possibilities of masculine identity and desire required by the patriarchal cultural order, and on the other hand, the psychosexual make-up of the male subject-hero" (1991, 85). The feminine "make-up" of film noir heroes and villains not only displays an anxiety over masculine identity and threats to it from women and femininity but also challenges the very stereotypes of masculinity and normality. At the margins of masculinity, film noir liberates alternative types of men and masculinity at the same time that it constructs these alternatives as dangerous or threatening. Just as the femme fatale both signals and contains the power, especially sexual power, of women, so film noir's feminine men both signal and contain the power of alternative types of masculinity.

In the film, Marlowe knows how to protect himself from femininity in women, but he is a sucker for femininity in men. Femininity in men is even more dangerous than femininity in women. The association between femininity and danger or evil displays an anxiety not only about women's potency but also about men's impotency. Insofar as femininity and masculinity are seen as opposites, not only is femininity a threat to masculinity, but ambiguity itself is a threat to the two poles that keep identity fixed. It is not just that masculine identity is in danger when subject to the evils of femininity because of castration threats. More than this, femininity in men threatens to undermine the very boundaries and borders of identity that keep it stable and fixed. Even greater than femininity's threat to masculinity is the threat of ambiguity to identity itself. It is not so much that femininity threatens to contaminate masculinity with its evil but rather that gender ambiguity threatens the boundaries of proper identity itself.

Framing Homosexual Desire

In addition to the threat posed by femininity and gender ambiguity in *Murder*, especially in terms of its male characters, the film is driven by an unconscious homoerotic desire, primarily between the male characters, but also between Ann and Helen. In the showdown between the women at the beach house, Ann rants that she hates men, all men, especially those men obsessed with Helen. She also says that she hates their women, "especially the big-league blondes, all moonlight and bubble bath." She continues to describe Helen using sensual metaphors until Helen laughs, saying, "Your slip is showing, dear." With this tongue-in-cheek maternal line, Helen dismisses Ann as a "strange child." She puts Ann in her place, and Ann storms out. Helen's remark also signals that Ann has made a slip, a Freudian slip, perhaps, in protesting too much over Helen's male lovers and displaying so much passion in her description of Helen's charm and sensuality. Ann is as obsessed with Helen as any of the male characters. While Moose can't seem to get close to Helen/Velma, and Helen's husband continually tells us that he is a helpless, pathetic old man who doesn't even try to keep up with Helen, Ann is on Helen's tail from beginning to end.

More explicit, and one of the main sources of humor and pleasure in the film, is the homoerotic desire between men. Both Marlowe and the audience (set up to identify with him) take pleasure in a series of one-liners that suggest homosexual desire between men. In the first scene, Marlowe calls Randall "darling." He calls Moose "a cute little fella." He asks Marriott if he wants him to go along and hold his hand. He calls Marriott "a pretty boy" and asks Helen if Amthor is a "bad boy." When Moose wants Marlowe to leave the Coconut Beach Club, he tells him to "ditch the dame" because he wants him to "meet a guy"; when Marlowe complains that Moose is ruining his love life, Moose

Marlowe (Dick Powell) and Moose (Mike Mazurki) in *Murder, My Sweet*.

takes his hand, and they hold hands for the rest of the scene. At one point, Marlowe asks Moose if he is "making love" to him. At another point, he asks Moose to stop "dancing" with him. And in others, he tells Moose to "keep his shirt on" and that "they were kidding the pants off you, son." He tells Ann that Helen fixed him up on a "blind date" with Amthor, who showed him a "real cute time" for three days. When he finds Amthor dead, in voice-over he says that Amthor had been snapped "like a pretty girl snaps a celery"—in this case, Moose is the pretty girl, and Amthor is the celery. In the end, Marlowe refuses the jade necklace, saying that he tried it on and it was wrong for his complexion. The biggest laugh, and one of the most pleasurable moments in the film, comes in the final scene in the cab when Marlowe (knowing that Ann is posing as the policeman Nulty) says, "Nulty, I haven't kissed anybody in a long time. Do you mind if I kiss you, Nulty?"

Throughout the film, Marlowe's relationship to the police chief Randall (Donald Douglas) is intimate. Their banter is reminiscent of

Amthor (Otto Kruger), Moose, and Marlowe in *Murder, My Sweet.*

screwball romantic comedies of the same period in which sexual tension between men and women was created through argumentative but flirtatious dialogue with which both parties pretend to dislike the other. Marlowe and Randall claim to hate each other, but in almost every scene together, they are intimately sharing cigarettes. In the scene in Ann's apartment, the exchange of cigarettes is most obviously flirtatious when Marlowe first grabs Randall's hand and then his package of cigarettes; Marlowe then removes a cigarette from the pack and offers it to Randall, who takes it and starts to light it when Marlowe takes his hand again and lights his own cigarette by holding Randall's match and Randall's hand up to his mouth. Within this context, the phallic nature of the cigarette becomes more significant as these men share and grab each other's cigarettes. Marlowe's flirtation with the police culminates in the final scene when Marlowe asks the policeman Nulty if he can kiss him.

Although the homosexual undercurrent of the film is contained and framed within the narrative structure "tough-guy-detective-gets-the-good-girl-in-the-end," homoerotic *jouissance* is the greatest source of pleasure for the audience. When the blindfolded Marlowe asks Nulty to kiss him in the cab, the film reaches its climax. Just as the image of the femme fatale overpowers the narrative within which she is killed at the end,[3] the homoerotic pleasure in the film's narrative and its images break out of its heterosexual frame. While the presentation of the femme fatale both articulates and attempts to control the wily power of femininity, especially feminine sexuality, the presentation of homosexual desire between men both taps into homoerotic *jouissance* and attempts to make a joke out of it. Like Marlowe, *Murder, My Sweet* is blindfolded when it comes to its own homosexual desire. If feminine sexuality and homosexuality challenge the authority of patriarchy—the authority of men over women—then *Murder* attempts to reinscribe them both within the controlling confines of patriarchy by killing off all evil femininity in both men and women and by making homosexuality into a joke. As we see in the film, the repressed is bound to return, and the return of the repressed is not only threatening but also pleasurable.

The Mother's Missing Jewels

Perhaps the most threatening, and therefore the most repressed, figures in the film are the ones that we never see, the ones that go missing, the jade necklace and the mother. The first time that we hear of the missing jewels is when Marriott hires Marlowe to help him "buy back the jewels." Marriott objects when Marlowe suggests that he is buying back the jewels for a "lady friend." The first time that we hear that the missing jewels are made of jade is when Ann Grayle poses as a newspaper reporter and goes to ask Marlowe if they recovered "the jade" when Marriott was killed. After Marlowe grabs her purse (what would Freud say about that?) and finds out her true identity, Ann tells Marlowe that the jade belongs to her father. Marlowe says that he thought that it belonged to a woman, and Ann tells him that her "father happens to be married." Marlowe says, "Oh yes, of course he would be. . . . It was your mother, then, who was wearing it the night of the holdup?" assuming that where there is a father and a daughter, there must also be a mother. Ann passionately objects, "She is not my mother!" It isn't until Marlowe visits Mr. and Mrs. Grayle at home that we learn that "the jewels," now "the jade," are an "irreplaceable" necklace of sixty beads of indeterminate value, possibly worth over $100,000.

The jade can be seen as a metaphor for the mother. The jade and the mother are not only introduced in the same scene but also both introduced as missing. They are both surrounded by mystery: what is so important about these missing jewels, and who and where is the mother? The history of both the mother and the jewels is a mystery, and although as the film progresses we find out more about the jewels, the mother remains a mystery. While in the end we find out that the jewels, like Velma, were never really missing, the mother is still absent from the film. Moreover, there is a suggestion that the other woman (Helen/Velma), who is most certainly not the mother, does not rightfully own the jade or the place of mother. In fact, with her first line in the film, Helen tells Marlowe that she was "reckless" to wear the jade in public and that she "never should have worn it out." After all, as she says, the jade—like the mother—is "irreplaceable." It is notable that in Chandler's novel *Farewell, My Lovely*, the character of Ann is not Helen's stepdaughter. There is no relation between Mrs. Grayle and Ann. In the novel, Ann Riordan just happens onto the scene of Marriott's death and gives Marlowe a lift. She is nosy and jealous of Helen, but she is not a "kid" or a "strange child," Mrs. Grayle is not a mother, step- or otherwise, and Marlowe does not assume that the missing jewels belong to the mother.

The mystery of the film, like the novel, is driven by Helen's attempts to conceal that she is an impostor, a "mug," who has no right to the name or the place of a "duchess." The jade necklace is a red herring that Helen uses as bait to lure the men in the film, Marriott, Amthor, and Marlowe. Even Ann and Mr. Grayle get caught up in looking for the missing jade. This search for the jade is supposed to throw them off the track of the real search, the search that will reveal Helen's true identity as the cheap mug, Velma Valento. Just as the jewels are not really missing—Helen has them all along—Velma has been right in front of our eyes the whole time, but like Marlowe, we are effectively blindfolded. In the final scene, Helen hands Marlowe a box containing the necklace, which we never see. Helen plans to use the necklace to lure Amthor (who is already dead at this point) to the beach house to kill him. She tells Marlowe that she lied about the necklace because she wasn't going to let Amthor get it. Moreover, she says that she still isn't going to let him get it. With great delight she says, "I'm just going to let him look at it.... and then he'll start to quibble." She delights in thinking about Amthor's reaction to just looking at the jade; she knows how to use her jade to get power over men.

The jade has a special power that men seek. Mr. Grayle explains that jade "isn't sufficiently known or appreciated in this country," but "the great rulers of the East treat it with a reverence accorded to no other stone." They spend years looking for a single piece. Fei Tsui jade is "extremely valuable," and as a "collector," he is "extremely interested." He tells Marlowe that it is difficult to fix the value of the necklace. Later, Helen tells Marlowe that she and Marriott guessed that the jewel thieves "didn't know the real value" of the jade. Jade, specifically this jewel from the East, is irreplaceable; it is of mysterious value and holds a power over the great rulers of the East who revere it and over the collectors of the West who buy it. Mr. Grayle is "anxious to locate the necklace without any publicity," and Amthor "wants the jade," because the one who possesses it possesses its mysterious powers. As we find out, Helen possesses the jade all along. Like the jade, she too has mysterious powers over men, powers that Ann describes as dewy moonlight and bubble bath. Like the jade, Helen is of questionable origins, she is dangerous and deadly. Men will die for her.

What is it about Helen Grayle that makes her so threatening, so deadly? Why must she die at the end of the film? Like other femmes fatales, her danger is associated with her sexuality. She uses her sexuality to manipulate men to get what she wants. And what she wants is to take a social position other than the one that she was given by fate. She wants to usurp the position of the duchess, and the "rightful beneficiaries" to wealth; she wants to become the rich aristocrat that Jules Amthor has trained her to imitate (he treated her for a speech problem). Amthor teaches her how to pass as an aristocrat, for which she dies in the end. Jules shows her how to use her jewels to take the place of the duchess. Treating her "centers of speech," Jules uses Helen like a jewel with which to lure her wealthy husband and then blackmail her. Jules is the real femme fatale, the poisonous jewels, the quack cum aristocrat who blackmails his female patients and manipulates men. He is a psychological trickster, Marlowe's "foxy grandpa."

In spite of what she learns from Amthor, Helen's powerful sexuality is in excess of the place that she tries to occupy, the place of the respected wife, mother, and queen. Underneath her jewels, she is Velma Valento, the cheap showgirl, "cute as lace pants," who again becomes associated with the East in the scene in the Coconut Beach Club where Moose ogles the Asian dancer, also "cute as lace pants." Helen must die because she tries to occupy a position to which she is not the rightful beneficiary; she tries to take the place of the mother and possess the jewels. Her excess sexuality, however, gives her away. After all, the mother's jewels are supposed to be missing, but it turns out that she has them all along. The mother's missing jewels remain hidden throughout the film even as they motivate the action. The mother's jewels, or the mother's sex, is missing, and yet it is their absence that gives them power over men. As Freud's theories suggest, the maternal sex threatens castration at the same time that it promises an uncanny return to the first home, the womb. It both threatens castration and at the same time reassures men that they aren't castrated—"She doesn't have it, but I do."

Feminine sexuality in the place of the mother is the true threat for this film. Maternal sexuality is threatening and mysterious. It is irresistible and deadly. The mother's sex is the poisonous jewel that both fascinates and terrifies the men in the film. Marlowe wants the jade because, as he tells Ann, he is "a small businessman in a messy business" and wants "to follow through on a sale"; but when he can't "finish the job," he won't take the jade. In other words, for Marlowe, getting the

Moose and Marlowe at the Coconut Beach Club.

jade is a test of his manhood—can he finish the job? Mr. Grayle wants the jade because he is an old man and having it makes him feel potent. He tells Marlowe that his only two interests in life are his jade and his "beautiful, desirable" wife (throwing his daughter in as an afterthought as if he didn't remember where she came from). Possessing the jade/Helen ensures his manliness by allowing him to pretend that he too is desired by Helen. But more than anyone else, Jules Amthor passionately wants the jade. He will stop at nothing to get it. He uses "psychological tricks" and injections of truth serum; like Helen, he manipulates Moose to do his bidding. Amthor identifies himself as a "quack" in a very sensitive profession, ahead of his time in psychological treatment. He uses the "tricks" of psychology to try to possess the jade for himself. Whereas Marlowe and Mr. Grayle want the jade/maternal sex to prove their manhood in a classic Oedipal situation, Jules's (note the name) relation to the jewels is as much an identification as an incestuous desire. He wants the jewels so that he can wield the power of the maternal sex, Helen's power to manipulate men.

It is significant that the jewels and jade in question take the form of a necklace, a necklace that in fact is never worn and cannot be worn. This jade necklace represents the maternal jewel, and as such it is reckless to display it in public; that never should be done. Maternal sexuality should not be displayed in public. This is why even Mr. Grayle does not want any publicity. The public display of maternal sexuality is threatening for men and reckless for women. Helen is asking for trouble if she wears the necklace. On the one hand, the necklace is threatening to men because it represents the power of repressed maternal/feminine sexuality; on the other hand, the necklace is threatening to women because it represents the restrictive chain of patriarchal control over maternal/feminine sexuality. Helen cannot wear the necklace and keep her power. She must possess the necklace but not wear it. As soon as she wears it, she displays what should not be seen: maternal/feminine sexuality. Paradoxically, at the same time, by wearing it, she displays her lack of control over it insofar as she is wearing the patriarchal chain around her neck. Certainly Mr. Grayle hopes and expects to use the necklace to keep Helen. That is why at the end of the film he says that it is "ironic" that he is losing Helen because of the necklace. When Helen describes the holdup, she says that the robbers gave her back one of her rings, a rather nice one, and shows Marlowe a giant stone on her left hand. This allusion to a wedding ring, returned to the femme fatale rather than stolen from her, again suggests patriarchal control over, and ownership of, her sexuality.

What then is the function and position of the maternal sex in *Murder, My Sweet*? In *Powers of Horror*, Kristeva associates the suppressed feminine with the maternal sex. Ultimately, what Kristeva calls the "abject" always comes back to the maternal body, specifically the maternal sex. As she describes it, the abject is what calls into question borders, most particularly borders of the self. In terms of personal development, the maternal body becomes abject in the infant's attempt to separate itself from it. For the infant, particularly the male, the mother's body becomes both fascinating (and a possible erotic object) and terrifying (insofar as an identification with it threatens the breakdown of borders). It makes sense, then, given Kristeva's analysis, that the moral, sexual, and gender ambiguity of *Murder, My Sweet* would recall the threat of maternal abjection with its blurred borders and threat to identity. In order for the male child to shore up his identity, particularly his identity as masculine, he must abject the maternal body. The maternal sex, from which the infant was born, becomes the fascinating and horrifying object of its repressed incestuous desires.

The missing, mysterious, fascinating yet deadly jade/mother in *Murder, My Sweet* can be read as the return of a repressed incestuous desire that both terrifies and excites. That the necklace is deadly is made explicit by Mr. Grayle at the end of the film when he passionately tells Marlowe that "it must stop," that a man is dead because of his necklace and now he is losing Helen because of it. Repeatedly Mr. Grayle yells, "It must stop!" almost as a warning that if it doesn't more will die because of the deadly necklace, almost as if the necklace could strangle on its own. The Chinese jade has a mysterious and fascinating, irresistible yet deadly, power, which, like Helen/Velma, is associated with questionable exotic origins.

At the end of the film, as if too hot to handle, Helen's precious Fei Tsui jade necklace is practically tossed back and forth between Marlowe and the police. Marlowe refuses to keep the necklace because it is "wrong" for his "complexion" (too green? too Oriental?) and because he didn't finish the job (he wasn't man enough to possess it). When Randall asks Marlowe what he expects him to do with it, Marlowe replies, "Give it to your girlfriend. Send it back to China. Strangle yourself with it. I don't care!" Marlowe makes it clear that he wants nothing to do with the deadly jewels. His reply suggests that the only choices are to give it away to a girlfriend who can wield its sexual power and perhaps still be restrained by the patriarchal chain, to send it back to its origin and those incestuous rulers of the East, or be strangled by its deadly powers. Marlowe, for his part, leaving behind the jade, prefers the "kid," the orphaned daughter, to the deadly mother. The kid's "Sunday school picnic" face and "cute figure" don't (yet) threaten with the abject excess of maternal/feminine sexuality. As long as he is blindfolded to her sexual difference and pretends that she is like him, one of the "boys," he isn't subject to the abject power of her sexuality.

We can diagnose the recurring Orientalism in *Murder*, from the Coconut Beach Club's allusion to the South Pacific to the jade revered by the rulers of the East, as the return of the repressed otherness and ambiguity inherent in the identity formation of "the West." While the rulers of the East know the proper value, the invaluable value, of jade, which they revere, this indeterminate jewel is a threat to the West. Within this Orientalist paradigm, the East represents a maternal/natural figure in relation to the West's paternal civilizing influence. "The East" represents not only something unknown and unappreciated but also an ambiguous threat. The fascination and terror evoked by "the East" in film noir in general (e.g., *The Lady from Shanghai*, *Chinatown*), and *Murder* in particular, are symptomatic of the abjection of the "other" as a defense against ambiguity necessary to form a fixed and stable identity. The West abjects its other to defend itself against the "Eastern" other within. By projecting the threat of indeterminacy, ambiguity, and otherness outside, both individual and national identity attempt to shore themselves up against the inevitable return of the repressed.[4]

Murder's Missing Race

It is noteworthy that in *Murder, My Sweet*, unlike the novel on which the film is based, with the exception of the dancer in the Coconut Beach Club and a couple of other Asian characters in Chinatown, all of the characters are white. Whereas *Murder's* Marlowe is hard-boiled in his cynicism about women and femininity, the novel's Marlowe is hard-boiled not just in his cynicism about sex but even more so in his cynicism about race. *Murder's* Marlowe appears the tough guy because he spouts quick-witted remarks about sex and "flirts" with the "bad guys"—calling them "cute" and "little," and referring to their harsh treatment of him as showing him a "good time" or "dancing" with him. *Farewell, My Lovely's* Marlowe, on the other hand, appears tough for the most part because of his hard-boiled attitude toward race and racial difference in a novel peopled with "dinges," "shines," "smokes," "niggers," "hunky immigrants," "Chinamen," "Japs," deferential "Mexican" bellhops, smelly "Indians" speaking "pig latin," and "short dirty wops." Here Marlowe's disdain for these characters is his defense; he isn't afraid of them because he isn't afraid to "call a spade a spade." These racial stereotypes protect him from racial ambiguity and racial difference by ensuring fixed racial borders between Marlowe and the other "smelly," "dirty," "ignorant" racialized abject characters that he encounters.

In an important sense, film noir is born out of the hard-boiled racism of Chandler's style. Several classic noir films were based on his novels (*The Falcon Takes Over* [1942], *Time to Kill* [1943], *Murder, My Sweet, The Big Sleep* [1946], *Lady in the Lake* [1947], *The Brasher Doubloon* [1947], *The Blue Dahlia*), and he wrote the screenplays for others (*Double Indemnity, And Now Tomorrow* [1944], *The Unseen* [1945], *Strangers on a Train* [1951]). Although it is arguably racial stereotyping that gives Chandler's protagonists their hard-boiled edge and contributes to their cynicism and the "dark" mood of his novels, in the films, this racial stereotyping is displaced onto sex or to the margins or condensed into complex racialized women or maternal characters or objects (the jade necklace in *Murder*).

Significantly, in the 1975 film version of *Farewell, My Lovely* the hard-boiled racism is displaced onto a corrupt cop played by Harry Dean Stanton, and Marlowe (Robert Mitchum) becomes so sensitive to race relations and racism that he gives all of his money and his favorite baseball to a fatherless mulatto boy (Andrew Harris). The 1975 protagonist does not use racial slurs, which are instead put in the mouth of an unsympathetic bad cop. Characters around him represent racist attitudes, but Marlowe rises above them with his sensitivity to race and racism. The Marlowe of the 1975 film maintains his integrity by rising above the explicit racism of those around him, but he continues to operate as a hard-boiled character by virtue of his hard and cynical attitude toward women and the law. In the novel, on the other hand, Marlowe's attitudes toward race and racial stereotypes are integral to his integrity; he is a straight shooter and doesn't mince words, which in Chandler's world entails using racial slurs and invoking racial stereotypes. It is telling that the film noir genre, in an important sense developed out of the stereotyped world of Chandler's novels, displaces the racism essential to the logic of that world and to the integrity of its protagonist onto sex, maternity, and a few marginal characters, along with its "dark" style.

CHAPTER 3

Stereotype and Voice in
The Lady from Shanghai

The Lady from Shanghai displays the ambivalent process of subject formation through which we produce cultural narratives and social and psychic identity.[1] The process of subject formation follows a logic of identity that produces stereotypes: figures shaped by normative difference, linguistic incommensurability, and maternal loss. Difference, incommensurability, and loss then return to produce melancholy and ambivalence in the subject. Like other film noir, *The Lady from Shanghai* manifests the ambivalence of that process in the intense struggle between its visual technique and its voice-over. Unlike other noir films, however, in this film the ambivalence is made audible rather than visible by the complexity and contradictions of its use of voice. Indeed, an argument can be made for the predominance of an ambivalent and melancholy voice in *The Lady from Shanghai* over its images.[2]

This chapter focuses on the predominance of voice and on its ambivalent operations in *The Lady from Shanghai*. The film will be read as a stereographic allegory for the struggle between a familiar Western, prophetic, literary voice (gendered male) and a foreign Eastern, proverbial, unintelligible voice (gendered female). If the struggle is resolved in favor of the surviving male voice-over at the end of the film, the resolution is a temporary fantasy. Although the Cantonese-speaking character Elsa Bannister (Rita Hayworth) is destroyed at the end of the film, in noir fashion, her voice continues to haunt us after the film's end, just as Elsa will haunt Michael O'Hara (Orson Welles): "Maybe I'll live so long that I'll forget her. Maybe I'll die trying." Indeed, the film as a whole will be read as a sustained ambivalent dialogue between these two voices, which sometimes displace each other and sometimes condense one into the other.

Drawing from Homi Bhabha's theory of colonial discourse, this chapter diagnoses the uncanny voice of *The Lady from Shanghai* as the symptom of the intense ambivalence produced and accompanied by differentiated but related acts of oppression. These acts are deployments of stereotypical discourses of sexuality and race, and their inscription into subjects and bodies. From this perspective, the haunting effect of voice in *The Lady from Shanghai* is both an aspect of what Bhabha has called "the return of the oppressed" and an acoustic site of unpredictability and promise. Marked both by gratification and terror, by hatred and desire, the haunting quality of that voice is an audible response to the desire to master life by fixing it into locations for the self and for the other.

The Elsa Effect

The Lady from Shanghai tells the story of Elsa Bannister's self-generated undoing. Hailing from Shanghai, the "wickedest city in the world," Elsa Bannister manipulates just about everyone in the film to get what she wants. Michael O'Hara is perhaps the most sympathetic of the film's characters, all of whom suffer the consequences of Elsa Bannister's ill-fated attempts to kill her husband and escape with the insurance money. Like everyone else in the film, O'Hara is duped by her Siren-like charms and ends up accused of a murder he did not commit. After the trial, while waiting for the verdict, O'Hara escapes, and the film famously follows him into San Francisco's Chinese theater and then into the Hall of Mirrors of the Crazy House. Once there, he miraculously escapes while Elsa and Arthur Bannister (Everett Sloane) shoot each other dead.

The film is determined by a logic of identity also made manifest in the ambivalent legal processes in the United States that produced differentiated American and Asian American national subjects. Lisa Lowe suggests that a contradictory set of stereotypes that includes the threat-ening "Yellow Peril" and the domesticated "model minority" was a mea-sure of the threat and the challenge posed by the immigrant from Asia to this process of national subjectification. This threat produced the Asian American citizen and an archive for its stereotypes even as it iden-tified the Asian American with a fantasmatic site of unfixed liminality. It produced an endless, ever-changing, and even contradictory archive of stereotypes that repeatedly fixed, stabilized, and disavowed that fluid site, defending the body politic against the anxiety caused by this ambig-uous state.[3]

Thus the logic of identity that drives the process of subject for-mation paradoxically produces difference. Bhabha's analysis of colonial discourse also emphasizes that the process of subject formation produces normative difference. It produces difference in relations that articulate them, that reconcile them, sometimes by means of hierarchies, some-times by means of contrast. It does not produce difference in a ludic relation, or a relationship of play that preserves the incommensurability of its registers. These normative differences are produced as antitheti-cal knowledge that can nevertheless be grasped as a unified zone for the other. Sometimes they are produced as contrasting fields (or lines of force) that nevertheless work toward a similar end, as when sexual desire is articulated with a fear of miscegenation producing the character of Elsa Bannister in *The Lady from Shanghai.*

Elsa, the film's female lead, is a good case study for the paradoxi-cal effect of the process of subject formation that manifests itself in film noir. On the one hand, Elsa is the daughter of White Russian parents and is conventionally marked with the iconography of the femme fatale (low-cut dresses, cigarette smoke, elaborate coiffure), making her the recognizable gun-toting white seductress of noir. On the other hand, she is a femme fatale with a literally dark or nonwhite past that binds her to her husband, Arthur Bannister. The film incrementally associates her darkness with the Orient's stereotypical incomprehensibility, with its entrancing power, and with the inhuman efficiency of its automatons. Elsa was born in Cheefoo and has worked in "the wickedest cities in the world": Macao and Shanghai (hence the film's title).[4] She mindlessly quotes Chinese proverbs (in English), speaks fluent Cantonese, and is familiar with San Francisco's Chinatown and its inhabitants. She is both a white femme fatale and an Asian, variously called Elsa, Rosalie (or Rosa Lee) by O'Hara, Xinlin Zhang by the Cantonese-speaking telephone operators, and Lover by her husband. Her evil stems from her dangerous duplicity to the second power, both as a wife displaying her outlaw sexuality by cheating on her husband and as the domestic and treacherous Asian.

The overt construction of Elsa as both white femme fatale and treacherous Asian is complicated by Rita Hayworth's ethnicity.[5] In fact, Rita Hayworth's evil Elsa as alien femme fatale unhinged the actress's carefully balanced and highly popular nonwhite persona.[6] The character of Elsa made manifest the implicit tensions in the actress's public persona, which proved too shocking both for her fans and for the moguls of Columbia studios. As Rita Hayworth (read Margarita Cansino), she was the "All-American Hooker" (quoted in Fischer 1989, 33). A tenuous balance of hot and cold, Latin sexuality and femme fatale frigidity, made Rita Hayworth into the ambiguous object of desire of moviegoers.[7] By all accounts, Rita Hayworth's metamorphosis into what is variously described in the literature as a "little boy," a femme fatale, "the whitest of women," a "platinum blonde," "a parody of a calendar girl," was a conscious effort by Welles to shock the public into seeing the source of its ambivalence toward Hayworth: the constructed, artificial, and even stereotypical nature of her public persona. Not only was the press invited to attend the moment when a master hairdresser cut her "long red-gold tresses," but there were "publicity stills for the film showing Welles himself 'clipping her trademark locks'" (quoted in Fischer 1989, 34).

The stunt was part of Welles's larger demystifying agenda. As Welles suggests in interviews with Barbara Leaming and in memos to Harry Cohn (one of the main executive producers at Columbia studios), Welles was interested in making an original film that would escape the cliché, that would depart from the whodunit, by means of the "shock effect" (Leaming 1985, 338). Welles used the "shock effect" to make strange what seemed natural, in an effort to see differently. Thus Elsa Bannister's alien femme fatale made audiences see Rita Hayworth differently by flaunting the artificial markers of her sexual and racial difference.[8] Welles was so successful that the release of the film was postponed for two years in order to give the film studios a chance to solidify Hayworth's image.

Through the manipulation and recombination of enhanced racial and sexual markers, Welles not only sought mastery and authority as a filmmaker. Through shock effects like the production of an alien femme fatale represented by Rita Hayworth (the American Love Goddess), Welles also wanted to be original in the sense of making a new beginning for the perception of the world. Like Brecht before him, Welles attempted to break apart the "realistic" representation of the world in the audience's mind. His purpose was to show an alternative reality, through a dialectical process that both shocked the audience into interrupting a natural identification with Elsa and left her image open to interpretation and criticism. But like Brecht, Welles did this through an intensification and repetition of unquestioned stereotypes that became more visible but whose attraction and repulsiveness remained unexamined.[9]

In an interview, Welles suggests his unexamined ambivalence about Hayworth's sexualized and racialized persona. "The whole wicked Gilda figure was absolutely false ... It was a total impersonation—like Lon Chaney or something. Nothing to do with her. Because she didn't have that kind of sex appeal at all. She carried it off because of her Gypsy blood. But her essential quality was sweetness" (Leaming 1989, 80). Welles's opposition of Hayworth's really sweet nature to her "false" but racialized monstrous sex appeal suggests both his own ambivalence toward Hayworth and his unquestioned identification of racial otherness with monstrosity and lascivious sexuality. This implicit identification is made manifest in the uncritical metamorphosis of Rita Hayworth into an Asian femme fatale to produce a terrified shock in the audience. It is also made explicit by Welles's use of the Chinese theater and the Orientalized Crazy House to produce the same effect in the viewer.

Elsa, the Chinese theater, and the Crazy House are examples of the normative sense of difference behind Welles's attempts to escape clichés and even stereotypes. Through the uncritical repetition and deployment of these normative differences, Welles managed to produce the unforeseen effect of another truth and another reality, not only in others but even in himself. Despite all of Welles's claims to originality, his combination of discourses of race and sexuality in the character of Elsa Bannister was, like the stereotype in Bhabha's definition, an "arrested, and fixated form of representation" (Bhabha 1994, 75). According to Welles, Elsa was not the "real" Hayworth, but Elsa's effect, the shock and terror produced by Hayworth-turned-alien-femme-fatale, was (and became) both real and true to him insofar as he saw her as a monster and felt shocked by it and was thus able to predict, manipulate, and exaggerate her monstrosity in the film.

Melancholy Voice

Bhabha's use of psychoanalytic theory is helpful to explain the effect of the sensual and threatening Elsa Bannister on the audience, and it goes a long way in explaining how the alienating effect to which stereotypes are put in *The Lady from Shanghai* paradoxically produces a temporarily stable reality effect. But the logic of the stereotype that produces the effect of reality (its truth) and the economy that produces "normative differences" also produce a master subject that is always a vacillating, menaced, ambivalent subject caught inside a self-fulfilling prophecy. Bhabha argues that the production of normative difference in a hierarchical relation is the necessary condition for the successful deployment of colonial power. It fixes the stable dominant location for the colonial master subject. But the stereotype's production of difference, even if it is normative, also produces an anxiety that accompanies the stereotype's affirmations and fixations, and opens up the space for the contestation (or for the challenge) to that colonial power by a subaltern subject. In other words, the stereotype always brings back the repressed material that produces anxiety. The stereotype results in the production of a master subject that is always in crisis, that is always anxious about its stability, that is always challenged, and that unsuccessfully tries to defend itself against this threat by deploying the stereotype.

A vacillating, menaced, and ambivalent master subject can be heard in the voice of Michael, the male protagonist of *The Lady from Shanghai*.[10] To hear its instability, though, one must first fix its prophetic and even biblical dimension. Midway through the story, Michael tells the story of a fishing trip where he encountered ravenous spineless sharks who devoured each other in a frenzy. The story is both a prophecy and a biblical parable. It fixes the privileged location of the hero firmly in Western culture. On the one hand, it is prophetic of the last and most memorable scene of the film, where Elsa and Arthur Bannister shoot each other to death in the Hall of Mirrors. (As if to drive home the importance of the parable, in this scene, Michael refers back to the sharks.) On the other hand, its performance locates Michael in a superior moral position opposed to the film's evil characters: Elsa, Arthur Bannister, and George Grisby. If Michael, an Irish character, acts the prophet and assumes the role of a fisherman, he towers over the infantilized Elsa, Arthur, and George, who resort to childish jokes to lighten the mood: "It's the first time anyone has thought enough about you to call you a shark," says Bannister to Grisby. The joke suggests the powerful effect of Michael's prophetic voice on the other characters, as is evident by Arthur's gesture to protect his face with his arm, by his joke, and by the melancholy and hurt expression of all the characters in the scene.

Thus Michael's voice is inflected with a prophetic tone that differentiates it from the voice of other film noir protagonists, also placing him at the center of a Western literary canon.[11] Michael's musical Irish brogue and fancy prose is one of the film's most memorable aspects, perhaps even referencing the continental modernism of James Joyce. Not surprisingly, his lines are peppered with symbolism and metaphor, as when he refers to Bannister as a "sleeping rattlesnake," to Acapulco as a "bright guilty world," and to Elsa as "the Princess of Central Park." The lyrical and metaphorical style of Welles's screenplay is far different from the clipped and literal prose of Raymond Chandler's screenplays.

Its mythical dimensions are in part the result of references to foundational continental Western texts such as *The Odyssey* by Homer, *Oedipus Rex* by Sophocles, and *Moby Dick* by Melville, all of which distinguish Michael's voice from the regional hard-boiled North American style of detective fiction.[12]

Given the screenplay's literary form and its multiple references, it is not surprising that the protagonist's voice-over is also larger than life. Similar to the voice-over of neo-noir films like *Devil in a Blue Dress*, it reaches well beyond the confines of the clueless private detective.[13] Unlike *Devil in a Blue Dress*, however, the scope of the voice in *The Lady from Shanghai* extends beyond the historical, into the literary, the mythical, and the biblical. In other words, the voice-over in this noir is not only the voice of an incipient novelist, of an omniscient narrator of prose fiction who refers to the film as a story, but also the voice of a prophet, and it even assumes the voice of continental Western literature itself.

The literariness of Michael's mythical, prophetic voice, however, also makes it unstable and free-floating.[14] Indeed, if his prophetic voice, biblical tone, and literary inflection place Michael in the center of Western culture, the literary, historical, and political dimensions of that same voice also dislocate Michael from that center and reposition him instead at its periphery. In the film, we are told that Michael is called "Black Irish" for his role during the War of the Spanish Republic. A fighter for the losing Republican side, convicted and imprisoned for killing a Fascist spy, Michael is a rebel and an underdog fighting for a lost cause. Not surprisingly, his fate is compared to the Passion of Christ. Early in the film, he is shown in front of a mast that looks suspiciously like a Christian cross as he rides on the boat that takes him to Arthur Bannister's yacht. This visual image, combined with Michael's commitment to Republican causes, associates his Irish background with the Irish struggle for Catholic identity and for political sovereignty. His thick Irish brogue is a statement of independence not only from a political state but also from the King's English.

Michael's voice occupies a peripheral position in yet another way.

It is also heard as a pretentious voice in the two senses of that word: it is as ostentatious as it is false. Within the film, Michael is ridiculed for thinking himself above the rest, and his voice is taken as a sign of this pretense. If Michael's sidekick Goldie (Gus Schilling) identifies Michael as a man who "talks fancy," Bessie (Evelyn Ellis), one of the Bannisters' servants, gives Michael the pejorative label of "Mr. Poet." Similarly, the wealthy Arthur Bannister derides Michael's pretention to literary independence from the economic forces that clearly rule over the small but representative world of his yacht. Not surprisingly, Michael's voice is even ridiculed by critics such as Lucy Fischer for being deliberately false, for being inflected with a "phony Irish accent" (Fischer 1989, 37).

Like Elsa's, Michael's voice is a site of struggle and contradiction. On the one hand, it is a stable and mythical voice: biblical, prophetic, literary. On the other hand, it is also an unstable voice struggling for its independence at best and parodic at worse. According to the film's narrative, the instability of Michael's presumed independent and authoritative voice is at least in part compromised by his social class and by his servitude to Arthur Bannister. Money talks powerfully in this film, and its threat to Michael is acoustically represented by the high-pitched, upbeat, cacophonous, and energized jingle of a radio advertisement for Laso, a product that promises to "tease your hair and please the man you love." Its volume, pitch, and rhythm are a challenge to Michael's bass timbre and soft, musical Irish brogue. Conversely, the consumer values of its capitalist culture stand opposed to Michael's literary ethos and Judeo-Christian morality.

But behind the catchy sounds of consumer capitalist culture there is another voice that represents a greater threat to Michael's independence. What compromises Michael's independent voice is not his desire for Bannister's money but his desire for Bannister's wife, Elsa. In a scene that represents the symbolic closed circuit in which Michael is trapped, Bannister goes on and on about the power of money while the sexual source of power is both visually and acoustically revealed. In contrast to Arthur's voice-over, the scene shows Elsa giving Grisby an unlit cigarette and asking him for a light. Grisby says he doesn't have a light and passes it on to Michael. "Big and strong," resourceful and passionate about Elsa, Michael lights the cigarette and passes it to Grisby, who gives it back to Elsa to smoke. The circuit of the cigarette is a visual metaphor for Elsa's explosive scheme and for Michael's scripted role as the fool who lights the match. Thus the forbidden desire for Bannister's wife becomes the weakness that traps Michael.

Michael's outlaw desire requires the assistance of an intermediary (Grisby), who facilitates Elsa for him but also exacts a price that will spell Michael's doom. True to noir, the abetting forces of evil are all associated with the feminine.[15] They either are feminized or identify with the feminine in the film. In the cigarette scene, for example, Grisby is represented as an emasculated character (not unlike the crippled Bannister, whose masculinity the voice-over explicitly challenges.)[16] Grisby can't light Elsa's cigarette; his high-pitched, even shrill, voice is as disturbingly theatrical and as unauthentic as that of the radio advertisement; and he begins the scene as a parody of Elsa's voice. In fact, Elsa will end the scene seductively singing the same song Grisby so successfully botches. Indeed, the power of Elsa's sexuality is in the inflection of the seductive and enchanting voice with which she sings the words to "Please Don't Kiss Me." Moreover, Grisby is identified throughout the film with the passive position of the voyeur to Elsa's acting, all of which suggests a continuum of perversity and evil sexuality that goes from Grisby, the theatrically handicapped, to Elsa, an experienced and effective seductress, actress, and singer. Significantly, Michael's voice will pay the price for his infatuation with Elsa's siren song. Michael will compromise his voice and identity by signing a confession he does not write, and by repeating the idiotic lines scripted for him by Grisby: "I'm just doing a little target practice."

The Mother as Other

In his study of stereotypes, Bhabha emphasizes their visual aspect (1994, 66–84). He is interested mostly in the processes of seeing and being seen and brings the discussion of the process of subject formation to the primal mirror stage discussed by Jacques Lacan. According to Bhabha, the stereotype is deployed (is seen and heard) in everyday sites of colonial society such as street scenes and sites of reading, which can easily be extended to include sites like movie theaters. In such sites, an imaginary visual and auditory performance occurs that is different from, but simultaneous with, the representation of the stereotype. Subjects are effects of this second drama.

Bhabha emphasizes the ambivalent nature of the dramatic process of subject formation. The scene where the stereotype is seen, heard, or read is a scene of disavowal and fixation. That disavowal and fixation refer the subject back to an earlier scene of the process. Bhabha argues that this primal scene is the scene of the mirror stage described in Lacanian psychoanalysis. In that scene, the subject fixes (or recognizes) and turns away from (or disavows) its own suspected fragmentation and motor instability and instead turns toward, and identifies with, an ideal ego that in Bhabha's analysis is not only white and whole but also maternal. "On one occasion a white girl fixes Fanon in a look and word as she turns to identify with her mother. It is a scene which echoes endlessly through [Franz Fanon's] essay 'The fact of blackness': 'Look, a Negro ... Mama, see the Negro! I'm frightened'" (Bhabha 1994, 76). According to Bhabha, the scene is primarily a visual scene (the "scene" is the "seen") that describes a problematic visual triangulation. In it, the girl desires to be turned into a fetish by the scopophilic gaze of the (m)other, at the same time that she fixes with her gaze the feared other into a stereotype. The combination of this perverse desire and fear produces the fantasy or mirage of self-stability and self-independence in a subject that suspects not only its fragmentation and instability but also its primal identification with, and link to, the body of the (m)other.

If the stereotype is a form of representation that "arrests a play of difference," then the process of "cultural negation as negotiation" sets in motion the play of difference. What Bhabha means by "negotiation" is the substitution of the disavowal of cultural difference for a process that opens a space for relations of incommensurable significations and knowledges instead of fixing difference into stable stereotypical sites or relations.

Bhabha draws from Walter Benjamin's theory of language and John Berger's meditations on the language of migrants to describe that opening process as "the foreignness of languages." Bhabha compares that liberating process to the complex acts of negotiation of the migrant with a second language. When arriving in a foreign country, dislocated subjects such as the migrant encounter a doubly opaque language that they must learn to negotiate, and that they translate in a melancholy voice. The meaning of that language is opaque to the subject not only because s/he is not acquainted with its vocabulary, syntax, and grammar but also because the second language is transformed when the migrant uses it, in the act of translation. "[The Turkish immigrant] asked for coffee. What the words signified to the barman was that he was asking for coffee in a bar where he should not be asking for coffee" (165). Voiced by the melancholy dislocated subject, the word "coffee" escapes the confines of the symbolic system that restricts it to mean a drink made by percolation, et cetera. An incommensurable dimension is opened and added to the word that triggers an anxiety and a fear in the barman of the scene and produces a stereotype. "He learnt girl. What the word meant when [the migrant] used it was that he was a randy dog" (165). Bhabha argues that this uncanny incommensurability is what produces the anxiety and the stereotype. The migrant's act of translation is uncanny because it opens up that incommensurable space by repeating the loss of the first language. Bhabha suggests that the translation not only conjures for the barman the image of a foreigner without a language but also raises the specter of a primal loss. He further suggests that like the dislocated subject, and unlike the barman, we must all learn to negotiate the foreignness of language or that incommensurability. Like Salman Rushdie in his novels, Bhabha asserts, we must all make of the foreignness of languages "the cultural condition for the enunciation of the mother tongue" (166).

As he does in his analysis of the stereotype, Bhabha again identifies the core of the process of estrangement represented by the act of translation with a stereotypical representation of the maternal body and the maternal experience. By making foreignness into the precondition

of what he pointedly calls the mother tongue, by referring to the foreignness of language as "a cleavage in the language of culture" (163),
by comparing its untranslatable nucleus to an overwhelming body both
protected and revealed by the folds of a flowing, majestic robe (164), by
suggesting that the opaqueness in the dislocated subject's language is the
result of an irreversible familiar abandonment (263) that as a national
body we are all obliged to suffer and forget (165), Bhabha unconsciously
identifies the maternal body and experience with the very core of the
uncanny that we must learn to negotiate. Bhabha's analysis of the stereotype both collapses and keeps apart two locations: the place of the other
and the place of the mother. Indeed, it suggests that the disavowal and
fixation of the stereotyping process is modeled after a visual and narcissistic primal relationship between the mother and the child.[17] By so
doing, however, Bhabha repeats and fixes the symbolic matricide that is
the precondition for the melancholy of the dislocated subject he diagnoses. Bhabha's unconscious matricide is also the condition of possibility
of the stereotype: the production and the repression of maternal loss.[18]

Bhabha's description of the disavowals that determine the stereotype, and his discussion of the foreignness of language as a linguistic
example of the disavowals that lie at the core of the process of subject
formation, are very useful to understand the manifestation of those
processes in *The Lady from Shanghai*. But it is also necessary to highlight
the displacement and condensation of the maternal in Bhabha's psychoanalytic account of the process of subject formation to suggest that
such disavowals are meant to cover over a loss that is different from the
foundational castration at the center of Lacanian psychoanalysis.

Welles's Lost Mothers

The Lady from Shanghai similarly produces, represses, and disavows
maternal loss. Its logic of identity produces a maternal loss meant to
hide an ambiguous site. Welles and the biographical literature about
Welles associated two personal losses with *The Lady from Shanghai* and
with the character of its title, although the connection between the two
losses has gone unremarked. It was well known during the production

of the film that Welles was loosing Hayworth, to whom he had been married for a number of years. Less discussed is Welles's association of the Orient in general, and Shanghai in particular, with the loss of his mother.

Welles was born in 1915 in Kenosha, Wisconsin. He was the second son of Richard Head Welles, a wealthy inventor, and Beatrice Ives, an advocate of women's rights, a literary intellectual, and a concert pianist. Welles lost both parents early in his life, in 1930 and in 1923 respectively, and remained in the care of a close family friend, Dr. Maurice Bernstein. A few months after his mother died (Welles was then eight), he embarked on a world tour that several biographers record took him to Europe and to the Far East, although there is some discrepancy whether he was accompanied by his father (Brady 1989, 8; Leaming 1985, 15), or by Dr. Bernstein (Higham 1985, 45). Seven years later, biographers again agree that Welles embarked on another trip to the Far East and to Shanghai in particular, although they do not agree on the length of his stay in that city (Leaming 1985, 30; Higham 1985, 52; Brady 1989, 15–16). On that trip he was a companion to his lonely and unhappy father, whose alcoholism Welles ascribed to his father's separation from his mother (Leaming 1985, 31). Richard Welles died soon after of heart and kidney failure, though Welles felt both that he "drank himself to death" and more mysteriously that he was responsible for his father's death (32). That mysterious guilt can perhaps be explained by a revealing reference to the effect of Beatrice's loss on him. While discussing his first trip to the Far East in an interview with Leaming, Welles says, "I was my mother, and I kept the flame" (15). The remarkable statement reveals Welles's ambivalence about his mother. It suggests his resentment against her absence because of its fatal effect on his father and on himself. But it also suggests his melancholy identification with her and his interiorization of her absence in an effort to rekindle her love, in an effort to "keep the flame" alive. Welles's personal history and revealing statements suggest that the Far East in general and Shanghai in particular are sites that contain, preserve, but also repress the lost mother for Welles. From this perspective, both the film and the lady from Shanghai are also repetitions and returns of that repressed loss.

As is characteristic of film noir, the mother figure is displaced to the periphery of *The Lady from Shanghai*. She appears in the guise of Bessie, the female servant on Bannister's yacht. While she appears to serve Bannister, she is mostly there to take care of Elsa. Described as a grandmother and a widow with a family, repeatedly pictured with Elsa's puppy dog cradled in her arms, Bessie is Elsa's maternal protector. When we first meet her, she convinces Michael to stay in the Bannisters' yacht by telling him, "Don't go. She need you bad. You stay." Later she acts the part of Elsa's mother by telling Michael, "That's why I can't leave the poor little child he married. Somebody's got to take care of her." Moreover, Bessie is a racialized character, her blackness contrasting with Elsa's whiteness (Kaplan 1998, 194–95). Indeed, as black mother to Elsa's "whiter than white" Asian femme fatale, Bessie appears to be a stereotype of Hollywood cinema in general, and of the so-called Negro

Elsa (Rita Hayworth) and Bessie (Evelyn Ellis) in *The Lady from Shanghai*.

problem films. Like Bea in Stahl's 1934 *Imitation of Life*, Annie in Sirk's 1959 version of the same film, but closest to Dicey in Kazan's 1949 *Pinky*, Bessie is the black mother figure of a light-skinned woman who tries to pass as white. As we argue in chapter 2 of this volume, these films manifest the same anxieties over crossing racial boundaries as film noir.

In *The Lady from Shanghai*, however, we have a film that reworks the stereotype. It traces the origin of racial anxiety, the ambiguity about borders, from the passing daughter back to her evil mother. Unlike the Hollywood "problem" films, the racialized mother in this film does not chastise her daughter for crossing the racial divide, nor does she act as policing agent enforcing and naturalizing racial difference. Instead, Bessie helps the Asian femme fatale survive and pass in the white world. She abets the forces that confuse the racial divide, ensnaring Michael with her pleading maternal voice to stay and take care of the evil Elsa.

Passing is similarly linked to an evil mother tongue in Welles's use of Cantonese in his film. In *The Lady from Shanghai*, Elsa is directed to move from the intelligible English of the first sequence to the apparently unintelligible Cantonese of the last sequence of the film. The ease with which she moves from one language to the other is an acoustic version of the visual passing in the "problem" films. The condensation of both languages compounds the condensation of both races in her evil character and has a predictable effect on the English-speaking audience. How, it asks, can Elsa look so white and speak an Asian language so fluently? The audience searches in vain for the stereotypical phenotype of the Oriental in her face. It looks closely at her makeup, unsuccessfully seeking traces that hint at her Chinese background. The absence of such traces makes it wonder whether Cantonese is supposed to be her first language, her mother tongue. If it is, the audience asks, why hasn't she spoken a word of it before? The audience feels suspicious and unsettled by the revelation of a foreignness for which there is no acoustic account.

Forgetting that the father of the actress Rita Hayworth spoke mostly Spanish, the audience can fall back on the comfortable fiction that her mother tongue was English. Similarly frustrated, and faced with the difference of the Cantonese of the character Elsa Bannister, the audience puts itself outside her in-between linguistic state, accepts the purity of her first language (English), and assumes the perfection of her Cantonese. Thus the audience silences the combined and excessive sounds of the distinct voices overflowing from both the character of Elsa and the actress Rita Hayworth: the sound of Cantonese inflected by English and by Spanish.

Moreover, the ease with which the evil Elsa moves from English to Cantonese can make the audience paranoid about language and voice. After she speaks Cantonese, the audience wonders how to listen to her English, and whether there are any revealing signs of Elsa's foreignness. Conversely, the audience wonders whether the absence of those signs is a terrible sign that they all have been successfully erased. Similarly, it tries to listen for any traces of an English inflection in Hayworth's Cantonese. It begins to listen for the slips in the acoustic performance of language, for the inflection of Cantonese with English, for the tricks that will betray the artifice of the passing evil character of Elsa Bannister.

But Elsa is not the only site where the in-betweenness of language play is arrested in the film. As Ann Kaplan has pointed out, the pidgin English of Elsa's Orientalized servant (Lee or Li, played by Wong Show Chong) is evidence of the film's many debts to Hollywood stereotypes (Kaplan 1998, 197). Lee has few lines in the film, and many of them are in Cantonese. His few lines, though, are revealing both in themselves and in counterpoint to Elsa's lines. After Michael decides to go along with Grisby's insane plan in order to keep Elsa, Lee transmits a message to Michael from her: "She said meet you at Aquarium. Nine o'clock. Before many people there." If Elsa's English seems impeccable, the English-speaking audience can now hear its foreignness indirectly, both in the inflections of Lee's heavily accented English and in his syntactical mistakes.

The displacement of an evil maternal voice, the femme fatale's dangerous condensation of languages, and the servant's incorrect English are all symptoms of the melancholy economy driving the film. They make the English-speaking audience long for a lost, original, first language, for an unambiguous identity based on the clarity of its mother tongue.[19] But that nostalgia is the result of a loss presupposed in the threat of Elsa's linguistic passing, in the danger of Lee's heavily accented English, and in the evil of Bessie's maternal voice.

Stereographic Identity and Performance

In an interview about his experience with Welles in the making of *Touch of Evil*, Charlton Heston gives an insightful account of Welles's style of direction, comparing it to the way people talk. He remembers examples of "counterpointed scenes in *The Lady from Shanghai*" where "you hear two conversations interwoven." Heston stresses that Welles had "a marvelous ear for the way people talk" and for "the degree to which people in real life overlap one another when they're talking." "In the middle of somebody's sentence, Heston continues, you will ... apprehend what he's talking about and you will often start to reply through his closing phrase. People do that all the time. Orson directs scenes that way" (Comito 1998, 221).

Perhaps more than any of his other films, *The Lady from Shanghai* represents Welles's acoustic style of directing: his displacement of voices that are racially, sexually, and culturally inflected, even as he condenses those voices into a memorable third sound that seems to escape the limits of the sound track. There are at least three moments in the film where Elsa and Michael speak to each other at the same time. The importance of this technique is emphasized by the fact that it is repeated in the most visually striking and memorable scenes of the film: during the opening sequence in the carriage drive through Central Park, at the Aquarium, and at the Mandarin theater. (It is one of these scenes that Heston remembers in his interview.) They are all moments or sites of sound similar to musical counterpoint or polyphony, when more than one sound (musical idea, melody, or voice) is expressed, making it impossible to grasp the sum or total of the composition, and setting up the necessary condition for some loss of sound. But they are also moments that make it possible to hear with distinctness each sound as it is added, and that dynamically reconfigure our sense of what is being expressed as well as erased.

The film's opening sequence contains the first example of Welles's contrapuntal style. Michael and Elsa have just met, and they are riding in a coach. Michael, the poet, doesn't know Elsa's name, but he playfully names her Rosalie. At the same time that he repeats that he will "have to call her Rosalie," Elsa, smiling and charmed, asks, "Rosalie?" interrupting him, subtly challenging him, and moving him to explain his choice as "a gorgeous romantical name entirely." His explanation is followed by his own introduction, "My name is Michael," which is simultaneous with Elsa's terse but gently ironic rebuke, "You're a character," which is in counterpoint to Michael's long-winded reply, a part of which is unintelligible, but whose point does not escape us as he distinguishes between himself ("a poor sailing man") and Elsa ("the princess of Central Park.") The acoustic counterpoint between Elsa's clipped prose and Michael's storytelling is visually complemented by camera angle and movement. The counterpoint is also transcribed into the scene's composition, which divides the space into the interior of the carriage (where Elsa sits) and its exterior (where Michael stands) even as the composition provides a small window that allows the camera to move from photographing each character individually to photographing them, not together, but in one frame. The fascinating and complex scene is as successful a representation as can be of the mutual seduction and interplay between these two very different characters, whose differences are dynamically added one to the other without wholly collapsing them into one sum. The scene simultaneously produces a sound that is unintelligible but whose unintelligibility is not so much a threat as an invitation to the viewer to add his or her own voice to the combined sound of Elsa and Michael's conversation.

Later in the film, Lee speaks English again in a scene whose complexity merits a shot-by-shot description because it too holds the promise of breaking the melancholy circle around *The Lady from Shanghai*. Elsa, who is backstage in the Chinese theater, goes to the phone and identifies herself to the Asian American telephone operators. "I am

Xinlin Zhang," she says in Cantonese.[20] The shot includes Elsa right front and a performer putting on makeup and an elaborate headpiece left back. The scene cuts to a room filled with telephone operators, all of whom speak to one another in Cantonese. They respond to Elsa's request with "It's Xinlin Zhang. What does she want this time?" There is a cut to the performance of a Chinese opera from Elsa's perspective backstage. It includes the opera singer, the theater's audience, and a man who is busily arranging the set as the performance is taking place. There is a quick cut to the face of Michael, who is in the audience. From his perspective, the camera then takes us back to the performance, this time showing us the front of the opera singer, but also exposing the musicians in back of him, and again including a man setting up the props on the stage. There is a cut back to Elsa on the phone, who says (over the voice of the opera singer), "Hello, Lee?" The shot once again includes a performer putting on a mask and headpiece and looking at Elsa from

Michael (Orson Welles) and Elsa (Rita Hayworth) in *The Lady from Shanghai*.

the left back of the screen. In a typically composed "telephone conversation scene," the camera takes us from backstage to Lee's apartment, where he answers, "Hello," in English and after a brief pause says slowly in Cantonese, "This is Lee Gong." The camera then cuts back to Elsa, who says very slowly and deliberately in Cantonese, "Please help me," while in back of her the actor puts on an elaborate robe. This is followed by a cut back to Lee, whose response, again in Cantonese, is now inflected differently. It is now as long and quick as it was brief and slow before. The viewer is encouraged to interpret both his words and their tone, which reflect impatience and familiarity with, as well as authority over, Elsa. He says to her, "Do I owe you something, red-haired foreigner [Hong Fan Tou]? You are giving me a hard time. Why should I help you?" The next scene shows Lee running out of his apartment into a car with other men.

The scene has many aspects in common with the sequence in the coach at the beginning of the film. Like that scene, there is a play of difference and interpretation that is encouraged by the complexity of the dialogue and the mise-en-scène. Much of the dialogue in this scene appears unintelligible to an English-speaking audience, but as in the coach scene, we are invited to decipher the dialogue through visual cues and cultural conventions. Also like the stereophonic scene in the coach, in this scene we hear words repeated by the two characters, but inflected very differently. The words "Hello Lee" leave as quickly from Elsa's mouth as they are slow to emerge from Lee's. While Elsa asks, Lee responds with the same words. The close comparison makes it easier to hear the differences in the voice between two characters that are presumably speaking the same language, even as they shift from Cantonese, to English, back to Cantonese. Perhaps Lee's first slow response to Elsa not only voices the erasures of his Cantonese in "Hello" but also suggests a gentle reminder (perhaps to Elsa, perhaps to Hayworth, perhaps to himself) of the pronunciation of his own name, "Lee Gong." Significantly, this reminder unwittingly reveals Elsa's foreignness to Gong, suggested by her English-inflected Cantonese and confirmed by Lee Gong's following impatient words. But the reminder does not silence her or impede his communication with her. Indeed, it is a scene where communication across languages and cultures is made possible but depends on the active participation and interpretation of the audience and its willing entry into the play of differences between the character's and the actors' languages, voices, and cultures. Participation is encouraged by comparing and contrasting sounds and voices while showing the listener the acoustic complement to the performance's secrets, the tricks of the trade, the masks off the face, the music on the stage, the makeup behind the scenes. Communication between the director and the audience depends on giving up the pretense of a natural, original, stable mother tongue whose clarity and goodness come at the price of producing the monster of a maternally inflected foreignness or unintelligibility.

Indeed, in the scene, we hear performed the process of identity. More accurately, the scene is an acoustic performance of a fluid identity. It invites us to interpret identity through a polyphony of sounds rather than assuming identity by the clarity or unintelligibility of the meaning of words. And yet the scene is also about the revelation of a "real" identity. Elsa reveals herself in Cantonese to be Xinlin Zhang, and her apparent servant reveals himself to be a leader of men, a man with a family and a last name, Lee Gong. The opera onstage is also about the forceful revelation of identity. It performs the trial of a woman accused of being a sinner by a judge who asks her, "What is your given name and surname?" When the woman answers, "Li Yulan," the judge asks, "Li Yulan, what is the origin of your story? Spit it out!" The English-speaking audience, the Cantonese-speaking opera singer, and Lee Gong share and voice identical concerns about the mysterious identity of a woman. But the harmony of their concerns is hidden by the apparent unintelligibility of the Cantonese, by the tendency to vilify radical difference in sound and sense, by the inability to embrace the polyphonic and contrapuntal nature of identity and voice. The anxiety over this inability leads to the production of the Asian stereotype and gives shape and strength to Elsa, the powerful evil femme fatale.

The film's final sequence follows this logic of identity to its logical conclusion. Right before the shoot-out between Elsa and Arthur

Bannister, Michael and Elsa have what barely resembles a conversation in the Magic Mirror Maze. Elsa says, "We could have gone off together—," and Michael interrupts and finishes her thought, "Into the sunrise. You and me or you and Grisby?" To this, Elsa replies in a "comatose" monotone, "I love you," to which Michael responds by quoting back to her one of Elsa's Chinese proverbs: "One who follows his nature keeps his original nature in the end. Or haven't you ever heard something better to follow?" (Fischer 1989, 37). After a long pause, Elsa replies almost inaudibly, "No."

In this scene, Michael's voice deploys the conventional authority of voice-over and appropriates Elsa's words to the point of using them against her. On the other hand, Elsa's clipped style of conversation has been emptied of all affect, and she speaks like an automaton, telling Michael what he wants to hear. If in the opening sequence the characters talk through each other's phrases as they communicate, here they finish each other's sentences or voice each other's thoughts while talking at cross-purposes from each other. If the dialogue loses its dynamism by emphasizing the differences between voices expressing the same thought, the scene visually achieves an eerily static quality even as it is crowded with the reflections of both characters. Unlike the versatile camera work of the first scene, here the camera focuses first on Elsa, then on Michael, and then on both. Conversely, the sense of balance conveyed by the first scene's effort to open and preserve an in-between space for both characters is here replaced by the dramatically uneven disposition of the characters, where Elsa always occupies the subordinate position. Thus the last scene is both an acoustic and a visual undoing of the promises of the opening sequence. It is literally an "arrested form of representation" that both deploys and makes visible and audible the operations of the stereotype.

The Lady from Shanghai deploys a melancholy logic of identity that produces and then displaces and condenses the foreignness of language in order to master a self-induced loss. On the one hand, the film condenses the strange and the familiar as an attempt to think differently about the self. As in Brecht's epic theater, the scene in the Chinese theater intends to open the door to the uncanny, to a new way of knowledge through the uncanny, knowledge that is both familiar and unknown, ours and foreign. It is a scene of cultural play, a moment of interruption and surprise, that should take us further than the agonistic struggle between opposites, that should relocate us and change the very contents of knowledge. But to make us think differently, the film depends on the shock of discovering the radical and archaic otherness that lies within us rather than on hearing the polyphonic harmony that is the process of identity. The true meaning of the Cantonese in the Chinese theater is the paradox that the desire for the strange is a circuitous way back to the mother tongue. The intensity of the scene's strangeness calls for the stereotypical process that produces the familiar, the origin, and the mother as lost.

CHAPTER 4

Sleeping Beauty and Her Doubles: *The* (Uncanny) *Secret beyond the Door*

The secret in Fritz Lang's 1948 noir/gothic film *The Secret beyond the Door* is the secret of most of the noir films that we analyze in this book: the absent mother, both fascinating and terrifying, motivates the murderous impulses of the film.[1] Lang's film explicitly suggests that the protagonist, Mark Lamphere (Michael Redgrave), suffers from a repressed trauma that lies behind his unconscious resolution to kill his mother in the person of his wife, Celia (Joan Bennett). Celia, acting as psychoanalyst, has to unlock the door of Mark's unconscious and bring this repressed trauma to consciousness in order to save them both. The psychic premises underlying the action are made explicit by a "brain psyche major" who, upon viewing Mark's collection of death rooms, remarks that "the murder of a wife or girlfriend has its psychological roots in an unconscious hatred for the mother," and "psychoanalysis would say that he had an unconscious resolution to kill in this room, but if he would have been able to tell someone like a psychoanalyst, then no murder would have been necessary." At the same time that Lang's film pokes fun at psychoanalysis—Celia's brother calls her psychoanalyst friend a "witch doctor," and at the party Celia jokes, "Paging Mr. Freud"—it uses psychoanalysis to diagnose Mark's murderous impulses and his neurotic relationship to his wife.[2]

The Secret beyond the Door opens with a dreamy voice-over of a woman talking about the meaning of dreams. The woman's voice tells us that if a woman dreams of boats or ships, that means she will find a safe harbor, but if she dreams of daffodils, then she is in great danger. But the woman tells us that she shouldn't be thinking of danger, since it is her wedding day. We see the woman wearing a wedding gown in an old church. She says that her heart is pounding so hard that she feels as if she is drowning, and that when you drown, your whole life passes before you like a fast movie. At this point, we get a flashback to the woman, Celia, in her brother's office. Her brother Rick (Paul Cavanagh) is chastising her for breaking off another engagement. He suggests that Celia is one of the most eligible bachelorettes in New York City and that she should find a husband because when his heart gives out, she will need someone else to take care of her.

The next thing we know, Rick has died, and his lawyer, Bob (James Seay), has proposed marriage to Celia. She accepts, but Bob insists that she take one "last fling" to Mexico with the Potters to think about marriage more seriously. While in Mexico, Celia meets Mark, an architect, and they fall in love at first sight. Within a few days, Celia writes to break off her engagement to Bob and marries Mark. In voice-over, Celia tells us that the trouble began on their honeymoon at a romantic hacienda in Mexico. We see Celia lock her door to tease Mark, and he leaves for Mexico City immediately to sell his architecture magazine.

At the Lamphere's Blaze Creek estate, Celia discovers that Mark was previously married and has a son, David (Mark Dennis). She also meets the mysterious Miss Robey (Barbara O'Neil), Mark's secretary, who wears a scarf over half of her face to cover a scar from burns she suffered while saving David from their burning summer house. When Mark arrives at Levender Falls, Celia meets him at the station, and they embrace warmly until Mark notices the lilac in Celia's lapel. When he sees the flower, he goes cold, abruptly withdraws from the embrace, and tells Celia that he has to go to his office in New York City. At this point, Celia considers leaving Mark and returning to New York. But she has an imaginary conversation with her brother Rick in which he asks her if she loves Mark and is willing to stand by him. She decides that she does and that she will.

At a party to celebrate their wedding, Mark shows his guests his collection of "felicitous" rooms. Celia has been under the impression that these rooms were the settings for happy events, but now she finds out that they are all the settings for murders. In gruesome detail, Mark describes the murders that took place in his collection of rooms. When he passes by room number 7, Mrs. Potter (Natalie Schafer) begs to see this room, too. But Mark insists that it is his secret. From this point on, Celia schemes to discover the secret behind door number 7, as she says, for Mark's own good. She thinks that by unlocking the door, she can also unlock the door to Mark's repressed traumas and release him from his tortured psyche and thereby save their marriage.

Celia makes a wax imprint of the key using a piece of one of the two candles in her room and has a key made. One night she waits until everyone is asleep and enters the room. She discovers that it is a copy of her bedroom. At first, she thinks that it is Mark's first wife Eleanor's room, but she soon realizes that none of Eleanor's things are there. When Celia notices that one candle is shorter than the other, mirroring the two candles in her room, she concludes that she is the intended victim for this death room. She hears footsteps and runs out of the house into the fog, where we see a man coming toward her and hear her scream.

In the next scene, we hear Mark in voice-over imagining his trial for the murder of Celia. Soon we discover that Celia is not dead; she returns to Blaze Creek to risk her life in order to "save" Mark from his psychological torment. She prepares herself and brings a bunch of lilacs to room number 7, where she waits for Mark. When Mark arrives ready with a scarf to murder her, she urges him to try to remember the repressed trauma set off by locked rooms and lilacs. Upon hearing the door to the room lock, he remembers one day when he was picking lilacs with his mother and putting them in every room. Afterward, she was preparing to go out on a date dancing. Mark remembers that he was jealous and didn't want her to go. She calmed him by telling him to get ready for bed and then come to her room for a bedtime story. When he went to leave his bedroom, he found the door locked and bloodied his hands trying to get out. He saw his mother leave for the dance with a man. When Celia tells Mark that it was his sister Carrie (Anne Revere), not his mother, who locked the door to his room, he drops the scarf. Celia and Mark notice smoke and realize that the house is on fire. Mark makes his way out and then returns to save Celia. The film ends with Celia and Mark back at the hacienda in Mexico, Mark with his head in Celia's lap. Mark tells Celia, "That night you killed the root of the evil in me, but I still have a long way to go," and Celia corrects him by saying, "We have a long way to go."

Although *The Secret beyond the Door* employs techniques familiar to film noir—voice-over, flashback, investigative narrative structure, sharp contrasts in lighting and camera angles—the effect of the voice-over is not typical of film noir. Most obviously, the voice-over is that of a woman and not that of a male detective. More than that, though, the voice-over is neither a rational description or explanation of past events nor distanced from those events. Celia's voice-over does not have the authorial distance of more traditional noir voice-overs. Traditionally, the voice-over provides a critical distance from the action. In *The Secret beyond the Door*, however, Celia's voice-over provides little critical distance, especially as the film progresses. Unlike Marlowe in *Murder, My Sweet*, or Michael in *Lady from Shanghai*, or even Corky in *Bound*, Celia does not explain the action that we see on the screen. Rather, most of the time, we hear the inner workings of her mind. Celia's voice-over operates more like an internal monologue, increasingly becoming stream of consciousness as the film progresses. The voice-over is not clearly located in the present of the film or in the future in relation to the flashbacks. The time and place of the voice-over shift between an internal and external location in relation to the action on the screen.

This use of voice-over as inner voice creates a sense of a psychological interior, an inner space of turmoil from which the narrator cannot distance herself or escape. The rational conscious mind cannot distance itself from the repetitions and desires of the unconscious mind. Rather, the voice-over is just as much at the mercy of the unconscious as is consciousness itself. In the beginning of the film, Celia's voice-over is an unsteady combination of critical distance from events ("I sent

Edith away because I wanted to meet him on my own ground," "Maybe I should have followed the dark voice in my heart and run away") and her interior thoughts and fears ("I'm afraid. I'm marrying a stranger," "Why had he gone? Why had he lied?"). As the film advances, she loses more and more of her critical distance until the voice-over becomes an almost delirious stream of consciousness. For example, when Celia interrupts a fight between David and Mark, we hear her thoughts: "Funny, why do I keep on thinking about red carnations? Maybe when pain becomes unbearable, one does not feel it any more. I came down to write Edith that the gardener found her husband's wallet. David is leaving. I shouldn't have let him go. I should have defended Mark. The gardener said he had the lilacs pulled out. I'm thinking in circles. The whole thing is ridiculous. David is oversensitive and high strung. How did Eleanor die? How did Eleanor die?"

From beginning to end, there is an almost obsessive repetition in Celia's voice-over that can be associated with the repetitious logic of the unconscious. Freud and his contemporary followers maintain that one of the primary patterns of the unconscious is repetition. Freud claims that we repeat what we cannot remember: "The patient does not remember anything of what he has forgotten or repressed, but acts it out. He reproduces it not as a memory but as an action; he repeats it, without, of course, knowing that he is repeating it" (1914, 150). In this way, a trauma that is repressed becomes unconscious but is repeated or reenacted in conscious life until we remember the now unconscious trauma that caused it. Until we remember the original trauma, we will continue to repeat it over and over again. Once we remember the trauma, however, we will have no need to continue repeating it. This is the premise set out by the psychology student who, when seeing the death rooms at the party, remarks that if the murderer would have been able to bring his unconscious resolve to murder his mother to consciousness and tell an analyst, then no murder would have been necessary.

The most striking example of repetition in the voice-over is when Mark abruptly leaves the hacienda on their honeymoon and Celia discovers that he lied about receiving a telegram. We see her frantically pacing her room, and the voice-over fiercely repeats over and over again, "Why had he gone? Why had he lied? Why had he gone? Why had he lied?" The music matches Celia's repetitious frenzy with a stark refrain to produce a repetitious beating inside the viewer's head to match that inside Celia's. "Why had he gone? Why had he lied?" becomes the throbbing symptom of Celia's psychological pain. In this moment in particular, the voice-over does not explain or describe the action or even the protagonist's motives; rather, the repetition of the same questions over and over again creates the effect of a stubborn psychological pain that will not let up. The repetitions in Celia's voice-over contribute to the creation of a turbulent interior psychic space.

In voice-over, Celia tells us that she knows Mark is the one for whom she has been waiting when he says that she is nothing like herself, that her face is like the calm before the storm of her inner thoughts. Celia is attracted to this man who can see her inner turbulence, the storm inside her. Mark sees two Celias, the composed and calm Celia whom she presents to the world and the stormy Celia who lies beneath, waiting to be revived, as he says, like a "twentieth-century Sleeping Beauty." These two Celias correspond to the split between conscious and unconscious. As Celia says, Mark sees behind her makeup something that she had not even seen herself, her unconscious desires. Mark sees another Celia whom no one else has seen, a Celia who is not even visible to Celia herself, a Celia behind the scenes.

As Elizabeth Cowie argues, the use of voice-over in the film also creates the effect of two Celias. Cowie explains that in the beginning of the film, the voice-over implies that what we are seeing is a flashback; soon after, however, the voice-over presents Celia's thoughts and fears in the present time of the film, suggesting that the film presents events as they unfold. We are at the same time privy to Celia's inner thoughts. Cowie concludes that "there are then two Celias, one who is the author of the flashback but who ceases to be marked as such and thus comes to be aligned with the omniscient narrator, and Celia the character in the film" (1998, 155). Unlike the omniscient voice-over of traditional film noir, where the detective telling the story has already lived it and already knows the outcome, Celia the narrator does not know what Celia the character will do. Again, the relationship between the two Celias mirrors the relationship between the conscious and unconscious. The conscious mind narrates and tries to understand events while the unconscious mind motivates the action. Like Celia's voice-over in relation to the action of the film, the conscious mind is always one step behind the unconscious.

Celia is doubled not just through the film's voice-over but also through her visual presentation. She is repeatedly seen doubled in a mirror, so that the viewer sees two Celias. In fact, the "trouble" starts when Celia is sitting in front of a mirror brushing her hair in her room at the hacienda. Taking Paquita's advice, Celia decides to make Mark wait and locks the door to give her hair two hundred strokes. As if enraged by the woman's pleasure in stroking herself beyond the door and out of his sight, Mark turns cold and leaves her. Just as this locked door denies him access to Celia, so the locked door from his childhood denied him access to his mother and to her desire, which was beyond him. The locked door triggers the hatred and matricidal impulses caused by his realization that he is denied access to his mother's pleasure. The locked door reminds him too that the gratification of his desire must be deferred: he has to wait.

Paquita (Rose Rey) tells Celia that women are patient and men are impatient. She suggests that women's patience makes them wise and women's wisdom makes a marriage a happy one. Sleeping Beauty (to whom Mark compares Celia), after all, waits one hundred years for her prince to arrive at just the right moment, and upon his arrival, she charms him with the words "You have waited a long while" (Perrault 1912). And though it seems that both Celia and Mark have waited to find love, they don't wait to consummate it with a hasty wedding. Mark is enraged when he has to wait for gratification. As the moral of *Sleeping Beauty* attests, while it may be wiser to wait, love will not wait:

> Now, our story seems to show
> That a century or so,

Late or early, matter not;
True love comes by fairy-lot.
Some old folk will even say
It grows better by delay.

Yet this good advice, I fear,
Helps us neither there nor here.
Though philosophers may prate
How much wiser 'tis to wait,
Maids will be a sighing still—
Young blood must when young blood will!

(Perrault 1912)

In Perrault's version of the Sleeping Beauty fairy tale, the moral should be that it is wise to wait until your mother is dead to marry. Although the prince marries the princess (Sleeping Beauty) immediately, he waits nearly two years until his father is dead to bring her back to his kingdom. Yet because the prince doesn't wait until his mother is dead, his marriage is threatened, and his mother must die so that his wife and children can live. In this fairy tale, the princess's mother is an ogress with infanticidal cravings who kills children and eats them. Castrating mothers don't get much worse than this queen of death, who must be killed so that Sleeping Beauty and her beautiful children can live. The bad mother must be killed off so that the good mother can live. Ironically, in the fairy tale, Sleeping Beauty's hiding place is discovered by the evil queen when the queen hears the sounds of this "good" mother beating her son—suggesting that behind every good mother is an evil one waiting to happen. Our twentieth-century Sleeping Beauty, Celia must kill the motherly ghost who is still haunting Mark so that she can escape his murderous plan. Behind the battle between Celia and Mark is the real enemy, the castrating mother with whom they both fight to the death. It is this castrating mother whom Mark sees beyond the locked door as Celia takes her two hundred strokes in front of her mirror.

Throughout the film, at the hacienda and back at Blaze Creek, Celia is shown doubled in a mirror. Even Mark acts as a mirror for Celia. She falls in love with him because he sees her; he sees beyond her makeup and tells her what she is behind her calm demeanor. She loves him for what he sees in her. From this perspective, *The Secret beyond the Door* chronicles a turn in Celia's narcissistic gaze originally directed at her own image reflected both by mirrors and by Mark, and now turned toward what lies behind Mark's matricidal desire, his own makeup. Along with Celia, the viewer is forced to turn her gaze from the body or image of woman so prominently displayed in film noir to the matricidal desires that constitute Mark and motivate film noir. *The Secret beyond the Door* calls on the viewer, along with Celia, to interpret what she sees as symbols for a secret unconscious desire/trauma. From the opening scene, Celia tells us that things have at least two meanings: boats and daffodils are not just means of transport and flowers but are also symbols for safety and danger. Celia's split or doubled persona is but

Paquita (Rose Rey) and Celia (Joan Bennett) in *The Secret beyond the Door.*

a reflection of the double meaning of all symbols. The most poignant of those double meanings and symbols is the "felicitous" room number 7. Celia misjudges Mark because she sees only one meaning of "felicitous," *happy*, and discounts the other, *apt*. Significantly, Celia's misreading of the meaning of the word suggests the way of revealing the secret beyond the door to these felicitous rooms: the act of transforming them into polysemous signs. Mark's room number 7 is a lucky seven, but it is an odd number that cannot be divided neatly in two and troubles the double insofar as it turns out that it is indeed the original.

The *Secret beyond the Door* is filled with doubles and mirror images. Even the film itself is in some ways an acknowledged double of Hitchcock's *Rebecca* (1940), which makes Ms. Robey all the more eerie in her resemblance to Manderley's Mrs. Danvers. Celia is not the only doubled character in the film. More obvious than Celia's double persona is Mark's Dr. Jekyll and Mr. Hyde double personality. Throughout the film, he goes from being charming and loving to being cold and cruel. Mark's hot and cold personality is the mystery of the film that the psychological detective Celia must decode. In Mexico at the wishing well, Mark tries to tell Celia that there is another Mark, the inner Mark, whom she has not yet met. He tells her, "There is another Mark that I wanted you to know," but Celia insists that she knows him. Still, she says that she is afraid that she is about to close the door to a quiet, familiar room and open a door to another room beyond which there is wind, sun, storm, everything. This set of double doors with the quiet and familiar on one side and the new and dangerous on the other again mirrors the split between the familiar conscious and the stormy unconscious. More than this, it foreshadows Mark's death rooms and the secret beyond door number 7. In the film *the door* and its *key* become metaphors for the unconscious, Mark's in particular, and its secrets revealed. The two Celias, then, seem to be mirror doubles of the two Marks.

Mark's secretary Miss Robey and his sister Carrie are also doubles in that they operate as two sides of stereotypical femininity. Miss Robey is masochistic; sister Carrie is sadistic. Miss Robey manipulates Mark by playing off of his guilt over her scars, constantly reminding him of her victimization with her half-hidden face, which in reality is not scarred. Carrie, on the other hand, dominates Mark, imposing her will on him "for his own good." Throughout the film, we find out that she locked Mark in his room and waited while he bloodied his fists trying to get out; she chose Mark's first wife to make him settle down; and

Celia at door number 7.

unlike Miss Robey, who claims that David is not a difficult boy but merely resents domination, Carrie insists that David needs discipline. Whereas Miss Robey exemplifies the stereotype of the masochistic woman who uses her victimization to manipulate men, Carrie exemplifies the stereotype of the domineering, sadistic woman who henpecks men into submission.

Mark's son David can be seen as a double for Mark, as the child Mark. Carrie tells Celia that as a child, Mark was like David, difficult and sensitive. Whereas Carrie wants to give David/Mark a "firm hand" for his own good, Miss Robey realizes that David/Mark resents domination. When Celia meets David, he looks like a little man wearing a suit and behaving in a formal manner—David is Mark's *Mini-Me*. Later, when Mark is scolding and hitting David, Celia tries to stop him. Mark's response, "You have sympathy for David, I wish you'd try to understand me as well," furthers the association between him and David. David tells Celia that she should not interfere between him and his father because she will never understand their relationship. David claims that Mark murdered his mother. The uncanny identification between Mark and David suggested by the film complicates David's claim that "he killed my mother." It is as if David is Mark's unconscious, telling him that he has killed his own mother, revealing Mark's unconscious resolve to kill his mother in her substitutes, his first wife Eleanor and now Celia.

The pairs of siblings are also doubled in the film. With Mark-Carrie and Celia-Rick, we have two sets of brother-sister relationships. In both cases, they are without parents. In both cases they have very close relationships, even living together as adults. Both Rick and Carrie take care of and protect their siblings. Underlying these close sibling relations is the suggestion of incest.[3] Celia suggests that she can't find a man as good as Rick and that is why she hasn't married. When Rick's lawyer Bob walks in on their embrace, Rick tells him that it is "strictly legal." And when Celia wants to run away from Blaze Creek, in voice-over she tells us that without Rick she has no reason to return to New York. Whereas Rick is the good father substitute, however, Carrie is the bad mother substitute. Mark and Carrie also live together as adults.

Carrie is the mistress of Blaze Creek and has taken that position over from her mother, from Mark's first wife, and from Celia. If Rick represents the loving yet stern father who lays down the law—or reads Celia "the riot act," as she says—Carrie is the overprotective and too stern mother whose affections and restrictions both suffocate and threaten castration. Celia loves passionately for the first time only after Rick's death, as if the death of the father of the law allows her to feel her desires for the first time. For Mark, on the other hand, love is associated with death because the suffocating love of the women around him has almost killed his passion; for Mark, loving women also means hating them and wanting to kill them in order to assert his independence from them. While for Celia, passion comes only after death, for Mark love and death amount to the same thing.

Elizabeth Cowie analyzes the connection between death and desire in film noir and in *The Secret beyond the Door* as the representation of desire "as something that not only renders the desiring subject helpless, but also propels him or her to destruction" (1998, 148). Desire is as irresistible and as fatal as fate. In fact, in many noir films, fate delivers its deadly blow in the person of the femme fatale, against whom the male protagonist is helpless in spite of his better judgment. In *The Secret beyond the Door*, from the beginning love is connected with death. On her wedding day, Celia is not only thinking of daffodils and danger but also imagining that she is drowning and that her whole life is passing before her eyes. Later she tells us that at the very moment when she knows that Mark is the man for whom she has been looking, she again thinks of daffodils; she enters an endless moment that floats like a feather, where time stops, and then she thinks of daffodils. The first moments of her love are beyond time and, like death, endless. After they leave the knife fight, Mrs. Potter tells Celia that she looked as if she had seen death (when staring at Mark), and Celia responds, "That's not how he looked." Repeatedly Mark, and Celia's love for him, are associated with danger and death. Eventually we find out that all of these daffodil moments have been foreshadowing Mark's obsession with death and deadly rooms.

The connection between love and death becomes most explicit in Mark's description of the last of his death rooms, the room of Don Ignacio, whom Mark describes as an educated and cosmopolitan man for whom murder, like love, was a fine art. Don Ignacio killed all of his lovers, Constancia, María, and Isabela. When the psychology student pipes up that the murders would have been unnecessary if he could have talked to a psychoanalyst, Mark replies, "Unless his love for his victims made it necessary." Love necessitates death. Don Ignacio becomes Mark's double, the representative of his unconscious wish to kill his mother/wife. Celia runs out of the house when she discovers the scarf with which Don Ignacio murdered his lovers on the stairs after she first visits room number 7. Later, when Mark imagines his trial for the murder of Celia, he is holding the scarf. And when he returns to Blaze Creek to murder Celia in room number 7, he again wields Don Ignacio's scarf, the scarf with which the Spanish don so bloodlessly killed the women he loved so well. For Mark, to love is to kill, and to be loved is to die. As he tells Celia, murder can be more passionate than love.

For Celia, on the other hand, love and passion are sparked only after death, after the death of her brother, after the deadly knife fight on the street in Mexico. For Celia, death is a turn-on. This is what attracts her to Mark and what attracts Mark to her. She is transfixed by the knife fight in Mexico because "death was on that street." And Mark is transfixed by her because she is so invested in the murderous passions of the fight. In the knife fight, love and death come from the same passion, and Celia is aroused by the strength of this passionate connection; it is unlike the barroom brawls she has seen in New York because it is a fight to the death with "naked knives." Even the knives, the instruments of death, become erotically charged for Celia. This fascination with the murder weapon and the crime of passion is what links her with Mark. The erotic charge from the passionate love demonstrated by murder in the streets is the "current" flowing between Mark and Celia when they are locked into each other's gaze. From the beginning, their attraction to each other is an attraction to death. For Celia and Mark, far from being opposed to each other, Eros and Thanatos are intimately and erotically connected. According to the film's logic, death is love's uncanny double.

In his essay "The Uncanny," Freud describes the uncanny as "nothing new or alien, but something which is familiar and old-established in the mind and which has become alienated from it only through the process of repression" (1919, 241). Freud identifies the double as one of the most uncanny experiences because it is the projection outward of something once familiar now as something external and alien (236). The experience of the uncanny is produced when something familiar that has been repressed appears and reappears without being recognized. Not having worked through the old trauma, the psyche will repeatedly act out the trauma without realizing it. This repeated acting out can create the experience of the uncanny, especially when it involves the double. With the manifestation of the uncanny in the double, "There is a doubling, dividing, and interchanging of the self. And finally there is the constant recurrence of the same thing—the repetition of the same features or character traits or vicissitudes, of the same crimes, or even the same names through several consecutive generations" (234).

In *The Secret beyond the Door*, we see this repetition of the doubling of the self and of the same crimes. Mark's rooms double the scenes of crimes. His rooms repeat the same crime, murder, over and over again. And Celia's bedroom is literally doubled with room number 7. This double room, and the moment that Celia realizes by looking at the uneven length of the candles that it is her room, is the most uncanny moment of the film. That the detail of the shortened candle is now reflected in this second room suggests not only that it is a double of Celia's room but also that it is dynamic and changes as she does. It is this coincidence of candle lengths, the mirror image of her own candles, that makes the scene uncanny. Seeing yourself, or in this case your room, mirrored or doubled, and then seeing that double take on a life of its own produces an uncanny sensation that you are split off from yourself. As Mark tells Celia when they first meet, "You aren't a bit like you." For Freud, this split self or double "becomes the uncanny harbinger of death" (1919, 235).

Death, dead bodies, and especially those that return from the dead, are themselves uncanny. Unlike most noir films, *The Secret beyond the Door* does not actually present any dead bodies. Rather, images of death abound, and the death rooms give Blaze Creek a haunted aura.[4] The stories of murder seem to take on a life of their own, against which our protagonists struggle for their own lives. To increase this sense of the uncanny in relation to death, in an odd twist, the film leads the viewer to believe that Mark murders Celia and then brings her back from the dead. The sight of Celia returned from the dead is uncanny both for the viewer and for Mark, who realizes that he cannot escape his fate, that as much as he resists his impulse, he will kill Celia. In Freud's analysis, it is this fate, this sense of inevitability, that makes for an uncanny experience. Even our uncanny relationship to death is a result of the inevitability of death (1919, 242).

It is our feeling of helplessness and subordination to a fate that we cannot control that produces uncanny sensations. Freud gives not only the example of death but also the examples of wandering lost and ending up in the same place over and over again, or repeating the same crime over and over again. The coincidence of the same, this repetition compulsion, gives us the uncanny sense that we are not in control of our destiny. This helplessness recalls the familiar but now repressed helplessness of infancy. Jacques Lacan's formulation of the mirror stage speaks to this helplessness (1977a). As Lacan describes it, the infant goes through the mirror stage when the infant encounters its image in a mirror (or the body of another) and realizes that it is a unified whole. The infant sees its own agency reflected in the mirror. So although the infant experiences itself as fragmented and out of control, the mirror image gives it the illusion of control. When the mirror double starts taking on a life of its own and ceases to mirror our own actions, then it becomes uncanny. The uncanny double does not reassure us of our agency or control but, quite the opposite, recalls our feelings of fragmentation and helplessness.

Film noir's fatalism can produce an uncanny effect when we see everyday people come to bad ends in spite of their best efforts because of this fate beyond their control. *The Secret beyond the Door* proposes a truly uncanny fatalism in Mark's theory that rooms can determine deeds. His theory of *felicitous* rooms, put forward in his magazine felicitously called *APT,* makes rooms responsible for what happens in them. The double meaning of the word "felicitous," both happy and apt, in itself becomes an uncanny double in the film. Celia believes that Mark collects rooms that make people happy, and she is bewildered when she discovers that by felicitous, Mark means not *happy* but its uncanny double *apt.* In Mark's theory of felicitous rooms, control of one's life and behavior is taken over by inanimate objects in the rooms and even by the walls of the rooms themselves. The idea that a room can close in on its inhabitants and determine their actions is the quintessence of film noir's claustrophobia. And the scenes at the Blaze Creek estate present the walls and physical presence of the structure as ominous and threatening; the stone walls tower over the inhabitants and lock them into a dark, damp world of a mysterious maternal past. It is after his mother's death that Mark installs his death rooms in the basement of her house, as if to signal the unconscious connection he makes between the maternal womb and death.

In his essay "The Uncanny," Freud suggests that the uncanny ultimately comes back to the maternal sex, which instigates castration fears, recalls the womb as a tomb associating the maternal sex with both life and death, and is both an "unheimlich place" and "the entrance to the former Heim [home] of all human beings" (1919, 245). Insofar as we are all born from the maternal sex or female genital organ, it is familiar; but insofar as we have repressed this apparently unseemly origin, it will reappear as uncanny and perhaps go unrecognized as the entrance to our former home. With its castrating mothers, association between mother and death, and the death rooms in the basement of the mother's house, Lang's film seems to echo Freud's problematic view of maternal sex as uncanny and threatening. The secret beyond the door turns out to be the secret of Mark's mother's desire for men; on one side of the locked door of his bedroom is Mark, and beyond the door is his mother, dancing and enjoying herself with another man. *The Secret beyond the*

Door makes explicit the uncanny maternal sex that secretly haunts much of film noir.

Hitchock's *Vertigo* also trades on the uncanny maternal sex represented by the figure of Carlotta as it haunts Madeleine, Scottie, and Judy. Carlotta comes back from the dead in the persona of the possessed Madeleine. In Freud's analysis, the idea of returning from the dead in itself produces an uncanny effect. Doubling also invokes the uncanny. And insofar as Carlotta is associated with the deadly pair of maternity and sexuality, she is a figure for the uncanny maternal sex. With Carlotta and her doubles in *Vertigo*, then, we get an intensely uncanny effect. The uncanny association between Carlotta and death also produces the connection between love and death throughout the film. Like Celia in relation to Mark's deadly desires, Scottie is attracted to Madeleine's death wish, and the film ends with him effectively killing Judy, Madeleine's double.[5] Just as the uncanny maternal sex as both love and death is figured as ethnically colorful in the ghost of the Spanish Carlotta Valdez in *Vertigo*, so in *The Secret beyond the Door* the connection between love and death is associated with "exotic" locations, especially Mexico.

The first death room is from Paris, in which a count murders his wife out of religious conviction. The second death room is from Barton, Missouri, in which a farmer kills his mother during the floods of 1913, the most unromantic of the murders, according to Mark, committed not out of passion but for a motive as "common as dirt," the insurance money. The third death room is from the jungles of Paraguay, where in spite of his "primitive" surroundings Don Ignacio is a cultivated man and a perfectionist in love and murder. He killed all of his lovers out of a passion greater than love itself. As Mark describes it, this is the most romantic and passionate of all of the rooms. Mark identifies with Don Ignasio and understands his need to kill for love. Mark's theory is that the passions and the crimes are determined by places, by their locations. Different rooms, different places, have different powers and evoke different emotions. According to his theory, it is felicitous that the jungles of Paraguay produce the most passionate instincts that link sex and death even in a cultivated man.

Mark's theory calls on us to interpret the significance of place in relation to feelings and actions. In his theory, different places produce different effects. For Mark, there is something inherent in the structure or the material composition of the place that produces its effects. Fate is determined by the physical presence of one's surroundings. Against this architectural determinism, the student of psychology proposes that one's actions and feelings are determined by psychic phenomena and then only secondarily associated with one's surroundings. It is not the rooms that determine the murders but something in the psyche that can become associated with, or even triggered by, the rooms. The key to understanding actions and feelings or murder is not understanding the architecture of buildings but rather understanding the architecture of the psyche. This is why the key that Celia has made from the wax mold is only a metaphor for the key to Mark's psyche, and the locked room number 7 represents Mark's locked psyche. Freudian psychoanalysis repeatedly trades on architectural and spatial metaphors. To counterbalance the fatalism of Mark's theory of felicitous rooms, Celia becomes a psychoanalyst who insists that finding the key to the psyche can change one's fate.

Just as *The Secret beyond the Door* makes explicit the uncanny secret of maternal sexuality that haunts film noir, so too it makes explicit the significance of place in film noir. Just as it reveals Mark's matricidal desires without interpreting them and yet calls on us to interpret them, so too it reveals the ways in which places motivate the action of the film without interpreting them and yet calls on us to interpret them. Like adherents of Mark's deterministic theory of place, several film theorists have argued that the dark and dank urban background of much film noir is a commentary on the post–World War II move from the cities to the suburbs; as cities are abandoned, they become associated with alienation, and as they become associated with alienation, they are abandoned.[6] Fewer critics analyze or diagnose the role of the "exotic" places juxtaposed to the cityscape in creating a sense of otherness that motivates the action of film noir.[7] Although the cityscape is central to much noir film, so too is the *other* space: for example, China or Chinatown in *Murder,*

My Sweet, Chinatown, and *The Lady from Shanghai,* or Mexico in *Touch of Evil, Out of the Past,* and *The Secret beyond the Door.* Although *The Secret beyond the Door* shows the life-and-death necessity of interpreting symbols, it reveals without interpreting the uncanny otherness of place at the heart of film noir.

In *The Secret beyond the Door,* Mexico operates as another kind of mirror double for the characters and the action of the film. The film begins and ends in Mexico; and as we find out, Celia meets and falls in love with Mark in Mexico. Although she can't find a suitable husband or love in New York, within days of her visit to Mexico, she finds a New Yorker to marry. In fact, it is only after the knife fight in the streets of an unnamed Mexican city that Celia's passions are awakened. The knife fight is a turning point for Celia that transfixes her with its violent instincts and "naked" passion. There is something different about this scene in Mexico, something "warm and sweet and frightening," death and pride, passion and honor, displayed violently on the streets

The fight scene in *The Secret beyond the Door.*

in public. This is not what Celia has experienced in New York. Passion and instincts are more visceral and immediate in Mexico than in "inhibited" New York. In Mexico, the bare-chested "gypsy" fights with naked knives to the death with a man who rips the shawl from a woman's neck to defend himself and his love for her. Both men carry knives, and the fully clothed man facing the camera yells (in Italian?), "Look at me!" and then throws his knife, which hits next to Celia's hand. It is as if the man is yelling at Celia and throws his knife at her. Just as the knife hits the table, Mark's gaze pierces Celia's "makeup," and she senses a tingling at the nape of her neck. She says that she felt like she was being watched, his eyes touching her like fingers. While everyone else is watching the fight, Mark is watching Celia living the fight vicariously. Just as her passion is ignited by watching the fight, his is ignited by watching her watching, and hers is in turn fueled by watching him watching her watching. Like Sleeping Beauty and her prince, they enter the great hall of mirrors, or desire itself.[8] As Lacan describes desire, it always operates through the refraction of another's desire. Like cinema's spectator, both Mark and Celia like to watch; their desire is engaged by the spectacle.

The film suggests that real passion is in that Mexican street; Celia's and Mark's passion is only an inhibited, even inverted, mirror reflection of it. At the hacienda on their honeymoon, Mark is thinking about the architecture of the place, with its built-in "distilled romance," when Celia tells him not to think but to "just feel." Mark expounds his theory about how women are closer to nature and instinct and thus feel and intuit more than men. He claims that it will take men longer to come to a conclusion reached immediately by women because men use their intellect whereas women use their instincts. Goading Celia, he maintains that as intelligence increases, instinct decreases, and this is why while "women are happy, we human beings are not." He says that human beings have become inhibited, and Celia playfully snaps back, "That's a word for you." All the while we hear a bird in the background cackling loudly at Mark's theory. Mark opposes instinct and intellect— when one increases, the other decreases. The increase of intellect is accompanied by inhibition; in Freudian terms, we could say that it is accomplished by repression.

The knife fight in Mexico represents uninhibited instinct. In this regard, Mexico, with its bare-chested gypsies, is depicted as being closer to nature. And this contact with uninhibited nature awakens desire in both Celia and Mark. The distilled romance of the hacienda is distilled passion, passion that leads Mark to think about his death rooms and murder. At the level of instinct, love and death are but two types of the same passion. It is only when the psychoanalyst uses her intellect to decode the inhibitions and repression of instinct that the two, love and death, can be separated from each other. It is only back in "more civilized" New York that the inhibitions kick in and instincts become tangled and mangled into a perverse necrophilia. On the streets of Mexico, death follows love out of honor and pride, and staking one's claim becomes a public act. In the secret rooms of New York estates, on the other hand, murder becomes an obsession, and only the frozen remains of passion become the spectacle. Whereas in the streets of Mexico the instincts are expressed openly (albeit in ritualized forms) and love and killing have a common origin, in New York the inhibited instincts turn inward, leading to the cultivated man's self-destruction when love becomes death.

If Mexico is New York's double, then it is analogous to the split between unconscious and conscious. Mexico is the land of uninhibited desire and instinct, the unconscious openly displayed, while New York is the land of desire and instinct inhibited, even perverted, by the conscious intellect, which forces them underground and through the back door. Visually, the scenes in Mexico—on the street, in the café, at the hacienda—are all open, light, and spacious. By contrast, the scenes in New York—in Rick's office, at the Blaze Creek estate, in the car—are closed, dark, and claustrophobic. In *The Secret beyond the Door*, Mexico represents the open and natural expression of instinct, and New York represents the claustrophobic inhibition of instinct for the sake of the higher intellect. To imagine itself as cultivated and civilized, as intelligent and lawful, New York must imagine Mexico as natural and primitive, as instinctual and outlaw.

Perhaps it is *apt* that after Mark's speech about women, nature, and instinct, he is the one associated with instincts beyond his control. Whereas Celia is trying to interpret the symbols of his neurosis, Mark is simply reacting to unconscious desires and acting out his old traumas. He is emotional and unpredictable, and Celia is levelheaded and steady. She embodies the analyst using her reason to unlock the secrets of Mark's psyche. Mark embodies the obsessional son unable to get any sort of rational distance from his emotions. He is like a savage animal led by instincts beyond his control. At different moments, both Carrie and Celia refer to Mark as a "beast," a beast who acts on natural instincts. He is the emotional one closer to nature and instincts, and Celia is the rational one relying on her intellect.

This gender reversal puts Celia in the position of asking if she should carry Mark over the threshold and insisting that she will meet him on her ground, not on his, and that she will choose the weapons and the battleground. She insists on "wearing the pants" even while she regards her beautiful evening gown in the looking glass. Like the "big gypsy" wielding the knife, Celia stakes her claims and fights to the death with the ghost of Mark's mother. Yet unlike the gypsy, Celia uses the tools of the intellect, the tools of psychoanalysis, to claim her victory. Mark is also like the big gypsy in that he is acting on instinct, but Mark's is a perverted instinct that does not allow him to "honorably" stake his claim. Still, in the end, like the big gypsy, Mark carries away his "spoils," and as Mark himself says, "To the victor go the spoils." In Mark's case, he literally carries Celia out of the burning house. Perhaps it would be more felicitous to identify Mark with the spoils, however, insofar as he is most certainly spoiled.

Celia uses her reason to liberate instincts and passions. Rather than pit reason against nature or instinct and thereby turn instinct against the self, Celia puts reason into the service of instinct. Celia does not accept Mark's theory that instinct and intellect are inversely proportional. Instead she makes the two work together to separate love from death. Relying on instinct alone leads to the fatalism, and ultimately the pessimism, of Mark's theory that rooms determine behavior and actions, that we are creatures determined by something beyond our control, that even our passions are not our own. This view resonates with the fatalism of film noir. Relying on intellect alone, on the other hand, leads to inhibition and repression, and ultimately neurosis and psychosis; it leads to the prison of Blaze Creek and self-destruction. Mark builds a crypt and then lies in it.

Celia seems to realize that we need both instinct and intellect in some kind of harmony or balance. Once Sleeping Beauty's passion is awakened, she is as ardent about knowing the truth as she is about loving Mark; for her, in the position of analyst, the two are intertwined: there is no love without the pursuit of truth. As Celia tells us in voice-over at the hacienda fountain, when two lovers drink from the fountain, then they will speak only the truth, and their two hearts will beat as one. Two hearts, two passions, become one only through the truth, through the intellect's search for meaning and the passion for interpretation. Passion and truth, instinct and intellect, must also become one. They cannot be cut off from one another. The split between unconscious and conscious that produces an uncanny double must be repaired. In other words, unconscious desires must find expression and articulation in consciousness. Only then can lovers drop their weapons and declare a truce and truth in the "battle between the sexes."

CHAPTER 5

Mad about Noir:
Hitchcock's *Vertigo*

With *Vertigo*, Alfred Hitchcock takes the logic of film noir to its limit. With his self-conscious use of style over narrative and his startling perversion of the investigative structure of film noir, the confusion and fragmentation of classic film noir become obsession and madness. The latent threat of the abject mother in classic film noir becomes the explicit threat of an identification with a depressed and ultimately mad mother. The return of film noir's repressed mother, and the detective's (and audience's) identification with her, throw the spectator into the position of the melancholic unable to mourn or lose this mother who threatens madness.

Vertigo opens with a chase scene. We see a man leaping across rooftops and two men following him, one in a police uniform. The plainclothesman slips and ends up dangling from a rain gutter. The police officer returns to help him and falls to his death. In the next scene, we see the plainclothesman, John "Scottie" Ferguson (James Stewart), balancing a cane in his friend Midge's (Barbara Bel Geddes) apartment. Midge is asking Johnny why he decided to leave the police force. Johnny explains that his vertigo prevents him from doing his job. Still, he says that he is determined to overcome it. Scottie is contacted by an old schoolmate, Gavin Elster (Tom Helmore), who proposes that Scottie do some private detective work following Elster's wife, Madeleine (Kim Novak), to help explain her strange behavior. Elster claims that his wife has become possessed by her dead great-grandmother, Carlotta, who committed suicide at exactly Madeleine's age. Johnny follows Madeleine to Carlotta's old haunts and eventually meets her when he rescues her from San Fransisco Bay. He falls in love with her and tries to break Carlotta's spell. But when Madeleine climbs the bell tower at the mission of St. John the Baptist, Johnny's vertigo prevents him from following her, and he is helpless when she throws herself to her death.

After some time in a mental hospital, Scottie is released but is still obsessed with the beautiful Madeleine. One day he sees a woman who reminds him of Madeleine. He follows Judy (Kim Novak) to her hotel room and makes a date with her. Once he leaves, in voice-over Judy tells us the details of Gavin Elster's plan to murder his wife. In flashback we see that Elster threw his already murdered wife off of the tower while Judy, dressed like Madeleine, watched. Still in love with Scottie, Judy decides to stay and try to make him love her for herself. Scottie insists on remaking Judy into Madeleine by changing her hair color, hairstyle, and clothes. Only once he has transformed her back into Madeleine can he love her. After her transformation is complete, she makes the mistake of wearing Carlotta's necklace, which Scottie knows belonged to the real Madeleine. Finally realizing that Judy was part of a plan to murder Elster's wife, Scottie returns to the scene of the "suicide" and forces Judy to accompany him up into the bell tower. With Judy in tow, Scottie overcomes his vertigo and makes it to the top. He makes her confess to helping Elster kill his wife. Still proclaiming her love for Scottie, Judy sees a shadow enter the bell tower and steps back in terror. As she steps back, she falls from the tower and screams, just as she did when Elster pushed his wife from the same tower. The film ends with Scottie standing out on the ledge of the bell tower, completely cured of his vertigo.

The Logical Limit of Noir Is Madness

Two common features of film noir are the investigative narrative structure of the plot and the emphasis on style over narrative. With *Vertigo*, Hitchcock takes both of these features to extremes. Noir's emphasis on style undermines the investigative narrative structure so that the truth behind the mystery under investigation often remains unclear at the end. The use of extreme lighting, flashbacks, and dramatic point of view shots leaves the spectator with a fragmented sense of the truth. As other feminist film critics have argued, these B movies were more concerned with killing off or punishing the femme fatale than with solving the mystery or leaving the audience with the truth in one neat package. Christine Gledhill argues that "rather than the revelation of socio-economic patterns of political and financial power and corruption which mark the gangster/thriller, Film Noir probes the secrets of female sexuality and male desire within patterns of submission and dominance" (1998, 28). The mystery of film noir, then, is not "whodunit?" but "what is the power of female sexuality?" The power of female sexuality is represented not primarily through the narratives of these films in which the women are killed off, but through the emphasis on visual style through which women often dominate on screen.[1]

Unlike Continental detectives such as Dupin or Sherlock Holmes, the American hard-boiled detective of film noir is stymied in his attempts to use reason to solve the crime. More often than not, these detectives resort to brute force or gut instinct to crack the case.[2] In his search for truth, the film noir detective is usually duped, most likely by the femme fatale. Within film noir, the use of reason does not lead to truth. Rather, the truth can only be found through the body and not the mind. Even then, what film noir shows us is that the truth is always compromised and ambiguous. The hard-boiled detective of film noir may have his principles and his own brand of tough integrity, but he is usually an ambiguous character playing both sides, somewhere in between the law and crime. We can't say between good and evil because in film noir there is no good that has not in some way been contaminated by evil. In film noir, life is tough, and the truth hurts; to survive, our protagonists must themselves become tough and skeptical.

Taking this noir logic to its limits, *Vertigo* teaches a harsh lesson in the futility of reason in the search for truth. More than this, it shows the ways in which truth is constructed and thereby unmasks even film noir's ambiguous commitment to truth, especially the truth of the femme fatale: in film noir, if the truth is a woman, she is man-made. In *Vertigo*, Scottie gives the resistant Judy a forceful makeover to turn her into the mysterious ideal of feminine beauty Madeleine Elster, who earlier had jumped to her death. This makeover is a repetition of the unseen construction of Madeleine by Gavin Elster as part of his plan to kill his wife, the unseen real Madeleine. Scottie brutally transforms Judy into the lost Madeleine, just as Elster had done before him. As Laura Mulvey argues, *Vertigo* is the story of woman cut to the measure of male desire (1975, 17). *Vertigo* shows us how the femme fatale is man-made, and by so doing, it shows us how the truth is created.

Scottie's insistence on reason and logic is ineffective in his attempts to bring Madeleine back from her trances. As the film later reveals, this is because Madeleine is not what she seems; she is an illusion, Gavin Elster's creation. Her trances aren't any more real than she is. Logic and reason are useless in relation to the fiction created by Elster and Judy Barton as Madeleine. Moreover, Scottie's faith in reason and logic accelerates his fall into madness. His faith in reason, and not his vertigo, is what ultimately prevents him from saving Madeleine. Blinded by his faith in reason, along with his desire for Madeleine, Scottie refuses to believe that something sinister is going on. His faith in reason blinds him to the sinister truth that Madeleine is nothing but an illusion created by Gavin Elster as part of his murderous plot. Because Scottie believes that he can use reason to save Madeleine, he is devastated when he can't. Hitchcock's *Vertigo* teaches the difficult lesson that reason is always undermined by the unconscious—Scottie's vertigo triumphs over his reason.

In *Vertigo*, the free-floating anxiety of classic film noir becomes explicitly associated with the detective's guilt, his guilt over the death of his fellow officer and his guilt over the death of Madeleine. When Scottie asks Judy, "Why me?" she answers that Elster knew of Scottie's condition, of his vertigo. If the answer to the question "Why me?" in classic film noir is "for no reason at all" or "because fate arbitrarily puts the finger on you," in *Vertigo* the answer is "because of your unconscious desires. You still can't overcome your fate." In *Vertigo*, however, fate is not an accident outside yourself but is determined by your own unconscious. Those uncontrollable factors that threaten your demise are no longer external but internal. It is not just that you can't control your fate, but that you can't control yourself.

In *Vertigo*, the truth of physical facts gives way to the truth of the psyche. The threat to the detective is no longer physical but mental. The investigative narrative structure of film noir becomes a psychological investigation whose physical hazards—falling, death—become metaphors for psychological hazards, metaphors for the fall into madness. The investigation into women and their sexual power over men is no longer the latent motivation of film noir; in *Vertigo* it becomes explicit. Madeleine herself, and her power over Scottie, is the film's real mystery. This is evident when the truth of the mystery is revealed two-thirds of the way into the film. Once we know the answer to "whodunit," the lingering question is "What will Scottie do when he finds out?" By perverting the investigative structure of film noir, Hitchcock invents the psychological thriller. The mystery becomes the secrets of the psyche, and the danger becomes madness.

Hitchcock's emphasis on the unconscious is most evident in his visual style. Like classic film noir, *Vertigo* seems to privilege style over narrative. In fact, in *Vertigo*, in a certain sense, style takes the place of narrative in telling the story. The film is full of towering buildings, bridges, and the hills of San Francisco conjuring vertigo. Much of the film takes us along with Scottie as he follows Madeleine in his car; this journey seems to take us in circles, mirroring Scottie's spiral into madness. Like other noir directors, Hitchcock uses lighting and shadows to create the mood of his film. The repeated images of Madeleine in profile or silhouette work almost like flashbacks, reminding us that she has been there before. Judy/Madeleine is often shot in shadow, even in silhouette. Madeleine is often almost glowing and ghostly in overexposed shots. The most striking use of lighting comes in the scene when Judy emerges from the bathroom dressed exactly like Madeleine, bathed in an otherworldly green light.

Color distinguishes *Vertigo* from classic noir. Hitchcock uses color, like other elements of his visual style, as a substitute for narrative because it more directly affects the unconscious, which operates according to images and associations. For example, the colors in which his women are clad say much about their characters: Midge is shown in pastel sweater-skirt sets; Madeleine wears black, white, and gray; and Judy wears bright greens and lilac. The color red is associated with Carlotta, especially her necklace, and throughout the film seems to threaten madness. Hitchcock's aggressive use of color suggests that color itself threatens madness. The beginning title sequence signals the move from black and white to color as a dangerous move. As a gesture to classic noir, the title sequence begins in black and white with music typical of film noir murder mysteries. Quickly, however, Hitchcock begins to introduce only the slightest color when we see the close-up image of a woman's face, so big that it exceeds the frame of the film. The camera moves into a close-up of her eye, and she is suddenly bathed in red light; at the same moment, her eyes look terrified, as if she has seen a ghost. The color red is associated with this threat from a world beyond, the threat of Carlotta's madness. As the opening sequence progresses, various colors take over the screen until the screen goes black and we have moved inside the eye of the woman, where brightly colored spirals move to the tempo of unsettling music. These colors and shapes are repeated in Scottie's bizarre nightmare of falling into Carlotta's grave.

The threat of color is again striking when Scottie follows Madeleine to the florist's shop. In this scene, Scottie follows Madeleine into an alley and through a back door. Inside, the corridor is dimly lit, and Scottie is seen in shadows wearing the uniform of a classic film noir detective. At this moment, we are thrown back to the classic noirs of the 1940s. Once Scottie opens the door—a door that does not move from inside to out but across the screen, as if to suggest that he is opening the door onto another world, perhaps the world of the unconscious, the world of madness—we are thrown into a world of color. Again we are confronted with an aggressive use of color when the reds, pinks, and purples of the flowers explode onto the screen. Scottie stands just on the other side of the doorway looking in at this other threatening world, which he will be unable to resist. Color represents the mysterious and dangerous world of feminine sexuality, a melancholy world haunted by the fascinating and terrifying abject mother, Carlotta.

The Melancholy Spectator

In her chapter on *Vertigo* in *The Women Who Knew Too Much*, Tania Modleski argues that Scottie identifies with Madeleine/Carlotta and that his identification is melancholic. Modleski persuasively cites Scottie's feminization throughout the film, which she interprets as evidence of Scottie's identification with Madeleine/Carlotta: zoom shots that Modleski interprets as Scottie's desire to merge with Madeleine, Scottie's search for the dead Madeleine just as Carlotta looked for her lost child, and Scottie's dream in which he falls into Carlotta's grave. Modleski's thesis invites us to diagnose Scottie's identification with Madeleine/ Carlotta in the dream as both his refusal to lose his love object by incorporating it into his own ego and his guilty self-reproach for letting Madeleine fall to her death. Scottie puts himself in the place of Madeleine looking into Carlotta's grave, and he is the one who falls from the tower instead of Madeleine. This substitution of himself for Madeleine signals both sides of his melancholic identity: identification with the lost object and self-punishment caused by a combination of guilt over the loved one's death and displaced anger toward the loved one for leaving.

Applying Freud's theory of melancholia to the film, Modleski describes Scottie's identification with the lost Madeleine as a melancholic identification that produces Scottie's sadistic attitude toward Judy, the Madeleine substitute. Leaving aside the problems with Modleski's underdeveloped thesis, and her distortion of Freud's theory—the melancholic substitutes the lost other for his own ego rather than find external substitutes for the lost other—her analysis suggests that the audience is also put in the position of the melancholic. Modleski argues that Hitchcock sets up the audience to identify with Scottie through dramatic point of view shots throughout the first part of the film, and then by discrediting his vision when he is released from the mental institution and mistakes several women for Madeleine. Modleski says that "we experience through Scottie the split that Freud says is characteristic of melancholia: on the one hand we identify with him, as before, but the repeated disqualification of his vision makes us wary; we become more judgmental than we had previously been" (1988, 96). She suggests that the audience is put in the position of the melancholic both identifying with Scottie and judging him and themselves harshly for his or their faulty vision.

Modleski's suggestions about the melancholic position of the spectator can be expanded and extended to explain Hitchcock's perversion of the investigative narrative structure of film noir and the return of the repressed abject mother. *Vertigo*'s most dramatic interruption of the classic investigative narrative structure of film noir is that the solution to the murder mystery is revealed long before the end of the film. More than this, it is revealed not by the male detective but by the femme fatale; she possesses the truth and decides to keep it from the detective, who discovers the truth so late in the film that spectators can't help wonder how he can be so dim-witted. Hitchcock uses the classic film noir conventions of flashback and voice-over to reveal the truth. But unlike traditional film noir, in *Vertigo* the flashback and voice-over are the property of the femme fatale. Hitchcock uses the conventions of film noir to undermine the investigative narrative structure on which the genre is based. If classic noir is satisfying because it appears to deliver the truth at the end of the film through the detective's investigative efforts and then becomes frustrating only upon reflection when all of the pieces don't fit neatly together, *Vertigo*'s premature revelation refuses the satisfaction of classic noir. Instead of giving us the illusion of a solution to the investigation as a climax to our pleasure in the film, Hitchcock turns the investigative structure back on itself and leaves us asking why he revealed the solution too soon. With Hitchcock's *Vertigo*, the real investigation begins only when the film is over. And it is not an investigation into the facts but an investigation into the motivations and psychic dynamics of the film itself.

Critics and viewers have been angry and confused by *Vertigo*'s premature revelation. When the movie was first released, a film critic at the

London Observer wrote, "The last half-hour is as dull as ditchwater, for there is no suspense, and no mystery remains except the mystery of who is supposed to care what happens."[3] It is precisely this premature revelation that throws the spectator into the melancholic position. Until the revelation scene in Judy's hotel room, the camera insistently gives us Scottie's point of view. With this scene, the camera leaves Scottie for the first time. The camera's insistence on showing Scottie's point of view, at times dramatically panning into what Scottie sees both with his eyes and with his mind's eye, forges a strong identification with Scottie on the part of the spectator. We see only what he sees and as he sees. In the museum, when Scottie realizes that Madeleine carries the same flowers and wears the same hairstyle as Carlotta in her portrait, the camera shows us the flowers or the hair, shows us Scottie looking at the flowers or the hair, and then a second time shows us the flowers or the hair, but now the camera dramatically zooms in as if to suggest that Scottie has made the connection between Madeleine and Carlotta. We see with Scottie's mind's eye. As Modleski argues, we are forced to identify with Scottie's desire to merge with Madeleine/Carlotta.

The persistence of Scottie's point of view throughout the first part of the film sets up the spectator's fall into melancholy in the second part of the film. With the revelation scene in Judy's hotel room, we lose Scottie's perspective. Scottie's perspective, with its faith in reason, is the lost object that sends the spectator spiraling into melancholy. The loss of Scottie's perspective combined with Judy's revelation tears the ideal from the real and exposes the ideal as mere deception.

Judy is a poor substitute for Madeleine because she is real. Madeleine, on the other hand, wanders wordlessly, like a ghost, bathed in white light for most of the film. Unlike Madeleine, Judy is not the ideal woman: she talks too much, and her clothes, makeup, and manners are crude. Whereas Madeleine is introduced with myths and mystery, Judy is introduced with proof and ID cards. Just before she runs up the tower, Madeleine warns Scottie (and the viewer) that "it's too late ... I'm already dead." Because ideals don't exist, as the ideal, Madeleine is already dead. Scottie echoes her warning when in the final scene he tells Judy, "It's too late, you're already dead." Once Judy reveals the truth about Madeleine, we know that she did not exist, that she was created by Elster to murder his wife. Our own faith in reason and in our own eyes, Scottie's eyes, is lost, and we are thrown into melancholy. In this moment, we lose both the ideal feminine and the ideal masculine. Madeleine's eternal feminine beauty is exposed as a man-made fetish. Scottie's phallic rationality is exposed as impotent and fallible. Witnessing the death of the ideal, the audience (like Scottie) is put in the melancholic position of both refusing to give it up and refusing to settle for less, and becoming angry at its loss. By opening the space between the ideal and reality, *Vertigo* throws the audience into a free fall.

The audience is set up to identify with Scottie, and we feel betrayed when we lose the privilege of Scottie's perspective and are forced to take Judy's in her flashback. We have been duped along with Scottie. We have been "ditched" in a way that provokes anger. Both the loss of

Scottie (James Stewart) with Kim Novak's two characters, Madeleine and Judy, in *Vertigo*.

the ideal and the loss of Scottie's perspective open up the abyss in the ego, the hole in the self, that Freud describes as melancholy: "The loss of the object became transformed into a loss in the ego" (1917, 170); "in grief the world becomes poor and empty; in melancholia it is the ego itself" (164). Melancholy is a type of vertigo insofar as it empties the ego and opens an abyss at the center of self-identity. Modleski begins her chapter on *Vertigo* with a quotation from Sartre's *Being and Nothingness:* "Masochism is characterized as a species of vertigo, vertigo not before a precipice of rock and earth but before the abyss of the Other's subjectivity" (1988, 87). Melancholy, then, is vertigo before the abyss of your own subjectivity become other.

Vertigo shows the repetition of melancholic losses and incorporations. Madeleine acts the part of the melancholic in her identification with Carlotta to the point of being possessed by the spirit of her dead grandmother and committing suicide. Scottie becomes obsessed with Madeleine, and when he loses her, he suffers from a melancholic identification with Madeleine and her identification with Carlotta. Finally, the audience is thrown into melancholy when we are forced to give up Scottie's perspective and accept Judy's as our own.

Carlotta Valdez loses her daughter and her lover. She suffers from melancholia to the extreme that she loses herself, and her losses lead her to commit suicide. Freud diagnoses melancholic suicide as the incorporation of the object within the ego followed by sadism directed at the lost/disappointing object. His description of the melancholic suicide fits the suicide of Carlotta Valdez. Freud says that "the analysis of melancholia shows that the ego can kill itself only when, the object-cathexis having been withdrawn upon it, it can treat itself as an object, when it is able to launch against itself the animosity relating to an object—that primordial reaction on the part of the ego to all objects in the outer world. Thus in the regression from narcissistic object-choice the object is indeed abolished, but in spite of all it proves itself stronger than the ego's self. In the two contrasting situations of intense love and of suicide the ego is overwhelmed by the object, though in totally different ways" (1917, 173).

The Melancholy Mother

If the mother is the fascinating and yet threatening figure repressed in film noir, then *Vertigo* stages the return of the repressed. *Vertigo* presents us with two mothers: the good mother Midge, and the bad/mad mother Carlotta. Midge is the nurturing, overprotective mother who is powerless to protect Scottie from the bad/mad mother, Carlotta. Midge is the castrated mother, whose attempts at painting herself into the place of the object of Scottie's desire turn him off completely; she cannot hold his attention and eventually disappears from the film. In her final scene, she tries to revive Scottie with the very Mozart music that he made her turn off earlier, complaining that it gave him vertigo. In this scene, she tells him not to worry because "mother's here." He doesn't even acknowledge her presence because he is in a trance induced by his melancholy relation to the bad/mad mother, Madeleine/Carlotta. If Midge has no power over Scottie, Carlotta through Madeleine has an otherworldly power over him that threatens him with madness. Just as Madeleine becomes possessed by Carlotta, so Scottie becomes possessed by Madeleine's identification with Carlotta.

Carlotta represents the abject mother, both fascinating and terrifying, whose maternal sexuality threatens madness. Her ethnicity is also abject in that it is the return of the repressed other; it threatens to break down the proper borders of the self, especially the borders of Madeleine's white-American identity. In Scottie's dream, the sound of castanets, associated with Carlotta's excessive ethnicity, threatens his fall into madness. There Carlotta becomes a caricature of a flamenco dancer (her Mexican identity is displaced onto Spanish icons in the film), presumably associated more with nightclubs than with motherhood. Behind Madeleine's staid grays, blacks, and whites lies her exotic "Spanish" grandmother dressed in bright colors, who like the overly made-up, garish Judy becomes the mistress of a married man.

As local historian and bookstore owner "Pop" Leibel (Konstantin Shayne) explains, Carlotta came from a mission south of the city and, like many such girls, became the mistress of a wealthy white man who cast her aside. Pop's story suggests that Carlotta was Mexican American and poor; like "so many" poor Mexican American girls she either tried to gain class mobility through sexual relations with a wealthy white man and/or a wealthy white man took advantage of her situation. Like Judy, Carlotta's class position, along with her ethnicity, ensures that she can never take the place of the proper wife or mother; rather, she is used and cast aside. Like Helen/Velma in *Murder, My Sweet*, Carlotta is punished for her attempt to pass for upper class. In Scottie's dream, Carlotta's sexuality is associated with her ethnicity; she is the flamenco dancer who tempts him to madness. She is the mother whose sexuality and ethnicity compromise her child and ultimately lead her to suicide. Her desirability as ethnic other, as exotic flamenco dancer, is also what dooms her as both beloved and mother.

Scottie both desires and identifies with the exotic Carlotta through Madeleine. Madeleine is quite clearly a mother substitute through her identification with Carlotta, the melancholy mother. The melancholy that defines her identity is as the childless mother and as the spurned lover. Once the lover becomes a mother, she is cast out because "men had the freedom and power to do that in those days." Yet through Madeleine's identification with Carlotta, the mother retains her sexual appeal and power. Madeleine's power over Scottie, who seems helpless to resist her, comes directly through her mysterious identification with the exotic, melancholy Carlotta. For Scottie, Carlotta is a mystery to be solved, the mystery of maternal sexuality. *Vertigo* teaches us, however, that this investigation into forbidden maternal sexuality leads to madness.

Maternal sexuality leads to madness because it is melancholy: the sad Carlotta becomes the mad Carlotta. If Scottie's identification with Madeleine, and thereby our identification with him, is melancholy, it is because of the mother's melancholy. The mother is melancholy because she is abandoned by the world of men, and at the same time, her child is taken away by that world. The world of men, who have the freedom and power within a patriarchal society to do as they please with her, first defines her worth in terms of sex and maternity and then robs her of her self-worth once she has served her purpose. Like Madeleine Elster's "suicide," Carlotta's suicide is just a cover for the murder she has suffered at the hands of patriarchy. Suffering from the loss of her self-worth as both lover and mother, she identifies with the sadism of patriarchy and directs its reproaches at herself: if she is undesirable, then she is to blame; if she has lost her child, then she is to blame. Just as Gavin Elster and Scottie both remake plain-old Judy into the mysterious feminine ideal Madeleine, so patriarchy remakes the mother into a melancholic. By so doing, the world of free and powerful men absolves itself of any responsibility for the treatment and suffering of its women and mothers.

As in *Murder, My Sweet*, in *Vertigo* the mother's necklace becomes the ambivalent symbol of her power and patriarchy's attempts to control her. Repeatedly the camera zooms in for close-ups of Carlotta's necklace, from Scottie's perspective. In his nightmare, Scottie again sees Carlotta wearing the necklace, and the camera goes in for a close-up that, as Modleski says, gives the impression of Scottie merging with the necklace. Something about this necklace fascinates Scottie and holds him in its power. And yet Judy's "slip" is putting on the necklace as she is preparing to go out dressed up as Madeleine. Out of love for Scottie, Judy doesn't tell him the truth, hoping that he can love her "for herself." She goes along with his obsessive desire to dress her up as Madeleine. But Scottie seems repulsed by Judy and cannot manage to kiss her. Only when she again embodies his ideal woman can Scottie finally kiss her and embrace her. After the famous kiss on the revolving pedestal, Judy is hungry and wants a "big steak." It is as if her appetite is unleashed through love. The necklace will serve as a leash for that desire. Earlier, Elster told Scottie that Madeleine had some of Carlotta's jewels (Freud says jewels symbolize women's sex organs), so once Scottie sees the necklace, in a flashback he remembers Carlotta's necklace and finally he realizes the truth.

Judy makes the mistake of wearing the mother's necklace. While possessing the necklace gives her power over Scottie, wearing it gives him power over her. The necklace reveals to Scottie that she has been possessed before, that she is not really his after all, but that she belonged to Gavin Elster. Perhaps this is what enrages Scottie: that she has already been had, that he never possessed her; that he never had the chance to possess her. The necklace is a symbol of the chain or leash of patriarchal control that already had Judy and that made her into Made-leine. In *Vertigo*, as in *Murder, My Sweet*, the mother's necklace signals the ambivalent power of maternal sexuality and patriarchal attempts to control it. Within the patriarchal imaginary, having sexual power gives the woman power over man, but displaying sexuality, particularly for-bidden maternal sexuality, turns the tables on her and deflates his desire. Sexually aroused by the forbidden desire for the mother, man becomes angry and blames the woman for provoking him. When Scottie sees the face of motherly Midge painted onto the mysterious Carlotta, he can no longer sustain his erotic attachment to the mother; instead he is repulsed by such a suggestion. When he sees Carlotta's necklace on Judy, his desire becomes anger. In both *Murder* and *Vertigo*, the necklace represents the ambivalent power of the abject mother: as both fasci-nating erotic sexuality and terrifying phallic/castrating power in need of control.

The Obsessional Son

There is a price to pay for abjecting the mother, especially for the son who can't quite lose her. The son who identifies with the abject mother becomes abject himself. This abjection can take various symptomatic forms: he can become a pervert, turned on by the abject, or he can be-come an obsessive in his attempts to separate himself from the abject mother. The rituals and repetitions of obsessive personalities can be seen as attempts to ritualistically purify the abject mother who contin-ues to haunt them. In *New Maladies of the Soul*, Julia Kristeva claims that a "veritable 'buried mother' resides at the core of the psyche of obses-sionals" (1996, 53). This "buried mother" is a depressed mother with whom the obsessional identifies and against whom he struggles for his life. As Kristeva describes it, the obsessional neurotic's identification with maternal depression leads him to deny this depression and to com-pensate for it with an overinvestment in the symbolic. Through his in-vestment in the symbolic, he takes the place of the paternal agent that he imagines to be the cause of his mother's suffering, what she lacks (62–63). In the case of Scottie, he tries to compensate for his identification with the depressed mother Madeleine/Carlotta with an overinvestment in the power of reason and logic. In a struggle with Carlotta, he tries to repossess Madeleine by occupying the place of paternal protector and savior; he is not going to let Madeleine suffer what her grandmother Carlotta suffered at the hands of men. And yet that is exactly what he does; he lets Madeleine fall to her death, and he nearly pushes Judy to hers.

Kristeva continues her analysis of the obsessional son's identification with his depressed mother by indicating that he eroticizes the wounded and depressive narcissism of his mother by taking revenge against her in sadistic relationships with other women. In this way, he both protects his mother, whom he loves/is, and punishes her through her surrogates. He both protects the purity of his mother's silent depression and eroticizes her suffering. Making women suffer, then, is what turns him on. The obsessional's ambivalent identity is supported by his identification with the depressed mother and his attempts to protect her, on the one hand, and his eroticization of her suffering, on the other. Certainly, Scottie is attracted to Madeleine's suffering. And in his attempts to make Judy into Madeleine, into the lost mother Carlotta, he becomes sadistic to the point of dragging her up the stairs of the tower where she will fall to her death. Thus Scottie becomes the obsessional son identifying with and eroticizing the mother's suffering through his sadistic relationship with the Madeleine/Carlotta mother substitute, Judy.

In Pursuit of Sexual Difference

In spite of its feminization of the detective and his identification with the depressed mother, *Vertigo* seems to present sexual difference with a vengeance in its characterizations of pursuit. *Vertigo* opens with a scene of pursuit when Scottie and the police officer who falls to his death are pursuing a criminal. As the plot continues, *Vertigo* repeats different stories of pursuit: there is Madeleine's pursuit of Carlotta, Scottie's pursuit of Madeleine, his pursuit of Judy, and Judy's pursuit of him. Madeleine/ Judy and Scottie adopt stereotypical passive feminine and active masculine positions in relation to the pursuit of love. In his pursuit of Madeleine, Scottie is shown metaphorically and literally in the driver's seat; we see him following her, saving her, undressing her while she is unconscious, holding her. Ultimately he is unsuccessful in his attempts to possess Madeleine; she is already possessed, and he isn't potent enough to win against the phallic mother. In his pursuit of Judy, Scottie is even more aggressive. He barges into Judy's apartment, insists on knowing who she is, forces her to change her clothes and hairstyles. He is active to the point of sadism, while Judy is passive to the point of masochism.

Both Madeleine and Judy, on the other hand, are passive in their pursuit of love. Madeleine does not try to possess Scottie but is herself possessed by Carlotta. Judy stays to try to make him love her for herself, but she "makes" him love her only by becoming his passive object of manipulation. Scottie wants to have or possess the object of his desire, while Madeleine/Judy wants to be possessed. She wants to be loved for herself, while Scottie wants to have her. The distinction between being and having in relation to sexual difference is Lacan's revision of Freud's distinction between passivity and activity. Lacan maintains that sexual difference is determined in relation to being or having, specifically being or having the phallus or desire and its satisfaction (1977b). Madeleine/ Judy wants to be satisfaction, while Scottie wants to have it. Even while *Vertigo* sets up this neat and traditional scenario of sexual difference, it also reveals that this version of sexual difference is an illusion created within the patriarchal imaginary. Scottie can't have it, and Madeleine/ Judy can't be it, precisely because Madeleine/Judy has already been had. In keeping with Lacanian psychoanalysis, *Vertigo* teaches us that desire is ultimately unfulfillable because the object of our desire is an illusion. The mirror recognition that sets up identity is always a misrecognition (Lacan 1977a). Scottie's identification with Madeleine/Carlotta is a misrecognition, and that realization drives him mad.

Vertigo's gender trouble throws us into a hall of mirrors that produces a dizzying spiral between desire and identification. Scottie's fear of heights is merely a metaphor for a more dizzying fear of the abject mother and her devouring threat. The collapse between desire for the feminine and for the mother, and identity with them, causes a free fall that produces the vertigo effect in terms of sexual identity. More dangerous than the looming heights of buildings, bridges, and staircases is the threat of the phallic/castrating mother. The spectator is forced to participate in this ambivalent desire that both fascinates and enrages. *Vertigo* takes us to the precipice of sexual identity and gives a glimpse of the dizzying delights and the madness of jumping into the abyss of sexual difference.

CHAPTER 6

The Borderlands of
Touch of Evil

It has been argued that *Touch of Evil* is not so much the end of film noir as it is the beginning of a new kind of border film.[1] This is a forceful and insightful reading of Welles's film, but one cannot help but think that to put such an emphasis on the intended or unwitting ambiguity of *Touch of Evil* in particular and film noir in general sometimes misses the significance of the intensity with which that ambiguity is resisted. Here we will argue instead that *Touch of Evil* is an example of an ambivalent film that intensely resists contact with ambiguity and insists on identity in ways that illuminate the relationship between race and sex in film noir.

Touch of Evil as Didactic Melodrama

Touch of Evil tells the story of a crime and its investigation, both of which take place on the border between the United States and Mexico. At the beginning of the film, Mr. Linnekar, a prominent and influential businessman of the region, and his girlfriend Zita (Joi Lansing) are brutally murdered when the car in which they are driving suddenly explodes as it crosses the border. The rest of the film is the story of the investigation of the murder by the film's protagonists, Ramón Miguel "Mike" Vargas (Charlton Heston) and Hank Quinlan (Orson Welles). It is also the story of Quinlan's corrupt methods, and his attempts to get at the truth by framing Manolo Sánchez (Victor Milan), Marcia Linnekar's (Joanna Moore) Mexican boyfriend, for the murder. Quinlan's methods are ineffectively resisted by the virtuous Mexican investigator, who finds himself the victim of Quinlan's smear campaign. At the end of the film, however, good appears to triumph over evil, although both Vargas and his wife do not emerge unscathed from the experience.

Despite the famously ambiguous ending, Orson Welles goes to great lengths in this film to distinguish good from evil. From this perspective, the film is a melodrama whose hero is the Mexican Mike Vargas struggling against the villain, his evil North American nemesis, Hank Quinlan. At the center of the melodrama is the smear campaign by the corrupt cop against the innocent detective. It is a battle between archetypes, characters who are larger than life, visually emphasized by the extended metaphor of the bullfight. Time and time again, Welles places Quinlan near the huge head of a bull that hangs on the wall of Tanya's place (Quinlan's former Gypsy lover, played by Marlene Dietrich). Throughout the film, we are constantly reminded that Quinlan is a creature of instinct, acting always according to the messages his "game leg" sends him. On Tanya's wall, we also find pictures of sharply dressed bullfighters. As if to drive home the metaphor, in the film's final sequence, Quinlan's death is visually foreshadowed by associating him with a bull, and by framing Vargas inside a small mirror that hangs beside the bullfighters' pictures. The film insists that the Mexican Vargas is the sequin-dressed good matador who risks his humanity to kill Hank Quinlan, the evil beast, the animal adversary, the archetypal bully.

In a reference to the famous 1957 book *The Untouchables*, *Touch of Evil* represents Mike Vargas as a Mexican Eliot Ness.[2] The head of a cleanup operation, Vargas's Eliot Ness–like incorruptibility is evidenced by his clean-cut looks, his three-piece suit, and his dark glasses. His name is also a reference to a detective of Spanish myth: "Vargas" is part of an old Spanish proverb ("Averíguelo Vargas," or "let Vargas find out"). It refers to Francisco de Vargas, a fifteenth-century Spanish courtier from Queen Isabella's reign famously known for his ability to crack difficult cases. Thus Welles goes to great lengths to portray Vargas as the proverbial cleanup man *(Nettoyer)* sent for when everything else has failed. He cleans up society from vice both metaphorically and literally:

he cleans those around him while keeping himself clean. It is no surprise that in the film, we see him cleaning his hands and glasses and even cleaning up after the dirty cop. When in a fit of rage Quinlan breaks two pigeon eggs and stains his jacket, it is Vargas who offers him a clean white handkerchief. Later in the film, Quinlan will tell Peter Menzies (Joseph Calleia) that he is carrying a halo for Vargas and will shortly be turned into Saint Peter complete with wings. Vargas's penchant for, and even obsession with, spiritual and noncorporeal cleanliness is evidenced in his chivalrous reaction to his wife's dishonor: "How can I leave here until my wife's name is clean? Clean!"

The struggle between the two men (Quinlan and Vargas) is played out over the innocent body of Susan Vargas (Janet Leigh). A white woman from Philadelphia, Susan is married to Vargas, who reminds us constantly of her innocence. Throughout the film, he calls her Suzie, and in a conscious effort to infantilize her, he tells the border patrol that he is "hot on the trail of a chocolate soda for (his) wife" at the beginning of the film. Quinlan doesn't buy this, however, and when Vargas complains about the fact that she was accosted by the Grandis on the North American side of the border, Quinlan insidiously suggests that perhaps she knew these shady characters beforehand and was willingly picked up by them. By the end of the film, Quinlan has succeeded in staining Susan's virginal image and has turned his insinuation into a reality. With help from the Mafia-like Grandi family, Quinlan frames Susan for murder, drug addiction, and prostitution. She falls into Quinlan's trap and dramatically loses her good-girl virginal looks. By the end of the film, she is picked up by the vice squad, drugged, and charged with possession of narcotics and murder.

As Schwartz (Vargas's ally throughout the film, played by Mort Mills) points out to Vargas, Susan is found half-naked. Undressed by the Grandi girls, her body has been exposed. Before she is found, we see her outside her hotel room, on the fire escape stairs, crying out for help to a crowd that mistakes her for a prostitute.[3] Covered only by a white sheet, and in plain view, she is unrecognizable to her husband, who drives by in a convertible right under her sight. Touched by evil, her half-naked and now polluted body is transformed and becomes invisible to her husband. Welles visually emphasizes the metaphorical distance between Susan and the untouchable Vargas by having the Mexican detective drive his car under a sign that reads "Jesus saves." While Vargas is associated with Jesus, the Christian savior of human souls, Susan's polluted body is associated with sin. Ironically, Vargas's saintly status makes him blind to his wife, whose body is now sinful and naked. Not surprisingly, later in the film, Vargas will leave Susan behind in a cell while he insists to Menzies (Quinlan's unwitting partner in crime) that despite Quinlan's smear tactics, Susan's family and good name must remain clean. "Her family! Her good name! Nothing's been touched by all this ... filth!" Vargas's outburst suggests that he is not as concerned with her earthly body as with her reputation and his name. As required by the melodrama that structures the film, Susan's body may have been touched by evil, but something both more ephemeral and more important is at stake and must remain unpolluted. Her soul is still susceptible of saving and must be saved. Significantly, her unpolluted soul is equivalent to Vargas's untouchable family name and to his pure Spanish Mexican heritage.

From this perspective, *Touch of Evil* is a film that visually and narratively insists on inverting the racial equation predominant during the forties and fifties in the United States that constructed North American whites as superior to so-called colored races. The film's inversion of the equation between a white race and goodness makes it a film critical of the institutionalized racism that put George Wallace in the governor's mansion in Alabama in 1963 under the platform of "segregation now, segregation tomorrow, and segregation forever." More to the point, the film demonstrates Welles's lasting commitment to the defense of Mexican Americans during the so-called zoot suit riots in Los Angeles and reminds the viewer of his participation as spokesman for the Sleepy Lagoon Defense Committee, which was in part responsible for the release (in 1944) of Mexican Americans unjustly accused and imprisoned after the riots (Wollen 1996). *Touch of Evil*'s melodramatic structure is thus conventional in its intimate association with a didactic purpose. The film aims at expelling evil from the social order while insisting on pure good and evil identities.

The Logic of Welles's Defense

Despite its melodramatic structure, however, the ambiguity of *Touch of Evil* has been a constant in the film's reception since its release, as is evident in the 1958 interview of Orson Welles by the film journal *Cahiers du Cinéma*. Focusing on the representation of Hank Quinlan, the corrupt cop and villain whose instincts nevertheless prove him to be right about the Mexican murderer and who is betrayed by his best friend at the end of the film, the interviewers press Welles on the film's apparent moral ambiguity. They ask him whether he is playing devil's advocate in this film. "You give the devil a chance for salvation. That's important after all!" (Comito 1998, 207). In the interview, Welles is clearly uneasy about the implications of this characterization of himself and actively resists such an interpretation of the film. Significantly, he responds to the suggestion of moral ambiguity in the film with references to the noir antihero fatefully in love with evil itself.

> All the characters I've played, and of whom we've been speaking, are versions of Faust, and I'm against every Faust, because I believe it's impossible for a man to be great without admitting that there is something greater than himself. This might be the Law, or God, or Art.... But ... an actor is in love with the role he plays. He's like a man who embraces a woman, he gives her something of himself. An actor is not a devil's advocate, he's a lover, a lover of someone of the opposite sex. And for me Faust is like the opposite sex.... I belong to the other camp, but in playing Faust I want to be true and faithful to him, to give him the best of myself, and the best arguments I can find, for we live in a world that has been made by Faust. Our world is Faustian. (Comito 1998, 207–8)

Welles's attempt to clarify his position regarding Quinlan is not lacking in ambiguity, but perhaps it is straightforward on two accounts. First, Welles wants to argue that to play a Faustian character like Hank

Quinlan, an actor must be true and faithful to the part. An actor must love Quinlan just as he loves someone "of the opposite sex." Second, Welles believes that the world is Faustian. Not only has it been compromised by Faust's pact with the devil, but the world "has been made by Faust." Faust, compared here to a woman, is the maker of the world and is responsible for the world's evil. Welles stresses that to claim that Hank Quinlan is a morally ambiguous character is not only to miss the difference between Quinlan the character and Welles the actor but to be unaware of the more important difference between good and evil, which is as clear as the opposition between the sexes for Welles.

The metaphors that Welles uses to describe acting are consistent with those he uses to describe directing in the same interview. If an actor is a chivalrous lover who embraces the maker of an evil world, a director is a conqueror of "uninhabited terrain" who "cultivates what lies fallow." The maker of the world, the uninhabited terrain, and the fertile soil are all metaphors for the body of woman. To act and direct is to embrace and dominate a body marked as primitive, wild, animal, and evil, but also to love a body both fertile and virginal. To act and direct means to be true and faithful to a body first marked as animal and sexual, and second marked as virginal and maternal. It also means to exercise absolute control over this body by replacing its "law of the jungle" with the Law of the actor or the director, both of which are marked as male. This is Welles's Law.

Thus Welles's melodramatic message about the justice of racial equality depends on condemning the femme fatale. To put it in another way, Welles displaces the blame of the melodramatic Fall away from a racialized body onto a sexualized body. He criticizes North American racism and defends Mexicans in Los Angeles by still maintaining the existence of a Manichaean evil force that he now places on female sexuality. Welles's *Touch of Evil* follows a similar logic, although the film's ending is somewhat at odds with moral clarity (whereby the good hero struggles with the evil villain and rides happily into the sunset). This tension results from the fact that the film is also the arena for a struggle between the saintly, untouchable image of a melodramatic hero and the fatalism and blindness that traditionally haunt the noir antihero. But this struggle too complements the logic of Welles's defense, since Vargas's fall from his status as an untouchable knight in shining armor depends on his wife's loss of virtue and good name.

Touchy to the point of explosion about Susan's virtue, Vargas loses control when he learns that his wife has disappeared from her motel room. He abandons his calm and polite exterior and tears into the Grandis' Rancho Grande, leaving it a complete wreck as he looks for Susan and shouts, "Listen, I'm no cop now, I'm a husband." Significantly, his loss of internal control is accompanied by the loss of his correct English and by his return to Spanish. It is also marked by the loss of his clean and neat exterior. Indeed, like his wife, we see Vargas gradually undressed and his skin exposed. Before the scene at the Grandis' Rancho Grande, we always see Vargas wearing a clean, pressed, and buttoned-up three-piece suit and tie. In the last scene of the film, however, he stands in front of Quinlan without a jacket, vest, or tie, with his shirt unbuttoned and his chest plainly visible. Skin exposed, he too has been touched by evil and has resorted to dirty ways of getting the evidence required to put Quinlan away, which includes turning Quinlan's partner not just into a traitor to his beloved friend but also into a walking "bug."[4]

As Vargas's odd statement makes clear, however, his descent or his necessary contamination with sexuality or sexual potency is in the name of honor. Vargas can come close to the film's source of evil as long as he remains wedded to this higher principle. As long as his motives remain honorable, as long as he is acting as a husband, his fall from the patriarchal law of order and politeness is not an indelible stain. Thus Vargas is protected from the responsibility of losing control even as he indulges in hysterical behavior and is at the center and origin of violent mayhem. Nevertheless Vargas's descent also suggests a crack in the logic of the film insofar as Mike's identity as policeman is in opposition to his identity as husband.

Leaving that sign of instability aside for now, it is fairly clear that Vargas doesn't so much follow Susan in her fall as he is brought down by Susan and her fall. Vargas doesn't so much heroically sacrifice his virtue to save his wife as he is the victim of her descent into vice and depravity. Like Adam in the story of Genesis, Vargas follows his wife out of the Garden of Eden. He is guilty only insofar as he is blind to her predisposition to fall, ironically suspected by Quinlan. The noir logic of *Touch of Evil* dictates that Vargas be brought down by the femme fatale, and only indirectly by the villain. Within this logic, his tragic flaw becomes his blindness to the evil that lurks behind his wife's good-girl looks.

Blind to the Evil Sex

Vargas's metaphorical blindness is suggested by the dark glasses he wears throughout the film and by the scene when he cannot see Susan half-naked and crying out to him from the fire escape. It is emphasized halfway through the film, when Vargas calls his wife at the motel where she is staying. He calls her from a grocery store attended by a blind woman who makes Vargas very nervous and who visually shares the picture frame with him during his conversation with Susan. On the other side of the phone line, and invisible to Vargas, we see a very different Susan from the one he infantilizes. Susan is in bed. Soft music is playing in the background. She is wearing a seductive negligee. When Susan is disappointed that all he wants to talk about is work, Vargas changes his official tone to a softer one and finally stammers his way into an "I love you," displaced to the end of a long sentence. He takes so long to say what are to him clearly embarrassing words that he worries that Susan might have fallen asleep. He emphasizes his embarrassment by covering his face and hiding from the empty stare of the blind woman minding the store. Susan, on the other hand, clearly enjoys the sexual overtones of the conversation. She sighs and comments on the sound of his breathing, calling him "my own darling Miguel." At her first suggestion that she might be sleepy, however, the relieved Vargas quickly changes back to his official tone and suddenly hangs up the phone, to Susan's great surprise.

The scene suggests that Vargas is as blind as the grocery store attendant to Susan's sexuality. He is blind, not so much because he cannot see but because he will not see, because he does not want to see something that he suspects might touch and contaminate him. His embarrassed shift away from a soft romantic tone that he nevertheless rehearses with Susan suggests that he knows that the sexual register is dangerous to him. Thus the scene suggests Vargas's blindness is related to his untouchable status, and to his concern about his purity. The scene suggests that at some level Vargas too suspects his wife's unclean sexual body. Unlike Quinlan, however, Vargas is embarrassed and even afraid of its effect on him.

The logic of noir gives Vargas good reason to be afraid of Susan's sexuality. The famous tracking shot at the beginning of the film ends with a kiss (solicited by Susan) between Vargas and his wife and the simultaneous explosion of Linnekar's automobile, which starts the film's central investigation. The explosion that follows from kissing Susan, or from touching her lips, is the first of a number of references first to her sexualized body and then to its dangerous nature. Quinlan is not alone in insinuating that behind Susan's good-girl looks there might be a provocative sexualized body. We are shown the truth of Quinlan's intuition when the Grandi boys metaphorically expose Susan's hidden sexuality by shining a flashlight into her dark room as she changes out of her day clothes.

Despite her innocent appearance during the day, Susan is presented differently at night. Not only do we see Susan in bed in her seductive negligee, but we also see her compared to Tanya, whom the film associates with prostitution. At the beginning of the scene of Susan's attack by the Grandis, "Pancho" (Valentín de Vargas) enters her room, faintly smiling. The camera shows us Susan clutching a sheet, staring wildly, as a shadow crosses her face. There is an abrupt cut to Tanya's place. As if to suggest a parallel with the sexual attack in the motel, a male voice calls out gruffly to Tanya. She is on the phone with Menzies, who is looking for Quinlan. "Now what would Hank Quinlan be doing here?" she asks knowingly. Menzies replies, "It used to be he'd hole up at your place for two or three days, with a case of whiskey." Tanya's heavily made-up face, the cigarette smoke that envelops her, and the male voice-over combine to suggest Tanya's kinship with the femme fatale. Menzies' implicit association between Tanya, vice, and Quinlan's fall, together with Quinlan's obscene references to Tanya's "chili," are all pointed allusions to her dangerous femme fatale sexuality.

The Grandis' obscene physical gestures to Susan parallel Quinlan's obscene remark. Susan is too hot (both too desirable and too dangerous) for the feminized Uncle Joe (Akim Tamiroff) and for the infantilized "Pancho." Twice we see Uncle Joe and "Pancho" lick their lips in anticipation of touching Susan. If Vargas is blind and does not touch Susan, the Grandis see too much and touch her with their eyes. In the scene where Susan is attacked, Pancho asks the gang leader (Mercedes McCambridge) to get something for him, and she refuses with the answer, "I like to watch." The scene further associates the danger of touching and watching with a gendered narcissistic pleasure and with a female sexuality, through a character who is a woman who likes to watch and touch other women. Not surprisingly, the effect of touching and watching women is fatal, as is suggested by the final shot of Uncle Joe strangled, eyes bulging out, tongue sticking out, as he faces Susan. Given her association with Tanya, as well as her deadly effect on Uncle Joe, Susan's screams "Let me go! Don't touch me! Let me go!" must be understood both as a cry for help and as a warning. It follows the noir logic of *Touch of Evil* that the title would refer to the touch of Susan's body, or the touch of the hidden femme fatale inside every good girl's body.

Vargas's blindness to his wife's evil sexuality protects him from bearing the responsibility for the fall, which, as in the story of Genesis, will be borne mostly by Eve: the true culprit of the tale. Thus Vargas's good name (and his stable Mexican identity) remains clean insofar as the film insists on Susan's evil. In other words, the goodness of Vargas's name, heritage, and race depends on the displacement of the root of evil to the sexualized body of Susan. *Touch of Evil*, then, challenges racist stereotyping. But once more, behind the figure of the exposed white American corrupt cop there is an even greater evil threatening the social order. The insidious nature of that evil is only fully revealed by tearing down the facade or the myth of the good American girl. The profound problem, the film suggests, is not the explosive mixing of races but the contact with an evil that transcends race and that the film firmly locates in female sexuality.

The point is driven home when Mike and Susan's story intersects the story of Manolo Sánchez and Marcia Linnekar, the other Mexican American couple in the film. The ethical problem that runs through the film is that Sánchez is presumed guilty because he is Mexican. Indeed, Quinlan believes that Ruddy Linnekar was right to object to her daughter "having a Mexican shoe clerk for a son-in-law." A racist to the point of caricature, Quinlan goes so far as to say that speaking "Mexican" (as he calls speaking Spanish) is to "speak guilty." Because of the death of his wife at the hands of a "half-breed," Quinlan is already convinced that Sánchez is a "fortune hunter that hypnotized Marcia" and killed her father to inherit a million dollars. But Quinlan's extreme racism blinds

Susie Vargas (Janet Leigh) and the Grandi gang in *Touch of Evil*.

him and his partner Menzies to another interpretation of the events, which Vargas also refuses to see. "Well ... instead of the man chasing the girl, suppose she was the one, suppose she asked him to marry her. What would he do? ... What would you do, Vargas?" The pointed question Sánchez puts to Vargas is not only whether he would marry a rich white girl but whether he would marry a woman who would chase him, who would be guilty of that of which Sánchez stands accused, a woman who would be the real agent behind the crime? Would Vargas marry the femme fatale behind the girl? Vargas answers with a question: "The question is, what did you do?" But if Vargas evades the question, it is because he doesn't want to face the answer. Like Sánchez, Vargas married the femme fatale who will bring him down just as Marcia Linnekar brings Sánchez down with her. The logic of noir thus complements the film's didactic and melodramatic structure insofar as Quinlan's racism makes him blind to the true culprit of the murder. Even if the Mexican shoe clerk planted the bomb (as he supposedly confesses at the end of the film), Sánchez is but a tool of the femme fatale, the true evil force behind his actions.

The Mother at the Border

The logic of noir, however, does not stop at the sexualized body of the femme fatale, as we argue in this book, and as is suggested by Welles's response to his critics from *Cahiers du Cinéma*. Behind the danger of the sexualized body lies an absence that makes Welles melancholy to the point of saying that the world itself is Faustian. Indeed, it is the melancholy search for an irretrievable loved object that makes Welles assume the sacrificial position of the noir antihero embracing evil and that drives the suicidal logic of *Touch of Evil*.

Welles's metaphors rehearse the traditional identification of the female body with nature, and the complementary identification of the male mind with civilization and culture. The lover of Welles's metaphors is a conquistador, a civilizing agent, while its love object is uninhabited terrain, and fallow ground, associated with a reproductive natural body both wild and virginal. This traditional view of the world splits humanity into binary oppositions like the two sexes (male and female) and their two corresponding forces (natural and cultural). It excludes both sexual and racial positions that lie in between these binaries. *Touch of Evil* follows these oppositions closely and practices its necessary exclusions. Thus Quinlan (the evil American cop) is the enforcer of a natural law, while Vargas (the good Mexican Eliot Ness) enforces a patriarchal law. If Vargas obeys "the fine print in the rule books," Quinlan works "like a dogcatcher" and obeys his instincts.

Quinlan is also a melancholy cop who has lost the object of his love. In the film, that love object is Quinlan's wife, but it is also a maternal figure represented by Tanya. Thus she has a calming effect on Quinlan. If outside Quinlan is a bully, inside Tanya's place he is passive, under control, and subdued. Inside we see him under the spell of nostalgia for a lost past, emphasized by the old sound of a pianola, and by the title of the tune played on it: "Avalon," an island from Arthurian legend thought to be an earthly Paradise (Comito 1998, 189). Like that music, Tanya is a remnant of that past. She is a maternal figure twice fallen from Paradise: she is a femme fatale, and she is a Gypsy, a member of a nomadic race of unknown origin.

When Quinlan looks at Tanya, and when the camera focuses on her face, we see her in soft focus, idealized. Quinlan's gaze goes through her in what seems a failed attempt to regain that lost Paradise. In the absence of this Paradise, the film warns us, we "will wish [we] had never been born." Abjected rather than born into a world of Gypsy femme fatale mothers, Quinlan's perspective turns Hobbesian. "Mean, brutish, and short," his life is determined by a struggle for survival of the fittest. This struggle is driven, in turn, by the competition for scarce resources, by an economy fueled by a primal loss, a loss of origins. The loss of Paradise, represented by Tanya's racial indeterminacy and by her sexually fallen body, is the force behind Quinlan's natural law.

In traditional Freudian psychoanalysis, the move from nature to culture requires a castration threat from the father delivered by the mother that will successfully move the male infant away from an identification with the mother to a subsequent identification with the father.

A film clearly influenced by psychoanalysis, *Touch of Evil* represents Tanya as the castrating enforcer of this threat. Thus Tanya denies Quinlan the protective and nourishing function of the good mother. Instead of a warm welcome, Tanya receives an infantilized Quinlan with disapproval: "You should lay off those candy bars." She also refuses to feed him and repeatedly tells Quinlan to go home. After Quinlan flatters her, she responds disapprovingly, "You're a mess, honey." She will not admit to loving Quinlan, even after his death at the end of the film. Not surprisingly, Quinlan will be visually associated with the severed head of a bull hanging from Tanya's walls. If Tanya represents a primal loss, she also represents the phallic power that disavows that loss and should move Quinlan out of nature's influence and into civil society and culture—a move that clearly never happens and instead leads Quinlan to the melancholy and even suicidal state partly responsible for his death.

This model of subject formation also forces the mother into an impossible, even suicidal, position. The enforcer of phallic power, she is made into both the guardian of nature and the origin of culture and civilization. Paradoxically, she is made responsible for eliminating herself and erasing her influence on the infant (Oliver 1997, 39). Thus an important aspect of the maternal function, according to this psychoanalytic model of subject formation, is to guard the infant against the noxious influence of the maternal body by warning him about its deadly force. This suicide is best represented in the film by Tanya's warnings about her own body. A maternal figure, she nevertheless warns Quinlan about her dangerous sex. "Better be careful. It may be too hot for you," says Tanya to Quinlan when he threatens to return for some of her "chili." Her chili, she reminds Quinlan, is red hot and bad for him; it is triply dangerous. Complicated by racial indeterminacy, her body is border food. Its material lies between the maternal and the sexual.

Thus the film's logic drives the mother to a suicidal self-image that will in turn produce the melancholy that haunts Quinlan. But the matricidal impulse is also riddled with symptomlike contradictions, and despite its erasures, the repressed mother insists on making her absence visible. Thus, despite itself, images of the absent mother multiply throughout *Touch of Evil*. From its margins, they touch everything and stain everybody like the pigeon eggs left abandoned by their mother. Another example is the mother who plays a part in a complicated ruse to photograph Susan in a compromising situation: smiling, in front of the Hotel Ritz, with "Pancho's" arm around her shoulders. To frame Susan, Uncle Joe distracts her with a Mexican woman who holds up a baby and says in Spanish, "Mire al niño" [look at the boy], as another gang member darts behind her to photograph Susan. Thus the mother is recruited by Uncle Joe to fabricate evidence about Susan's outlaw sexuality. But the scene incriminates Susan by condensing the maternal and the sexual into one image, paradoxically making the repressed maternal sex visible again.

Of equal importance is the fact that the mother returns speaking another language, a language that is presumably unintelligible to Susan and to the English-speaking audience. The foreignness of language

Tanya (Marlene Dietrich) and Quinlan (Orson Welles) in *Touch of Evil*.

intensifies the dangerous threat of the sexual mother. The Spanish-speaking mother at the borders of the film is meant as a haunting reminder of Susan's decision to marry Vargas, and in so doing to leave her English-speaking mother behind. "I can just imagine your mother's face if she could see our honeymoon hotel," Vargas says to her. Susan now lives in a suspicious border town where foreign languages threaten the mother tongue—or do they?

Border/Mother Tongue

In an autobiographical essay, Julia Kristeva states that "there is matricide in giving up the language of one's birth" (2000, 169). Reflecting on the "bifid" state of her exiled mind and body (166), and calling herself "a monster at the crossroads" (167), Kristeva describes the uncanny return of her mother tongue during moments in her life "when the plot thickens" (167): in dreams, when she hears her mother talking, when she gets into trouble in an artificial linguistic code, when she is tired and can't remember her addition and multiplication tables. She calls this linguistic return "the warm corpse that can still speak of her maternal memory" (170). In another autobiographical work, Gloria Anzaldúa describes a similar linguistic experience, though she describes the mother tongue somewhat differently. Anzaldúa tries to listen to what she calls "the voice at the edge of things" (1987, 50), a voice erased by the dual shadow cast by what she calls the masculine order, the maternal voice that existed before the dualism of light/darkness became a symbolic formula for morality. She calls the ongoing attempt at recovering that voice the struggle to overcome a tradition of silence and shame of even existing: to be "free to write bilingually and to switch codes without having always to translate," to "speak Spanglish," to speak in her "serpent's tongue" (59).

Both Kristeva and Anzaldúa associate their language with a process of erasure and return. They both speak in a forked tongue: the bifid tongue of a serpent that has been killed and returns to haunt them. Described as the memory of a warm corpse, and as a voice at the edge of things, what violently returns from a violent erasure is the mother tongue. Kristeva's and Anzaldúa's bifid serpent mother tongue is a far cry from the single mother tongue articulated by the logic of identity of noir. Its process of subject formation can ill afford a mother tongue as unstable as Anzaldúa's and Kristeva's. Instead Welles's noir films *The Lady from Shanghai* and *Touch of Evil* deploy singularity in language to stabilize the borders of normative identity. In both of these films, the mother tongue is one language: English, Cantonese, or Spanish. Passing from one to the other is suspicious; indeed, it is the mark of the evil femme fatale (see chapter 3 of this volume). If another language must be spoken, it will be spoken with a heavy accent and will be left untranslated to preserve its foreignness. The mother tongue conceived as Kristeva and Anzaldúa describe it, as a bifid edge, is repressed in noir. And yet despite its drive to linguistic singularity, linguistic ambiguity returns with a vengeance to the scene of noir's linguistic matricide.

One of Vargas's many problems in the film is the question of when to speak or not to speak Spanish. It is a complex question with many ramifications. As Quinlan says in the scene where he interrogates Sánchez, to speak Spanish is not only "to get hysterical" but also "to speak guilty." Indeed, the scene performs for us a fearsome lesson in language learning. Sánchez, fearing for his life at the hands of the racist Quinlan, shifts back and forth from English to Spanish, in what seems like an attempt both to answer and annoy Quinlan and to gain the sympathy and enlist the help of Vargas, his Mexican compatriot. With each language shift, however, Quinlan gets angrier and angrier. He insists on English being spoken in his presence, and he slaps Sánchez in the face.

At first, Vargas responds to Sánchez in Spanish, but perhaps conscious of the consequences this will have for the shoe clerk, he joins Quinlan in asking Sánchez to use "English ... English." Vargas has mastered the art of speaking English in such a way that he can avoid shifts into Spanish, but more significantly, he has managed to erase all traces of his Spanish accent (we will speak to the fact that Vargas is played by Charlton Heston presently). The polite nature of this double erasure is best captured during a scene when Vargas and his ally Schwartz get into Vargas's car, where the radio is set to a Spanish-language station. The broadcast is about the case on which Vargas is working and even mentions Quinlan by name, but Vargas turns off the radio out of consideration (one presumes) for his English-speaking friend. Indeed, the effect of Vargas's successful erasure of Spanish is so significant that at the beginning of the film, Quinlan is forced to pay him a compliment, if backhanded, when he says, "You don't talk like one, I'll say that for you. A Mexican, I mean."

Vargas's polite and strategic erasures of Spanish are very different from Sánchez's language shifting. Sánchez is either unsuccessful at erasing or unwilling to erase his Spanish. In fact, Sánchez's code switching makes it hard to tell what his mother tongue is: English, Spanish, or code switching itself, a border language, a bifid edge? He cannot or will not follow Vargas's example and advice, especially under circumstances of physical abuse. True, in one sense, the linguistic shifts during the interrogation scene are emotionally laden responses over which Sánchez has little or no control. They are uncontrollable emotional outbursts in the face of his victimization. These outbursts foreshadow the moment when Vargas too will lose control over his polite, reasonable, and calm exterior and will storm the Grandis' Rancho Grande shouting, "Dónde está mi esposa?" [Where is my wife?]. But in another sense, Sánchez's code switching is also a rebellious response to Quinlan's command to stick to English. Instead Sánchez wields language like a defensive weapon. He shifts from Spanish to English as if he were shifting gears. He uses Spanish selectively, to get Quinlan's goat, both to get Vargas on his side and to chastise him privately when Vargas displays an evident lack of power or motivation to help him. Indeed, Sánchez speaks bilingually in the sense that Anzaldúa gives to that word: he switches codes freely and willfully without feeling the need to translate.[5]

In the film, such language shifting earns Sánchez no friends. When the dynamite sticks are planted in his bathroom, Sánchez proclaims his innocence first to Quinlan in English and then to Vargas in Spanish: "Soy inocente, lo juro que soy inocente sobre la tumba de mi madre." Significantly, Vargas replies to Quinlan, not to Sánchez, and expresses disgust for Sánchez's code switching, for his "unpleasantness in any language."

Vargas even tells Quinlan, "You'll have to stop him [from speaking Spanish] yourself." In the same spirit of revolt against Sánchez's bilingual performance, Quinlan answers that he doesn't care what language Sánchez speaks, "From now on he can talk Hindu for all the good it'll do him." At which point Vargas surprises the viewer by politely translating Sánchez's words for an uninterested Quinlan: "He swears on his mother's grave that there has never been any dynamite in this apartment."

Vargas's polite translation is part of what Kristeva calls a "rhetoric of recognition" (2000, 173). It is a rhetoric meant to elicit recognition from Quinlan, who is assumed to be one of Vargas's own insofar as Quinlan shares the same authority and ideas with Vargas. Vargas may be racially different from Quinlan, but Vargas shares the same linguistic values (if not the same language) with Quinlan. Like Quinlan, Vargas believes that it is impolite not to translate into English what Sánchez says in Spanish. Indeed, in this scene, Vargas goes so far as to translate even after Quinlan makes it plain that he doesn't care what Sánchez is saying. Vargas's insistent translation suggests that he translates not so much to be polite but to uphold politeness itself. It is as if Vargas can assert his difference from Quinlan only by claiming allegiance to the higher authority of linguistic purity. From this perspective, Vargas's translation suggests that he believes in linguistic identity and singularity, like Quinlan. Here translation and the English-only command are the same in their opposition to Sánchez's messy and impolite language shifting and border language.

Quinlan doesn't believe anything Sánchez says ("From now on he can talk Hindu for all the good it'll do him") because for Quinlan, origin determines truth, and the fact that Sánchez is from Mexico, or rather that he is not from the United States, invalidates anything he says. He can swear all he wants on his mother's grave, but Quinlan will never believe him because Sánchez and his mother "speak Mexican," and therefore they "speak guilty." For Quinlan, there is only one language of innocence and truth, one believable mother tongue, one original language, and that language is English. Quinlan believes English is truthful and innocent because it is the language spoken in the United States, and not the other way around. For that same reason, Quinlan doesn't believe anything Vargas says, either. He may not "talk like one ... a Mexican," but he still is Mexican because he looks Mexican (read black), and most importantly because he is from Mexico, according to the narrative.

The Return of the Repressed

Despite Quinlan's characterization in the film as an intolerant racist, despite the film's criticism of Quinlan's visceral distrust of anything Mexican, including Mexico's official language (Spanish), *Touch of Evil* repeats Quinlan's blind trust in singular national identity, and his belief in the singularity of the mother tongue. Welles's belief is evident in his deployment and reliance on what Kaja Silverman has called "Holly-wood's sonic vraisemblable" (1988, 45). The sonic vraisemblable is the acoustic organization that subordinates the auditory to the visual and to the narrative tracks. It is the organization that circumscribes the human voice both to the image and to the film narrative to "suture the viewer/ listener into the ... safe place of the story" (45). Perhaps the most evident example of this is Welles's casting of Charlton Heston in the role of Mexican detective Mike Vargas. Like Quinlan, Welles assumes that Heston can play a Mexican even though he "cannot talk like one." He assumes we will believe that Vargas erases his Spanish accent, when we know that he didn't have one to begin with.

Indeed, to the listener it is embarrassingly clear that Heston had trouble speaking Spanish in the film. His trouble becomes audible when his performance is compared to Victor Milan's (Sánchez) clear delivery and seamless shifts in and out of both languages while conveying complex emotions in both. Heston himself feels this embarrassment, as is made clear by his subdued tone and restraint during the interrogation scene.[6] His tone and restraint seem like symptoms of his discomfort at playing this crucial scene in Spanish. Indeed, his embarrassment lasts fifteen years, as he remembers his reticence at playing the part of a Mexican detective ("I can't play a Mexican detective!") and qualifies his performance, which he describes as "plausible enough, I suppose."

Significantly, Heston also remembers that Welles soothed him by emphasizing the power of the visual stereotype over everything, including the voice. To Heston's reticence, Welles responds, "Sure you can [play a Mexican]! We'll dye your hair black, and put on some dark makeup and draw a black moustache, sure you can! We'll get a Mexican tailor to cut you a good Mexican suit" (Comito 1998, 214).

Welles overestimates the force of his identity logic, and he assumes that the unsettling effect of casting Heston as a Mexican Spanish-speaking detective will be lost on the viewer. But the irony of scenes like Heston's passionate intrusion into the Grandis' Rancho Grande is not lost on the viewer. Indeed, the scene conveys the noticeable return of a repressed border language. The strangeness of the language in this scene is meant to convey the return of Vargas's passionate Mexican nature. But more than that, the sound track conveys the uncanny music of English joining with Spanish: the bifid sound at the edge of things. If at the level of the script his outburst is meant to represent the return of the repressed Spanish (as mother tongue), at the level of the performance, the same outburst reveals the return of a border language that Vargas's English translations and polite Spanish try to repress. This uncanny sound is the music that accompanies the return of "the warm corpse of the maternal memory that can still speak" (Kristeva 2000, 3). That voice surfaces to unsettle the safe place produced by the "sonic vraisemblable." It is an acoustic obstacle to Welles's imperative gesture; his visual and narrative imposition of something that remains acoustically implausible: the conceit that Vargas's/Heston's mother tongue is Spanish and that his outburst is a loss of control over English learned as a foreign language.

The gap between the acoustic track and the visual track and narrative script is widened by the scene's exchange between Vargas and Risto Grandi. Risto says to him, "Talk English, can't you?" Within the film's narrative, the statement suggests that Risto (a border subject) does not even understand Spanish. It is the acoustic equivalent of the gang's visual abandonment of Mexican values. It follows the film's criticism of the gang's perverse love of the music, fashion, and language of the

United States. It is meant to be funny because Risto can't speak his own language. But instead, the exchange is funny because it is Heston who can't speak his character's language. Indeed, the listener has a difficult time understanding Vargas/Heston because of his English-inflected Spanish. From this perspective, Risto seems to escape the film's narrative and its visual frame when he asks Heston to speak English. A border subject indeed, Risto switches language and place. Despite his Mexican identity, Risto complains that he cannot understand Heston's Spanish. Despite his place in the film, Risto echoes the listener's complaint that s/he cannot understand Heston's Spanish. Risto's outburst then emerges from an identity that is neither Mexican nor American, from a language that is neither English nor Spanish, and from a place that is neither inside nor outside the film. Risto's outburst is the return of the border/mother tongue.

In sum, Welles's resistance to the emergence of ambiguity in his film is manifest in his resistance to border subjectivity, maternal sexuality, and code switching. Paradoxically, the function of this resistance, like the function of his combination of didactic melodrama and the logic of noir, is to protect a racialized subject, to permit the entrance of the Spanish-speaking Mexican into the imaginary of civil society. To do so, however, Welles invokes an identity logic that is matricidal and has a melancholy effect. Because of her affiliation with the borders of identity, the mother is sacrificed and must even sacrifice herself, but at too high a price. Maternal sexuality, border identity, is sacrificed in *Touch of Evil* for the paradoxical purpose of creating racial equality while maintaining racial identity. But this identity entails the creation of a dangerous borderland that must be kept out of touch from the stable ideal subject. Thus Spanish-speaking Mexicans become citizens as long as they stay on one side of a border that marks the place where evil border language and border subjectivities (like maternal sexuality) are produced, sacrificed, and interred. The problem is that they don't stay buried for long. Boundaries are constantly crossed, and the repressed returns to haunt us in the voices of Risto, Heston, and the mother at the border of the film.

CHAPTER 7

Jokes in *Chinatown*:
A Question of Place

Jokes are the means through which the anxieties about race, gender, and place are screened and transformed in Roman Polanski's *Chinatown* (1974). Not only is Jake Gittes (Jack Nicholson) a smart aleck in the style of Philip Marlowe and Sam Spade in such classic noir films as *Murder, My Sweet* and *The Maltese Falcon*, but the mechanism of his off-color, obscene, racist, and in general off-putting jokes is the key to understanding the logic of *Chinatown* and its attention to place, an attention that is not just topical as in the geographically determined Chinatown and Mexico or the socially determined class and family structure but stylistic as well. As Virginia Wright Wexman has pointed out, Polanski manipulates location and place stylistically to influence the film's content. Through his critical attention to composition and his creative use of deep focus, Polanski undercuts the viewer's expectations by shifting the power away from the figure of Jake Gittes and onto the figure of Noah Cross, for example (Wexman 1985, 96). It is important to add, however, that by manipulating the difference between foreground and background, and between what is inside the frame and what lies outside of it, Polanski simultaneously moves us in and out of a place that is impossible for us to see but that is necessary to visualize if we are to overcome the symptoms of film noir.[1]

Successful Jokes and Bad Jokes

In *Jokes and Their Relation to the Unconscious*, Freud describes successful jokes by comparing them to, and differentiating them from, dreams. Like dreams, the primary material of jokes originates in the unconscious (Freud 1905, 168) and is transformed by processes that include "condensation, displacement, and indirect representation" (164). Freud calls these processes the dream-work and the joke-work respectively. Unlike the material of dreams, however, the material of jokes is not so much a wish as it is a primal play (179). Consequently, the function of the joke-work is not the dream-work's predominant avoidance of unpleasure but the development of play and the yield of a primal pleasure. Freud describes this old childish pleasure as a pleasure "in nonsense and in words that finds itself inhibited in normal moods by objections raised by critical reason" (171).

Moreover, unlike the dream-work, the technique of displacement is subordinate to the technique of condensation in the joke-work. In his description of the dream-work, Freud emphasizes that the principal difference between condensation and displacement is that the latter is "the work of the dream censorship" (Freud 1916–1917, 174), while condensation "does not give one the impression of being an effect of the dream-censorship. It seems traceable rather to some mechanical or economic factor" (173). The dream-work displaces the psychical energy within the material of the dream-thought to an innocuous element of the dream, and in that way the inhibition from the censorship is overcome (Freud 1905, 165). The primary function of the joke-work, however, is not to censor a compromising wish and displace its psychic energy but to mechanically uninhibit and develop a primal pleasure. Thus its principal process is condensation, which accounts for the brevity of jokes, and for Freud's description of jokes as a return to a primitive state of language and thought, an ambiguous primal state when one word and one concept conveyed a meaning and its opposite.[2] The aim of recovering the old pleasure in nonsense also explains the fact that whenever displacement is used in the joke-work (as when allusions are made, or internal associations are replaced by what are known as external ones), play with words appears uncompromised. Displacement in jokes insists "on maintaining play with words or with nonsense unaltered" (Freud 1905, 172). But Freud also points out that displacement in jokes only appears within restricted conditions, when they are allowable or sensible, because unlike dreams, jokes are social mental functions that require the participation of a third person for the joke to be successful (179).

Of course, all of this is true of successful jokes, but things stand differently with what Freud will call bad jokes in his essay on the dreamwork (Freud 1916–1917, 174). Bad jokes violate the restricted conditions of successful jokes. Rather than seeming sensible or allowable, bad jokes appear arbitrary. Moreover, their apparition is also arbitrary. Bad jokes are impertinent; they are out of place; they are displaced rather than condensed. A bad joke "does not belong" but is nevertheless "dragged in by the hair of its head" (174).

Freud's image for the bad joke significantly conjures the visual joke of the caveman dragging his woman into his cave. Like so much of Freudian psychoanalysis, the image not only puts woman in her place but also puts her in the place of the bad joke: the out-of-place that interrupts pleasure. The context in which Freud makes this remark reveals the anxiety he feels about trading places with the displaced woman in the joke. Both in his early work on jokes and later in his essay on the dream-work, Freud repeats his anxious concern that psychoanalysis might be taken for a bad joke. In fact, even though there is no significant section on bad jokes in *Jokes and Their Relationship to the Unconscious,* Freud suggests that they were the reason why he took up the problem of jokes in the first place (1905, 173). He declares that whenever he has undone the work of the dream through analysis for a person who is unaccustomed to, or uninformed about, his technique, the person declares that he must be joking. Freud then explains that when a person says this, the person does not compare dream analysis to a successful joke but compares psychoanalysis to a bad joke that violates its own rules. Curiously, this response to analysis leads Freud to write a whole book whose unacknowledged purpose seems to be to distinguish not so much the dream-work from the joke-work as the work of analysis from joking in general and from bad jokes in particular. But bad jokes that violate the rules of joking nevertheless come back to haunt Freud, and he is forced to devote some pages to what he calls broken humor at the end of his book (232).

A version of bad jokes makes its appearance in the book in the context of a discussion of humor. According to Freud, jokes are a species of the comic genus.[3] Like jokes, the comic also depends on restricted conditions: not only must the comic be allowable and sensible, but it is also contingent on the absence of a distressing affect such as pity, anger, pain, horror, contempt, indignation, or disgust (Freud 1905, 220). Humor is also a species of the comic. Its differentiating quality is that unlike jokes, its pleasure comes not from "an economy in the expenditure of inhibitions" but from "an economy in the expenditure of affect" (229, 236). Thus humor capitalizes on the restrictions and rules imposed on the comic. Humor works by interrupting the threat to the comic of an impending distressing affect. By putting itself in the place of the distressing affect, humor renders the prepared affect useless and produces laughter at the cost of the affect (228).

Humor works principally through displacement, unlike jokes, which work principally through condensation. Humor displaces the psychic energy away from the distressing affect and directs it elsewhere onto something of secondary importance. By displacing the affect's energy, humor transforms the release of unpleasure into a pleasurable discharge. Thus, like displacement in dreams, or repression in psychoneurosis, humorous displacement is a defensive and censoring process aimed at "preventing the generation of unpleasure from internal sources" (Freud 1905, 233). Moreover, like displacement and repression, humor is only partially successful and more often than not produces broken humor. Broken humor is a type of humor that does not work properly, that only partially stops the generation of the affect and produces a contradictory effect that combines pleasure with the repressed affect: "the humor that smiles through tears" (232). This failure, Freud perhaps prematurely concludes, is the operative mechanism for "the development of psychoneuroses," and it "turns out to be detrimental and must be subjected to conscious thinking" (233).

Broken humor in particular and humor in general are not only the black sheep of Freud's family of jokes insofar as they ultimately lead to unpleasure; they also stick in Freud's craw insofar as they undermine his attempt to put a distance between dreams and jokes.[4] Humor is like dreams not only because it deploys the process of displacement and seeks to prevent unpleasure but also because it is not social. "It completes its course within a single person; another person's participation adds nothing new to it" (Freud 1905, 229). If humor, broken humor, and bad jokes are like dreams, then humor analysis or interpretation should work by undoing the displacement, by pointing to the place where the psychic energy originated: to the unpleasurable affect. Analysis should interrupt the temporary and ultimately unsuccessful interruption of affect by humor. Analysis should work like an intensified and self-conscious version of broken humor. From this perspective, Freud's resisting patient is right to compare Freud's analysis to "a bad joke or ... an arbitrary and forced explanation dragged in by the hair of its head" (1916–1917, 174). The comparison, however, seems to have led Freud to distinguish between joking and dreaming, between bad jokes and psychoanalysis, when perhaps it could have led him in the opposite and more productive direction. The resisting patient suggests an interesting insight into psychoanalysis, which can indeed be said to operate like broken humor, or bad jokes, and some attention to the consequences of that comparison might illuminate both some of Freud's comments on psychoanalytic treatment and the effect on the audience of a film such as *Chinatown*.

Like broken humor, analysis and interpretation are also only partially successful, and in fact the success of analysis would seem to depend on this very limitation. As Freud remarks in his essay "Remembering, Repeating, and Working-Through," analysis carries the risk of putting the patient back in the place of trauma. It conjures a piece of real life, "and for that reason it cannot always be harmless and unobjectionable" (Freud 1914, 152). By the same token, however, analysis also "creates an intermediate region between illness and real life through which the transition from the one to the other is made" (154). In this region, a "place is found for a certain tolerance for the state of being ill" (152). This intermediary region is the ground that makes the cure possible, according to Freud. In this in-between place, patients can direct their attention to the phenomena of their illness; they can redefine and reinterpret it, both as "an enemy worthy of [their] mettle" and as "a piece of [their] personality" (152). This place is the out-of-place of bad jokes, and the film *Chinatown* holds the promise and the risk of paying it a visit.

Chinatown's Joke

Chinatown is a bad joke, and Jake is the butt of the joke. Like Freud, however, Jake Gittes resists being put in that position. Indeed, he appears to be as successful a joker as he is a detective. Both joking and detective work seem to come easily to him, and they both depend on his being one step ahead of his clients. At the beginning of the film, we meet him smartly dressed, in his office, in apparent control of his business and his life. Not only is he a smart dresser, but he is also a smart aleck who puts people in their place with a successful joke. In the first scene, after the character Curly (Burt Young) has been given painful, irrefutable evidence of his wife's unfaithfulness, he goes to the window of Jake Gittes's office and makes gestures that suggest that he wants to get out of the embarrassing place he has ironically put himself. By having his wife investigated, Curly has become the butt of his own joke. Jake Gittes, unmoved and without missing a beat, tells him, "You can't eat the venetian blinds, Curly. I just had 'em installed on Wednesday," and thus keeps his client firmly in place as the butt of the joke.

Despite our first impression, however, we quickly learn that Jake Gittes often gets ahead of himself and falls into traps for which he is ultimately responsible. Set up by a woman impersonating Evelyn Mulwray, he complains to the real Evelyn Mulwray that he "doesn't want to become a local joke"; but of course, that is just what he becomes by the end of the film. Set up by Ida Sessions (Diane Ladd), Jake Gittes is sent on a wild goose chase for the lover of Hollis Mulwray (Darrell Zwerling), the chief engineer of Los Angeles's Water and Power Authority. It turns out, however, that Jake Gittes has been unwittingly working for the powerful and power-hungry Noah Cross (John Huston), who is driven by unrestrained passions. On the one hand, Noah Cross is set on revenge against his erstwhile business partner Hollis Mulwray. Through an illegal real estate venture, slander, and then murder, Noah Cross gains back the power he lost when his former business partner turned Los Angeles's water reservoirs over to public governance. On the other hand, Noah Cross is also set on regaining control over his family, which he also lost to Hollis Mulwray after the sale of the Water Department. The all-important revelation at the end of the film is, of course, that the missing Katherine (Belinda Palmer) is Evelyn Mulwray's daughter by her own father (Noah Cross). Katherine is both Noah Cross's granddaughter and daughter, the result of an incestuous relationship, a secret that is known by almost everyone involved in the case (Hollis and Evelyn Mulwray, their servant Kahn [James Hong], Katherine, Noah Cross) except, of course, by Jake Gittes, who is taken for a ride along with the audience.

But this is only the first part of Jake Gittes's ride, which clearly does not end when he learns the truth. After Evelyn Mulwray's dramatic revelation, she gives him the address of her Chinese servant's home, where Jake Gittes wants her to hide and wait for him. "He lives in 1784 Alameda," she says, "Do you know where that is?" After a brief pause, Jake Gittes answers, "Sure." He knows the address is in Chinatown, and his meaningful look suggests he realizes that his tragic past is about to repeat itself. We know that he was a cop in Chinatown, and that despite the district attorney's advice to do as little as possible while there, he nevertheless tried to keep someone from being hurt and "ended up making sure she got hurt." But Jake Gittes does not seem to learn from his mistakes, and he does not change plans; instead, like a classical hero handicapped by his own hubris, he tries to do too much. Repeating a more subdued version of Curly's gesture at the beginning of the film, Jake Gittes watches through the venetian blinds as Evelyn and her daughter follow his plan and drive away to Chinatown. He then gets his partners on the phone and tells them to meet him at that address, which command is followed by his partner's surprised response, "Jesus, that's in Chinatown, ain't it?" and by Jake Gittes's somber reply, "I know where it is, just do it." Jake Gittes's arrogance guarantees that he will display his great ignorance, that he will repeat his mistake, and that he will make a joke out of himself.

Condensing and Displacing Race and Sexuality

One of *Chinatown's* running jokes is that Jake Gittes suffers from motormouth disease. An inveterate joker, he tells jokes out of habit and doesn't think before he speaks. He is out of place even in the one line he speaks in Cantonese close to the film's end: "Get out, damn it," he says to Kahn, who tries to keep him out of the house where Katherine is hidden.[5] This condition is a source of constant embarrassment to him. We hear him apologizing to Evelyn Mulwray several times throughout the film for repeatedly being out of place: for his automatic translation of otherwise innocuous references to speed, to his own neck, or to women, into obscene jokes. To Jake Gittes, these references are all occasions to make a joke; they offer him opportunities to feel the pleasure of returning to primal words that condense two antithetical meanings, as is made evident by his reply to Evelyn Mulwray's attempt to get him off the case: "Look, you sue me, your husband dies, you drop the lawsuit like a hot potato, and all of it quicker than wind from a duck's ass— excuse me."[6] But each time Jake Gittes tells his joke, he also censors himself, inhibiting the pleasure of telling it. Presumably, he interrupts the joke because he is in the presence of Evelyn Mulwray. In the scene when we meet her, she appears to turn Jake Gittes's off-color and racist joke about a Chinaman into broken humor. But in fact the sequence of which the scene is a part reveals that Jake Gittes's interruptions are as much the result of an internal agency as they respond to Evelyn Mulwray's external influence.

The joke is told twice early on in the film.[7] It is first told by Barney (George Justin), Jake Gittes's barber, as a means to interrupt a fight that is about to break out between his customers. It is a device that displaces the intense anger Jake Gittes feels against a man whom we first hear say (in soft voice-off, just out of range of Jake Gittes's hearing, and out of the visual range of both the detective and the camera), "Fools' names and fools' faces." Jake Gittes has been discussing with his barber the publication in the newspaper of his exposing photographs of Hollis Mulwray and his lover. Interpellated by the customer's comment, Jake Gittes replies with a seething "What's that, pal?" which is in turn followed by the customer's reply, "Nothing—you got a hell of a way to make a living." Jake Gittes reads an implicit accusation into the comment that makes his anger reach a great pitch. The gradual process begins with his repeated protestations that he makes an honest living, is followed by insults to the customer, whom he calls a bimbo and a bum, and culminates in a macho challenge to step outside.

Over Jake Gittes's protestations and interruptions, Barney insists on telling the Chinaman joke, which is so successful that in the following scene we see Jake Gittes enter his office with a broad grin on his face, telling again the off-color joke, revisiting its pleasurable sensation. Conscious of the salacious nature of the joke, he patronizingly tells his

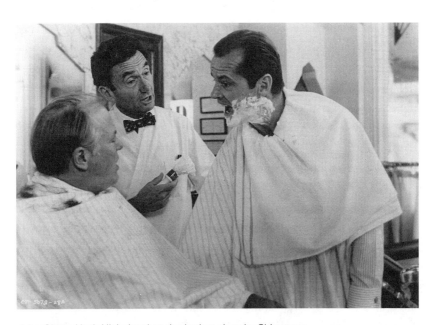

Jake Gittes (Jack Nicholson) at the barber shop in *Chinatown*.

secretary (while touching her) to "go to the little girl's room for a minute." Upset, she is nevertheless forced to comply, and as she absents herself, she apparently sets up the proper men-only stage for telling the joke. Despite his partner's efforts to stop him, Jake Gittes tells the joke, to his own great amusement. As he tells the joke, Polanski uses deep focus to show us what lies beyond Jake Gittes's range of vision. We are shown Evelyn Mulwray standing behind him listening to the joke clearly to the embarrassment of Jake Gittes's partners. After he finishes the joke, Jake Gittes laughs uproariously and turns around to face Evelyn Mulwray. When he sees her, his pleasure is abruptly interrupted; he stops laughing, looks at his partners, and becomes very serious.

The joke, then, is part of an economy of affect that goes from anger, to pleasure, to embarrassment. It also traces an affective circuit from inside to outside Jake Gittes, from Jake Gittes to other characters including Evelyn Mulwray, and back to Jake Gittes in the end. First it works as humor, interrupting the unpleasurable affect of anger through displacement. In the first scene, Barney works like displacement itself and successfully interrupts Jake Gittes's anger by displacing it away from him to the character in an off-color and racist joke. In the second scene, the joke-work is interrupted. The humor broken, the original unpleasurable affect returns to Jake Gittes, though now it is turned into embarrassment. In that scene, Evelyn Mulwray also works like displacement, but unlike Barney, she undoes the joke-work. She turns the affect or psychic energy in the opposite direction: away from the characters in the racist and off-color joke and back to Jake Gittes. She turns the Chinaman joke into a bad joke and turns Jake into the butt of the joke.

She does this twice over, in fact, because the reason why she is visiting Jake Gittes is to turn her anger about the publication of the photographs into pleasure by exposing him as an inept detective who doesn't even verify the authenticity of his sources. By the end of the scene, she puts him in his place with a smile on her face and a joke. After she tells him that he is now "going to get it," the detective tries to stop her and appease her by telling her as she walks past him, "Now wait a minute, Mrs. Mulwray. There's some misunderstanding here. There's no point in getting tough with me." Evelyn Mulwray caustically replies, "I don't get tough with anybody, Mr. Gittes. My lawyer does." Her intervention complicates the economy of the joke by opening it up to her own floating affect. The scene has the double effect of interrupting Jake Gittes's attempts to displace his feelings of anger away from himself and of turning his closed affective economy into an agonistic exchange of affect and competition for pleasure with Evelyn Mulwray.

The content of the joke repeats a similar interruption and opening of a closed circuit or economy of affect where pleasure is in short supply. Through the phrase "screwing like a Chinaman," the joke displaces internal anxieties about adultery, miscegenation, and dissimulation to racial and sexual stereotypes while simultaneously exposing the internal source of the anxiety. Built on a sexist and racist economy, the joke's success depends on a blindness and a disavowal. The man is "tired of screwing his wife." But instead of facing up to it and directly addressing his tiredness (by talking to his wife about it, for example), he interrupts his discomfort by displacing his wife into the object of the Chinaman's sexual practices. He displaces and changes his discomfort into pleasure by turning his old wife into something new, and by decontextualizing, appropriating, and imitating the sexual practices of another culture made secretive and mysterious. Not surprisingly, the odd secret of that unfamiliar culture turns out to be the production of pleasure through the interruption of pleasure. In other words, thinking that he is trying something new, he in fact repeats the original interrupted pleasure, to the great displeasure of his wife, who asks him, "What the hell do you think you're doing? . . . you're screwing like a Chinaman."

Angry at him for interrupting her pleasure, she interrupts him by accusing him of screwing "like a Chinaman," and in so doing she returns him to a version of his original position. Her comment suggests that she has seen through his efforts to displace his anxiety by screwing her like a Chinaman, and by turning her into the Other woman, the object of the Chinaman's desire. It also suggests that he might be closer to the truth and to the Other than he would care to admit. From within the joke's racist economy, she suggests that he might be "like a Chinaman" in more ways than one. First, he is "screwing like a Chinaman." Second, he is "like a Chinaman" in that he is an Other to himself, a deceived husband. Third, he is "like a Chinaman" in that he has no authority; his law is broken by his own wife. Finally, he is "like a Chinaman" in that he covers over or dissimulates the fact that he is tired of screwing his wife. By accusing him of being a Chinaman, the wife displaces the disturbing effect of her husband's games on her, and of their underlying self-centeredness and egoism. By unilaterally displacing his feelings of inadequacy away from himself and onto a Chinaman, he has also made her strange, turning her into a silenced Other, one who plays the part of the object in sexual intercourse. She gets back at him by pointing to the implications of his displacement, thus avenging his objectification of her: she suggests that she has indeed had a Chinese lover and that he isn't her only lover. Through wordplay, she turns her own anger into pleasure. In a turn of the screw, she liberates herself from the place of the Other where her husband's sexual experimentation puts her, and she turns her husband into the butt of his own joke, making him occupy her previous position. Like Gittes, the man at the center of the joke trades places with his wife and replaces her as the butt of the joke.

Thus this sequence criticizes the self-centered, narcissistic affective economy behind Jake Gittes's jokes and reveals both its destructive potential to others as well as its self-destructive potential by setting off competing affective economies that will not remain so easily displaced. It presents the struggle for pleasure that takes place between two characters locked in similar economies. But the script is also blind to the cul-de-sac where it has left not only its characters but the Other of the joke, the indeterminate, invisible object of the Chinaman's desire who remains doubly trapped within the perverse economy of the joke. Gittes's sexism is combated with a racism that remains unquestioned. Evelyn Mulwray's success as a joker depends on preserving the position of the racially and sexually othered even as she puts Jake Gittes in that position. Consequently, the characters' disturbing affects are either returned to them or exchanged momentarily for a pleasure that will not last long. The best of worlds from this perspective would see Jake Gittes locked in perpetual combat with Evelyn Mulwray or with himself, displacing and absorbing ad infinitum the disturbing affects produced by the unquestioned racism and sexism that creates the Other object.

Through style, however, Polanski opens up a space that remains closed in Robert Towne's script.[8] In this sequence, Polanski overcomes the limitations of the script and provides an in-between space that escapes both the narcissistic economy of Jake Gittes and the agonistic economy of the return of the repressed. This is a version of film noir's struggle between its visual and narrative aspects (Gledhill 1998, 30; Place 1998, 48). It is a space that has the potential of interrupting the competing economies of *Chinatown*'s successful and bad jokes. Stylistically, the two Chinaman joke scenes echo the bad joke. The scenes emphasize the vengeance of the return of the repressed. In the first scene, Jake Gittes's ambivalent feelings about his increasing popularity become fantasmatically displaced into a half-heard and half-understood remark about fools that could mean just about anything. That remark, told by a character outside the frame of the take, becomes intensely charged for Jake Gittes. Indeed, it is precisely the fact that it is mumbled by someone who is invisible to Jake Gittes that seems to set him off. Similarly, in the second scene of the sequence, the film's aggressive first-person perspective is again challenged from the margins. This time the first-person perspective is challenged by Evelyn Mulwray, who moves from the invisible space inside Jake Gittes's office to the background of the take, where she stands in focus but motionless, waiting for Jake Gittes to turn around to startle him.[9]

But Polanski combines the technique of deep focus with attention to the space outside the frame of the film to expand and open up the horizon of the visual plane for more than dramatic effect.[10] Through style, the film suggests an intermediary space between the visible and the invisible. In that space, the absences within the visual plane become visible as erasures and exclusions: spaces such as the empty chair left by the secretary who is forced to leave the scene for the joke to be successful. The process of displacement that makes visible the traces of the erased, however, competes with a process of condensation that has the opposite effect. The drama of both scenes is stylistically intensified through a process of condensation. This process takes the viewer from a shot divided into three spaces with a foreground, a middle space, and a background, to the flat space of opposition between two fighting characters, to a shot where we find the characters isolated and alone. The process of condensation also reduces to ridicule the complexity of the mood produced by Jake Gittes's sudden turn from unrestrained laughter to embarrassment and interrupted silence (perhaps a version of "the humor that smiles through tears"). It is that complex space, with its accompanying mood, that the film's style repeatedly opens up only to flatten out.

The Fate of the Third Space in *Chinatown*

Another example of the flattening of space is the memorable scene where Jake Gittes is attacked by "the man with the knife," played by Polanski. As in the sequence before, this scene has a narrative and a visual component. In this scene, however, the joke and the visual element work together from the beginning to produce a sense of intense claustrophobia and pain. The famous joke is told by Polanski's character: "You know what happens to nosy fellas? Ah? No? Wanna guess? Ah? No? They lose their noses." Visually, the scene is filmed to trap Jake Gittes in the front plane of the frame. Not only is the scene shot at night, making the background invisible, but Jake Gittes is twice restrained and kept in the foreground plane by Claude Mulvihill (Roy Jenkins) and by the chain-link fence behind him. There is no escape to a literal or figurative third space here.

The scene's visual entrapment is enhanced by the inside quality of the joke. The man with the knife asks Jake Gittes a number of questions to which they both know the answer. Given the circumstances, however, Jake Gittes cannot or will not answer the questions that lead to the all too literal punch line of the joke: "They lose their noses." He is unwilling to give the punch line because he is in the uncomfortable position of being both the third person and the object of the joke. Claude Mulvihill should be the joke's structural third person (the person receiving the joke), and Jake Gittes should be the nosy fella at the butt of the joke. But instead the joke is addressed to Jake Gittes, making him both the receiver and the object of the joke. That ambiguous position changes the figurative punch line into a literal cut that Jake Gittes is trying to prevent by remaining uncharacteristically silent.

Freud argues that successful jokes are different from dreams, from humor, and from bad jokes insofar as they are "the most social of all mental functions" (1905, 179). Successful jokes require the presence of three persons: the person making the joke, the object (or butt) of the joke, and the third "in whom the joke's aim of producing pleasure is fulfilled" (100). The first person makes the joke so that the third person laughs at it, and in so doing induces laughter in himself on the rebound (155–56). Freud significantly calls such a joke "a double-dealing rascal who serves two masters at once" (155). A servant of two masters, the joke serves the first person who makes it. It serves the purpose of uninhibiting a primal pleasure in that person. But the joke must also serve the

Jake and Claude (Roy Jenkins) confronted by a man with a knife (Roman Polanski) in *Chinatown.*

passive third person who stands in judgment of it (144). The decision to laugh is passed over to the third person first (144). This characteristic of jokes is absent from bad jokes, the comic, humor, broken humor, and dreams, all of which are structured around binary systems involving only two positions: the position of the subject and the position of the object.

From this perspective, the scene only seems to perform a success-ful joke while actually making a bad joke that collapses or condenses the place of the second and third persons into the place of Jake Gittes. Thus Jake Gittes cannot laugh, and neither can the man with the knife. Pleasure is interrupted, and pain takes its place. The scene is an inside joke insofar as it prevents an escape, affective or otherwise, to an out-side space. The claustrophobic and self-enclosed character of the scene is heightened by the fact that Polanski plays the role of the thug, feed-ing the sense that the scene (like the joke-work) reaches outside the nar-rative, grabs ahold of the director, and drags him inside its mysterious pit. This effect is underscored by Polanski himself in the interview at the end of the Paramount Pictures release. Referring to the decision to play this cameo role, he says, "If I remember correctly, it was Robert Towne's idea. He said, You must play that part, or something like that. And then I thought it would be fun for the crew and everybody. It was rather a sort of inside joke." The inside joke was Polanski's famous cru-elty to his actors and actresses, played out in the character's cruelty to Jake Gittes (Biskind 1994). But Polanski seems to undo the work of the inside (bad) joke in the interview by making public the private joke, exposing himself and liberating laughter even as he seems to open up a space for the viewer to judge him.

> I thought of a knife that would have a swiveling tip on it and I asked them to build it for me and they did it very well. It worked of course swiveling in one direction and not in the other. And I said to Jack "Please, you have to remind me each time before we rehearse or before do that to hold it knife in the right direction because if I turn it around like this I just rip your your nostril." And it was very good because that added drama to Jack's expression, I think [he laughs].

Polanski's self-exposure would suggest that the third space of the successful joke opens up the closed economy of the comic, humor, or the dream by including a third person: the audience as judge. Could this third space complement "the intermediate region between illness and real life" opened performatively by analysis through interruptions that work as bad jokes (Freud 1914, 154)? Could analysis and interpretation also work like successful jokes insofar as they constitute this third space? It would be a mistake to compare the space of the third person of the successful joke to the intermediary space opened performatively through breaks, interruptions, and bad jokes. Indeed, the inside quality of the joke of this scene is far deeper than Polanski would care to admit, as is suggested by the stuttering that inflects his confession, and by the self-induced laughter that accompanies the joke.

Freud's analysis of jokes makes clear that the first person occupies a space that cannot be occupied by the third person. The first person makes the joke, but the joke is not completed until he sends it to the place of the third person. Once there, through its presence and its nature as a fait accompli, the joke mischievously saves the third person the effort or psychic expenditure of inhibition, which economy renders that energy superfluous and produces an excess, a surplus of energy, which is spent through laughter (Freud 1905, 148–49). Only if the second master of the joke is thus well served will the joke ricochet to the place of the first master and produce an analogous surplus, thus completing the circuit and in so doing liberating the energy that is the joke. But why is the joke compared by Freud to an unprincipled and dishonest servant, a "double-dealing rascal that serves two masters at once" (Freud 1905, 155)? Freud's description makes sense only if the two masters served are not so much the first and third persons as they are the ambivalent tendencies within each to suppress and liberate psychic energy.

Freud's description of the workings of the successful joke suggests that it works similarly behind both masters' backs. It works in a roundabout way to oppose (from different positions) the tendency to suppress the unconscious material and cathected psychic energy. The joke's mischievousness is ultimately the master's own. It depends on a secret trapdoor, a trick the master performs on himself. It depends on the master's access to his background, to the back of his mind. This not only gives the master access to the inhibited impulse lying there within, but like the trick of a ventriloquist, the successful joke gives that inhibited impulse another voice and another place: the voice and place of a "third person." This "third person" is in fact more than just the accomplice and collaborator Freud imagines. It is actually a mirror image of the first: the ventriloquist's dummy, the other object. Thus the successful joke is a "double-dealing servant" to his master in at least two ways. On the one hand, it turns one ambiguous master into what appear to be two in order to uninhibit and satisfy the master's hidden desires. On the other hand, in so doing, the servant mischievously becomes and overcomes the master. The master's ambiguity, a part of himself, is now dealt a forceful blow by the servant-become-master. Polanski achieves and suffers the same double effect by telling the inside joke. On the one hand, it doubles him into a second evil twin (the man with the knife and the Polanski of the anecdote), which liberates him from the psychic energy required to remain true to his ambiguity and severs him from his ambiguous core. On the other hand, the joke condemns Polanski to a solitary existence, reducing him into his own spectator, making him occupy the position of the viewer-judge whose implied approval is ventriloquized through his laughter.

The Place of the Servant

The use of successful jokes to dissimulate and hide the ambiguity at the core of the self is perhaps best represented in the scene where Jake Gittes first meets Noah Cross. In that scene we also see the most intense use of displacement and condensation, the deployment of humor and jokes, as a means of defense, interruption, and postponement by both characters and by the film itself. As can be expected, however, the result of these defense mechanisms is only temporary. The jokes will be interrupted, and the humorous interruptions will be broken. Noah Cross's unspeakable incestuous secret (the mystery at the core of the film and the scene) will be revealed with a vengeance, not only despite but also because of the intensity of the initial foreclosures.

Narratively, the scene is a double cross-examination where Noah Cross tries to find out as much about Jake Gittes as the investigator tries to learn about the powerful landowner. The conversation over lunch is peppered with questions all of which are either answered by evasive jokes or followed by jokes.[11] Noah Cross makes the first in the series of jokes to an ambiguous effect. Jake Gittes has just told him that he was the person who suggested to Evelyn Mulwray that her husband might have been murdered: "I think I gave it [the idea] to her." Clearly taken aback by the suggestion (and perhaps by the double meaning of the line), Noah Cross interrupts his own telltale surprise and displaces Jake Gittes's attention from himself to the fish by means of a cruel joke. The detective is clearly disgusted by being served broiled fish with the head still on, and Noah Cross capitalizes on his disgust by calling attention to it, saying, "Oh, I hope you don't mind. I believe they should be served with the head." Jake Gittes's repulsion by the food taboo (the fish's head), however, can also be said to be an oblique reference to the disgusting effect of the incest taboo. Consequently Noah Cross's cruel joke to a disgusted Jake Gittes does more than interrupt Jake Gittes's incriminating suggestions. It also stands out as a significant displacement of Evelyn Mulwray, to whom Jake Gittes has just alluded with the phrase "I think I gave it to her." The joke stands out as a memorable transition and displacement from Evelyn to the fish. This displacement then also works like a slip of the tongue by unwittingly bringing attention to Evelyn Mulwray's proximity to the abject, the out-of-place, the repulsive fish served with the head. The broken food taboo displaces the broken incest taboo, and Noah Cross unconsciously exposes himself as abject, as a taboo violator.[12]

The last joke in the series is a direct consequence of the first. Jake Gittes becomes increasingly suspicious that Evelyn Mulwray is somehow the displaced center of the mystery, and by the end of the sequence, he insists on pursuing this line of inquiry and confronts Noah Cross with the compromising pictures he took of him arguing with Hollis

Mulwray. The revelation draws a long silence from Noah Cross, suggesting that he has been put off-balance again. Jake Gittes presses the point and asks, "What was the argument about?" to which Noah Cross curtly and seriously replies, "My daughter." Jake Gittes suspects that Hollis Mulwray and Noah Cross were fighting over Evelyn Mulwray, and the answer seems to confirm this. Clearly both the question and the answer touch a sore spot in Noah Cross, who makes Jake Gittes even more curious, and he asks, "What about her?" At this point, Noah Cross stops all attempts at cunningly, gracefully, or artfully evading the question and rudely ignores Jake, bringing the interrogation and the lunch to an abrupt and suspicious halt. Like the displacement to the fish, Noah Cross's answer both holds and hides the deeper truth: the fact that the daughter to whom he refers is not only Evelyn Mulwray but also Katherine. The answer works as a dark inside joke, a joke that cannot be shared, that condenses the two daughters into one word while displacing the unpleasurable truth. The joke turns against Noah Cross, who tries to keep this truth hidden inside but is unable to. Instead he calls attention to what he is trying to hide.[13]

The key to the visual composition of this scene is its repeated collapse of deep space into close shots and close-ups synchronized with the characters' evasiveness in the script.[14] The most dramatic of these is the shot of the fish head that sticks out of the scene like a sore thumb but whose meaning is extremely difficult to interpret. The image of the fish that begins the scene is both an example of the flattening of space to foreclose analysis (or investigation) and an example of the intense curiosity that the foreclosure produces in Jake Gittes and in the viewer. Thus despite injury to his nose, or perhaps because of it, he persists on acting like the "kitty cat" of the earlier scene. Curiosity brings him (and the viewer along with him) to the bottom of the fish pond in Evelyn Mulwray's house, where he finds the all-important clue to the mystery, but the discovery also gets him figuratively eaten by the Midget's (Polanski's) piranhalike goldfish. Thus even though the close-up of the fish is more hermetic than the close-ups of Jake Gittes and Evelyn Mulwray in the earlier scene of the Chinaman joke, the intensity of its foreclosure works to create a desire in the viewer and in the detective to solve the puzzle, and to interpret its meaning.

Moreover, the scene plays itself out visually like a complex dance by Noah Cross and his servant while Jake Gittes remains fixed in the center of the moving composition after his initial threat to leave. Like the third person in the successful joke, the servant is the passive witness of Noah Cross's dissimulations and evasions. He also helps Noah Cross by putting Jake Gittes in the state where Noah Cross wants him: lulled into a false sense of security. The servant is Noah Cross's accomplice in his attempts to pull the wool over Jake Gittes's eyes by making him comfortable, by serving him well, by tending to his every need. Together with his master, the servant surrounds Jake Gittes, literally making circles around him.[15] But Polanski also makes plain the illusory nature of this "third person" and "third space" through a number of visual cues including the similarity of the servant's attire and gestures to his master's own (they both wave and smile at the Mexican musicians when they begin to play). An exaggeration and even a parody of Noah Cross's gentility, the servant hovers over Jake Gittes but remains silent throughout the scene, exhibiting no individuality or any sense of independent purpose. Indeed, the servant in this scene is the visual correlative of the Other object in the Chinaman's joke fixed firmly in place by the narcissistic economy of the master's successful joke.

In his suggestive account of the role of racialized place in film noir, Eric Lott compares film noir to a "whiteface dream-work of social anxieties with explicitly racial sources, resolved on film [by] the criminal undertakings of abjected whites" (1997, 90). Like the dream-work, Lott suggests, film noir subsumes or displaces the unconscious anxiety felt by whites in their "dubious" struggles with other races in the United States during the forties (he mentions the so-called zoot suit riots and the internment of Japanese Americans during World War II as examples). The displacement, he suggests, is also a splitting of the white self into two interior spaces, producing and villainizing an other within. Film noir, or black film, takes this other within "all the way to the end of the line," erecting in this way a *cordon sanitaire* around a pure white self: a "refuge of whiteness" (85, 88). Thus, according to Lott, "the self-conscious end point of noir and its racial tropes" is the Asian or Mexican urban landscape and underworld, insofar as they are an external figure for an evil and a death displaced from a racialized interior" (84).

Lott's comparison of film noir to the dream-work is convincing. His account of the production of the white self first through a condensation of the other and the same, and second through a displacement of the other outside the self, rings true. And yet perhaps it is a better description of the mechanism of the successful joke-work and its production of doubles like the servant in the lunch scene. This mechanism is one of at least two similar but importantly different processes or economies operating in film noir in general and neo-noir films like *Chinatown* in particular. The difference is important because on it rests the alternative to the enclosed, self-centered, and narcissistic economy proposed by Lott, an economy that can only see the other as a fantasy and a projection of the self and consequently collapses the other into an indistinct compound of races, evil, and death. The second mechanism works against the first by opening the intermediary space of analysis. Like bad jokes or broken humor, this process interrupts the joke's defensive mechanisms by traveling backward through them creating the space of analysis and interpretation. Perhaps a different voice can be given to the unspeakable from this place. The film ends with an emphasis on just such a process.

Envisioned by Polanski as an "opera's finale in which the cast reappears on stage" (Leaming 1981, 147), *Chinatown's* ending was made famous by the disagreement between director and scriptwriter. Towne wanted a romantic ending that would not take place in Chinatown, which for him was principally a metaphor (Biskind 1994, 72). He wanted Evelyn Mulwray to escape and Noah Cross to be killed amid a downpour that ends L.A.'s drought. Over his protestations, Polanski gave the film the dramatic ending it now has. "'Make me a Chinese street,' he told production designer Richard Sylbert, 'a street in Chinatown'" (Leaming 1981, 147). On that street, Evelyn Mulwray is killed, and Noah Cross keeps Katherine as Jake Gittes looks on. Towne called Polanski's ending "the tunnel at the end of the light" (Biskind 1994, 72), a joke whose success is evidenced by the one-sided commentary on this ending, which invariably interprets it as the triumph of film noir's "nihilistic resolution" (Belton 1991, 947–48).[16] If Wexman describes the ending as the exposure of the "dark side" of "our own fantasy lives" embodied by the scene's spectators—described as Oriental voyeurs "gawking at the spectacle of Evelyn Mulwray's blood-smeared body" (1985, 101, 102)—Leaming reduces it to "Polanski's travesty of the genre [of detective stories]," where "violence and desire triumph" (1981, 147).

In contrast to the narcissistic closed economy these critics read into *Chinatown*'s ending, it need not be read solely as a version of film noir's "end of the line" for "noir's abject" subject (Lott 1997, 88). Instead it can be interpreted as a choice the film urges the viewer to make. Chinatown is both Evelyn Mulwray's destination and Jake Gittes's destiny, but these are not the same thing. Chinatown (the place) is the end of the line for her. In the spirit of classic film noir, the film's closed economy violently kills the femme fatale and keeps her in the place of the Other object. But *Chinatown* (the film) is also the continuing saga of Jake Gittes and of his memory of those violent erasures. It is not the end of the ride for him. The last line of the film ("Forget it, Jake, it's Chinatown") both locks Jake Gittes inside the film's traumatic cycle of repetition and sets the stage for future repetitions of the trauma that haunts Gittes, by urging Jake to forget.[17]

And yet Walsh's (Joe Mantell) statement also suggests that the vicious cycle depends on a displacement, a defensive mechanism, a forgetting and a repression that is also a tendentious and willful choice. This displacement substitutes *Chinatown*, the neurotic series of jokes flattening the space of interpretation, with Chinatown defined as the mysterious place of the unknowable and the unconscious.[18] But the displacement of the neurotic mechanism to a place beyond one's control (destiny, fate, Chinatown, the unconscious) only temporarily interrupts the disturbing affect of Jake Gittes's shame and pain and in fact prepares the ground and brings about the repetition of the disturbing material that Jake Gittes is trying to repress. This mystifying displacement is contingent on Jake Gittes's choice to forget Chinatown, to reduce Chinatown to a metaphor for fate, to reduce it to the obscure and the mysterious, to the other, rather than facing up to his actions and to the jokes he uses to cover over them.

This choice is emphasized by the ambiguous and intermediary space that the film leaves open for the viewer at the end. The final scene inverts the series of relentless visual collapses of deep space that orders the rest of the film. Instead, the film's last scene takes us from the claustrophobic condensation of space during the discovery of Evelyn Mulwray's body to a deep-focus shot where the characters slowly recede into the dark but visible streets of Chinatown. Although the shot certainly suggests the "end point of noir and its racial tropes" (Lott 1997, 85), its perspective also opens a place that could begin the analysis that might undo them.

Chinatown's logic partly derives from the mechanism of bad jokes and broken humor as Freud understood it in *Jokes and their Relation to the Unconscious*. The film works like a bad joke insofar as it screens (hides and reveals) the unconscious through displacement. Attention to the film's bad jokes helps us to focus on the film's interruption of the competing closed circuit of successful jokes, which operates as a defensive mechanism that both protects from the out-of-place and guarantees the subject's return to the original anxiety. In other words, *Chinatown* is a film at odds with itself. On the one hand, its bad jokes make visible the unconscious (the extremely out-of-place) while paradoxically keeping it off the screen; the film takes us to the region of the unconscious through displacements that obliquely show us what we are not meant to see. On the other hand, the film's successful jokes collapse that region with the place Chinatown, and this condensation interrupts the film's revelation of the unconscious processes.

Perhaps this tension between its different jokes explains the film's kinship with a shaggy-dog story, which, like *Chinatown*, is not funny and has no punch line. Viewing the film, however, we learn to travel its interrupting circuit, and like Gittes at the end of the film, we emerge from the experience as displaced and dislocated subjects. It may be that our dislocation will predispose us to displace our anxiety by repeating the joke regardless of the cost of doing so to ourselves, to our listener, and to others. But perhaps we also emerge from the film's dislocating experience having learned to open an intermediary space between our unconscious anxiety and the uncritical repetition of the joke. From this out-of-place place, located at the corner of Polanski's eye/camera, we half see the terrible consequences of assigning discrete and even opposed places, locations, and positions to ourselves and to others, and the liberating pleasure afforded by keeping these places open to interpretation.

CHAPTER 8

Franklin's New Noir:
Devil in a Blue Dress

Noir is a visual form of a model for subject formation driven by a logic of identity that has matricide and the exclusionary deployment of an intersection of race and sex as its principal mechanisms. The violent nature of the principal mechanisms of this model of subject formation ensures that crisis is inherent to its logic of identity. What we violently exclude violently returns. Moreover, our investment in the process of subject formation and stable identities ensures that when it returns, what we exclude returns transformed into something unrecognizable, amorphous, overwhelming, and external, like fate.[1] In fact, in deploying this model of subject formation and its logic of identity, we are responsible for our own haunting monsters.

Cultural forms of this process such as film noir contain both the mechanisms and the crises inherent to its logic. Noir transposes the mechanisms and its crises to its specific cinematic language. In this book, we diagnose the mechanisms and the crises in noir as symptoms of that process of subject formation. A recurrent operation of both noir and this logic of identity is the condensation and displacement of the threats to an identity-in-process. This dual mechanism of condensation and displacement is the main object of our study. More specifically, we describe the logic of identity as the condensation of race and sex to manage the precarious process of subject formation, and we highlight the displacement of the mother as a crucial element of this logic.

Some criticism about noir, however, and in particular racially inflected criticism, sees noir differently. For these critics, noir is a mirror of social changes in the United States.[2] Similarly, film critics of black neo-noirs such as Manthia Diawara turn the genre into a reflection of a unique African American experience, which in turn gives shape to a singular (if sometimes contradictory) response to the racism implied in noir.[3] These critics speak of noir and neo-noir as if they were mirrors that reflect an identity that is threatened in the case of noir and fighting for survival in the case of neo-noir. The uniqueness of the black experience and racial identity is what is at stake for these critics. Insofar as this is true, the monsters that undo the logic of identity in noir also haunt these critics. It is not surprising, for example, that Diawara would see a formalist approach to film noir (an approach that focuses on figures like the femme fatale) as a threat to the stability of the identity mirrored in black neo-noir.[4] Diawara suggests that focusing on figures like the femme fatale draws back from the more relevant and supposedly encompassing experience of black rage. But Diawara also acknowledges that black rage is aimed at women and effectively silences them by killing them. Thus Diawara is faced with the impossible task of choosing between a competing sexual or racial identity for a subject that is both, and of choosing between competing methodologies to study an aesthetic event that cannot be split neatly into form and content.

Mark Berrettini's essay "Private Knowledge, Public Space" is another example of an identity-based model of film criticism that is riddled with similar problems. Citing Ruby Rich, Berrettini describes black noir as noir "with a difference." Drawing from Stephen Soitos's study of African American detective fiction, Berrettini also emphasizes the central importance of a black experience to understand changes to the genres of noir and detective fiction. Berrettini discusses figures such as the femme fatale, but always as a function of racialized challenges to the convention. He argues that both in Walter Mosley's novel *Devil in a Blue Dress* and in Carl Franklin's film of the same title, the femme fatale becomes a tragic mulatta. But underlying this difference is the common tragic fate of both the femme fatale and the mulatta in both noir and in neo-noir, as well as in both detective and black detective fiction. It is this common tragic fate that Berrettini's account fails to explain. While the problem of racial identity accounts for the change from femme fatale to tragic mulatta, the identity model cannot explain why the new figure must also die. In fact, the death of the tragic mulatta, a figure of ambiguous racial identity, seems necessary given the nature of Berrettini's analytical model.

In both Diawara's and Berrettini's account of neo-noir in general, and of Carl Franklin's *Devil in a Blue Dress* in particular, race and sex compete for the attention of their identity-driven models. There is, however, another way of approaching this film and the novel that precedes it. This approach does not set race and sex against each other but rather highlights the exclusionary condensation of race and sex, as well as the displacement of the maternal figure in the novel and in the film. These mechanisms are then diagnosed as the symptoms of the identity logic that drives the constellation of noir novels, films, and criticism. The making of Easy Rawlins, a new noir detective and a new identity for noir, is a process that stabilizes and naturalizes a black subject by easing some of the tensions that have characterized noir. The slips in this process of identity building, however, reveal its operation and its artificiality. These slips are made manifest in the impertinent return of the characters of Mouse and Daphne, both of whom condense and displace the maternal threat that lies at the center of the identity logic that drives the film.

Building Blocks of a New Stable Authority

Fatalism is not a part of *Devil in a Blue Dress* in two significant ways. For Franklin, the answer to the question "Why me?" is "because of the color line." *Devil in a Blue Dress* transforms the fatalism of the 1940s into racism. In other words, if there is any fear and anxiety in his film, it is not due to a dangerously senseless, violent world over which the characters have no control. The source of the nervousness of the film's protagonist is as plain to the viewer as it is to Easy Rawlins (Denzel Washington). "Nervous? Here I was in the middle of the night in a white neighborhood with a white woman in my car. Naw, I wasn't nervous. I was stupid." Easy's dark skin threatens to determine his fate at a time when "the color line in America worked both ways and even a rich white man like Todd Carter [Terry Kinney] was afraid to cross it." By making racism the agent of Easy's misfortunes, Franklin demystifies North American filmmaking during the forties. In other words, he brings out the noir in film noir; he raises to the surface the racial aspect of noir; he makes explicit the threat to authority represented by the racially othered and contained by widespread racism.[5]

But fatalism is not a part of *Devil in a Blue Dress* in yet another way. Although fear may be what drives Easy, Franklin also makes it clear that his film is about a journey to self-determination. In a master seminar held in the American Film Institute, Franklin describes *Devil in a Blue Dress* as "kind of about a guy who makes a pact with a Faustian kind of character and then gets exposed to the real American dream behind the facade where the cogs and pulleys exist and where the back room deals are made and somehow is able to navigate through those subterranean waters and comes out the other end with his principles fairly well intact and still alive" (Franklin 1998). In the seminar, Franklin says that "if you're somehow in control of your own self-determination, your own business, if you somehow have a self-determination of some kind, then you can work as much as you want, as little as you want or whatever. That's the real American dream. That's what I was trying to get across" (Franklin 1998). Self-determination, owning a business, being your own boss, the real American Dream (going from employee to self-employment) is what *Devil in a Blue Dress* is all about, according to Franklin. And indeed, *Devil in a Blue Dress* shows us the making of a self-determined individual. Easy becomes a private detective with a double difference. Unlike many detectives of film noir, Easy sees behind the facade and can navigate the subterranean waters of the corrupt system in order to survive. Also unlike the detectives of film noir, Easy is black.[6]

However, the process of making this new noir is not without its problems. In its struggle to subvert noir conventions and to bolster and naturalize its black subject, Franklin's *Devil in a Blue Dress* also bolsters the genre by erasing, covering over, and easing the contradictions and tensions that feminist critics of noir have effectively made visible as strategic points of intervention.[7] In other words, there is a markedly nostalgic air to Franklin's self-determined black detective. Easy is a figure who harks back to a simpler time in many ways. Indeed, Diawara remarks that Franklin's films belong to a conventional and nostalgic trend of black neo-noirs of the Reagan/Bush era that restore the femme fatale to the traditional position of wife and nostalgically pine for a Southern simplicity (Diawara 1993b, 275–76). But again, Diawara's account cannot explain this apparent contradiction in black neo-noir film. The contradiction can be explained, however, as the result of the very identity logic that makes of Easy Rawlins a new noir. By that logic, the coherence of the private detective is returned to a time before the instability of the figure became visible to feminist critics.

One of the ingredients commonly associated with film noir is its expressionistic use of lighting. The film noir of the forties and fifties possesses a unique intensity of both darkness and light through which the characters move. Despite its simple black-and-white format, film noir

Easy Rawlins (Denzel Washington) in *Devil in a Blue Dress*.

has a striking painterly quality. The intensity with which the images are lit or shadowed gives them a visual incoherence. Sometimes the characters are drowning in shadows, sometimes they suffocate in the light, and sometimes they are divided into black and white horizontal lines. But lighting is never a leitmotiv in film noir. It is never a visual cue for the moral nature of a character. Intense black-and-white lighting pervades all the characters, good and bad.[8] The intense lighting of film noir's femme fatale is in stark contrast to the use of soft focus. If soft focus gives us a visual ideal of beauty based on the homogenization of the surface of the body, the intensity of the lighting has the opposite effect: it multiplies and fragments the same surfaces into incoherent pieces. This visual incoherence is one aspect of these films that undermines the identity logic of the noir narratives by complicating its insistent drive toward a coherently evil woman.

In contrast to noir's intense black-and-white look, *Devil in a Blue Dress* is filmed in muted colors. In the master seminar at the American Film Institute, Franklin discusses this choice and significantly associates it with his nostalgia for a simpler time:

> 1948 was three years after the end of World War II and for four years, 1941 to 1945, the United States was pretty much caught up in a war effort so there wasn't much new in the society—new cars, new clothes. There were some things that were new but for the most part you wouldn't find people dressing in their finest that much because it was a humble time.... It was an optimistic time but we weren't as commercially enslaved as we are now and the ad industry wasn't quite as effective as it is now in making us dissatisfied with everything we have.... What I didn't want to do was what I've seen in some period pieces where it takes place in 1935, 36 and it's everything from that year. That's just not the way the world looks to us. (Franklin 1998)

One striking aspect of this description is Franklin's use of the metaphor of slavery to describe the present relationship of a collective "we" to material things. Franklin suggests that the forties were a time of freedom from the chains of materialism that bind that collectivity today. Franklin suggests that the intensity of primary colors (yellow, red, and blue) are signs of modernity and of its slavery to consumerism. The soft colors of *Devil in a Blue Dress* are then not unlike the soft focus with which women were filmed in the forties to appear beautiful, attractive, and ideal. Color in *Devil in a Blue Dress* also has the homogenizing effect of the category of noir. It nostalgically sets apart and categorizes the time in which film noir was made as a better time, clearly better than a present of slavery to consumerism.

Another striking aspect of this description is the "us" with which the passage ends: "That's just not the way the world looks to us." Who is this "us"? Is Franklin, an African American director, describing the black community? Is he describing the community of filmmakers? Perhaps it refers to both. What is clear is that "us" refers not only to something bigger than Franklin but also to something that seems to travel through time, back to the real past, to the real forties, that allows Franklin to know how the world really looked. It is an "us" that knows the way the world looks, and by extension, the way the world looked then. This "us" is not only a collective voice; it also speaks from a time outside of time, an eternity from which the present does not represent a threat.

Devil in a Blue Dress's voice-over is a version of this collective voice from a safe and all-seeing place. Is this the place of a divinity or of a spirit? Not really. Instead, this is the voice of history. In a film like *Murder, My Sweet*, the voice-over functions as an ordering device. The noir convention is that the separation between the voice and the body of the detective gradually disappears as the film comes to an end, when we are gradually brought to the present of the narrative and to the reunion of the voice and the body of the detective, whose complete persona we see end the film. Despite this ordering imperative, however, there are times in film noir when the voice-over cannot retain its objectivity and becomes an interior monologue trying to help the body overcome a painful situation, a moment like the one in *Murder, My Sweet* when Philip Marlowe's body is drugged and out of control and the voice-over becomes an interior monologue in its attempts to help him recover. In contrast to this convention, the voice-over in *Devil in a Blue Dress* never comes back to the present of the narrative; it always remains objective. By doing so, *Devil in a Blue Dress* strengthens the authority of the voice that stands apart from the body on the screen throughout the film and is never vulnerable to the harm sometimes done to that body, and never steps down from its objective status. Neither is it like the haunted voice-over in a film such as *Sunset Boulevard*, which eerily speaks from a metaphysical other side. Instead, the voice-over of *Devil in a Blue Dress* stays safely ensconced in a time beyond time and beyond the suffering or the death of the body significantly telling us the history of the United States while locating within its larger frame the story of Easy. "Like me, a lot of colored folk from Texas and Louisiana had moved out to California to get them good jobs in the shipyards and aircraft companies."

There are two moments in the film when the voice-over seems to abandon this objective plane. Those two moments, however, differ significantly from similar moments in film noir, such as the one described from *Murder, My Sweet*. At the beginning of the film, Joppy (Mel Winkler) tells Easy that the job offer Dewitt Albright (Tom Sizemore) has just extended to him "ain't nothing to worry about." This statement is followed by the voice-over that says, "When somebody tells me ain't nothing to worry about, I usually look down to see if my fly is open." Later on with Daphne Monet (Jennifer Beals), we see a similar scene when she asks Easy if he is nervous and the voice-over answers, "Nervous? Here I was in the middle of the night in a white neighborhood with a white woman in my car. Naw, I wasn't nervous. I was stupid." All three of these scenes are humorous, but the humor is the result of different things. In *Murder, My Sweet* the audience laughs at the confusion in the voice-over, which first talks about the comfortable bed and quickly shouts at the body of Philip Marlowe, telling him to stay off it. It is the authority of the voice-over that is at stake here, but the audience feels as if it can laugh at it. In *Devil in a Blue Dress*, the voice-over does not trip. We laugh with the voice-over at Easy's stupidity and innocence. Unlike Easy, the voice-over knows better than to trust Joppy or to be caught in the compromising situation in which Easy finds himself. We identify with the voice-over's authority and separate ourselves from the flawed Easy.

Flashback is also in authoritative mode in *Devil in a Blue Dress* and operates similarly and as a complement to the voice-over. In film noir, flashback tends to be in tension both with the narrative (which it temporally derails and sends abruptly into the past) and with the voice-over (which loses some of its control over events).[9] The result is that the visual style of film noir unsettles the narrative. But in *Devil in a Blue Dress* flashback is used to a different effect: it clarifies the narrative. In the middle of the film, Richard McGee (Scott Lincoln) is found dead in his house by Easy and Daphne. We haven't seen him for a long while, so when we see him on the floor dead, the film conveniently provides a flashback to our first encounter with McGee in an effort to clarify for us who this person is, when we saw him last, and what his role is in the film. A similar use of flashback is made later on after Easy gets ahold of the photographs of Matthew Terrel (Maury Chaykin) with naked children. Rather than fragmenting the temporal line of the plot, as happens in film noir, in both of these cases, the flashbacks instead keep the time line intact. Indeed, these flashbacks are superimposed on the image of the film's present, and they are photographed in soft focus in what seem like efforts to give clarifying information harmlessly, without significantly disturbing the present of the film. Neither do they take us outside the time line framed by the beginning and end of the film. Thus the flashback has an important stabilizing effect. It maintains the film's coherence even as it keeps the audience, the filmmaker, and the voice-over outside the film's temporal flow. It contains the flow of time within the boundaries of the events and narrative of the plot. It emphasizes that our time and the time of the characters in the film are different.

So far, we have seen how Franklin seems to harmonize or homogenize the very visual and narrative devices that are in tension in film noir. He manipulates color, voice-over, and flashback in such a way as to create for us and for his narrator a perspective that is safe from the flow of time, a perspective that ensures an objective point of view, a perspective of a collective voice that seems bigger than Easy. The collective voice that stands outside time is the voice of a community of African Americans that has its visual correlative in the bird's-eye view of the utopian neighborhood with which the film ends. Berrettini rightly remarks that the final shot of Central Avenue in *Devil in a Blue Dress* is in significant tension with what he calls a threatening future L.A., more violent and corrupt, marked by Red hunts, increasing racial tensions, corporate-urban sprawl, and government corruption (Berrettini 1999, 85). In the promotional material for the film, Franklin describes that space as "the heart of the city's black community ... Central Avenue in 1948 was tantamount to Harlem during the Harlem Renaissance of the 1920's and 1930's." It is not surprising that Franklin would choose to end his film with this utopian image and with the voice-over that stresses the importance of friendship. An image of a community of self-determined male black friends who are responsible and who are not violent provides the necessary stability for an ideal community of families not unlike the one we see at the end of the film. This tranquil, objective, stable, harmonious, coherent bird's-eye view seems very different from the violent, subjective, unstable, fragmented perspectives of noir, but at what cost?

Chandler and Mosley

Franklin's *Devil in a Blue Dress* is to *Murder, My Sweet* what Walter Mosley's novel of the same title is to Raymond Chandler's novel *Farewell, My Lovely*. Indeed, Mosley's narrative style is a nostalgic transformation of the violent hard-boiled style preferred by Chandler. Fredric Jameson calls Chandler "the least politically correct of all our modern writers" (Jameson 1993, 37). He says that "Chandler faithfully gives vent to everything racist, sexist, homophobic, and otherwise socially resentful and reactionary in the American collective unconscious" (37). He then adds that these feelings are "almost exclusively mobilized for striking and essentially visual purposes, that is to say, for aesthetic rather than political ones" (37). Jameson's comments on Chandler's political incorrectness, and on the aesthetic function of his racism, sexism, and homophobia, are left undeveloped as a provocative aside. And yet it is possible to develop Jameson's point by revisiting an earlier essay on Chandler (published in 1970) and Jameson's 1979 book on Wyndham Lewis. The reader of these works understands that according to Jameson, Chandler's political incorrectness is a matter of neither political nor personal opinion. Moreover, it is not the political stance or the personal opinion of a stable subject or ego. Instead, Chandler's racism and sexism are symptoms of a fundamentally divided subject, a subject that can both "observe local injustice, racism, corruption, educational incompetence, with a practiced eye, while he continues to entertain boundless optimism as to the greatness of the country" (Jameson 1970, 632). If in this essay Jameson associates this condition with an American obsession and dissociation, he puts his own identity claim into question in his later book, where he makes similar claims about the British writer Wyndham Lewis. If Jameson associates this condition with a historical moment of advanced capitalism, he also puts his own historicism into question by arguing that Chandler's and Wyndham Lewis's racism, sexism, and homophobia are principally aesthetic problems: symptoms of modernism.

As should be clear to readers of Jameson, modernism for him is not a fixed moment of literary history. Instead, modernism must be understood as a mode of the aesthetic itself, that which reveals and revels in the accidental nature of the historical. For Jameson, Chandler's violently racist and sexist hard-boiled style goes beyond sexism or racism, historically, politically, or personally understood, and into a mode of writing and living that puts into question the very notion of identity, stable subjectivity, and authority: a language and life that puts into question the very possibility of a stable historical perspective. From this perspective, what lies at the core of Chandler's racism, sexism, and homophobia, indeed at the very core of his attractive and popular violent hard-boiled style, is an unreconcilable, if familiar split, in language and in being. Following Lyotard's *Des dispositifs pulsionnels* and *Economie libidinale*, Jameson argues that such racist and sexist moments are moments of libidinal escape from conventional forms of respectability, moments of unconscious liberation from repression, moments when the subject's desire is unrepressed and rises to the surface. In short, these are moments when the unconstrained aesthetic is working at its most intense against the repressive forces that surround us, contain us, tame us, and give us stable identities. They are profoundly heuristic moments, moments of profound pleasure, because they allow us to glimpse the arbitrariness of our language, because they put us in tangential contact with the similarly split nature of our philosophical being and of our psychological self.

Clearly, there are some problems with Jameson's interpretation of these moments, especially insofar as the libidinal escape may be harder for, and even incompatible with, readers whose identities are already compromised, indeed whose consciousness and subjectivity are socially, culturally, and politically constructed as fragmented, divided, disassociated, and pathological. But taking into account the limits to Jameson's argument, his characterization of Chandler's style is still useful to understanding the attraction of its destabilizing potential for an African American reader and writer of detective fiction such as Mosley. Indeed, Mosley will appropriate some of the liberating and heuristic force in Chandler's hard-boiled style while eschewing some of its racially determined violence. Unlike other black detective novelists, Mosley returns to Chandler's hard-boiled first-person narrative style.[10] Also like Chandler, Mosley deploys racial slurs like "nigger" and "zebra," using them (together with slang) to escape the prison house of language. But Chandler puts racial slurs and racist ideas in the mouth of his detective protagonist and narrator, Philip Marlowe: "I was with him yesterday—when he killed the nigger over on Central" (Chandler 1976, 96), or "Heads turned slowly and the eyes in them glistened and stared in the dead alien silence of another race" (4). Such slurs and ideas are displaced to the periphery in *Devil in a Blue Dress*.

This is not to say that racial slurs never appear in Mosley's novel, but they never appear in the voice of its narrator Easy Rawlins, a fact that strengthens the authority of the protagonist's voice. Only secondary characters like Dewitt Albright, Mouse, and Daphne use racist insults to an effect that is similar to that produced in Chandler's work, and then only in scarce and choice moments. Given the novel's black narrator-detective, Albright's use of racial slurs against Easy does not have the liberating effect diagnosed by Jameson but rather serves to expose him as the white racist that he truly is. The case of Mouse and Daphne, however, is closer to (if still different from) Marlowe's. They are black and mulatto characters, respectively, so their appropriation and use of the racial slurs "nigger" and "zebra" have the potential of highlighting the duality of language and of their psychological selves without simultaneously destroying them or others. These slurs help these characters escape from the identity-driven logic of their racialized world in both facilitating and debilitating ways. When a black character like Mouse uses the word "nigger" to insult another black character, the effect is comical, and the humorous possibility of its appropriation denaturalizes a racist language by suggesting instead its pliable and artificial nature.

Daphne's use of the racist slur "zebra," however, is debilitating. Daphne uses this word to describe the animal itself, which she sees in a zoo where she has a sexual encounter with her father. Daphne, it turns out, has a black mother and a white father, making her a mulatta. Thus "zebra" in this passage is an allusion to someone like Daphne with a biracial background. It is used to suggest disgust with the character of Daphne because of her mixed race. It liberates the writer's desire much in the same way that Chandler's desire is liberated from the constricting bonds of social convention, suggesting a psychological rift in the writer himself. And yet the slur is made indirectly in Mosley's novel. Daphne, not the narrator, makes the slur, significantly displacing the disgust the word is meant to produce onto the novel's femme fatale. Moreover, Daphne uses it not to describe herself but to name an animal in front of which her father first begins to sexually approach her. The scene is told as if to suggest that the slur is firmly lodged in Daphne's unconscious and comes out indirectly as the memory of an animal in the zoo. Daphne's unconscious is then saddled with a disgust for herself that the writer dares not put in the words of the narrator. Such moments in Mosley's novel also make visible the identity logic that drives *Devil in a Blue Dress* and that displaces its disturbing ideas to the psychological margins of its characters, even as it displaces these characters to the margins of the narrative.

Significantly, Easy Rawlins's voice is free from such splitting ambiguity. Not only does the narrator of *Devil in a Blue Dress* never use such racist slurs, but his account of the relations between blacks, Jews, and Mexicans is intensely idealized to convey the feeling of a shared and unambiguous unity of experience. Upon visiting a commercial establishment owned by two Jewish men, Easy remarks, "That was why so many Jews back then understood the American Negro; in Europe the Jew had been a Negro for more than a thousand years" (Mosley 1990, 138). Later in the novel, Easy again takes the reader back to a time "before Mexicans and black people started hating each other. Back then, before ancestry had been discovered, a Mexican and a Negro considered themselves the same. That is to say, just another couple of unlucky stiffs left holding the short end of the stick" (177). Easy's nostalgic evocation of a utopian moment of racial identification through shared suffering and identical hardship forces upon the reader a vision of hope, of a stable future, and of racial understanding that is hard to visualize. Not only is the gesture possible as a willful disavowal of the racial conflict that surrounds Easy, but its nostalgic tone also performs a leveling of the experience of suffering that makes suffering lose much of its meaning. Moreover, the nostalgic gesture flies in the face of Mosley's own displacements, of his racially and sexually determined exclusions, for the sake of building Easy's stable identity.

Mosley similarly sutures the split voice of Chandler's *Farewell, My Lovely*. In the novel, Marlowe hears his own voice during drug-induced trances or after being knocked unconscious. "I balanced myself woozily on the flat of my hands, listening. 'Yeah, that was about how it was,' the voice said. It was my voice. I was talking to myself, coming out of it. I was trying to figure the thing out subconsciously. 'Shut up, you dimwit,' I said, and stopped talking to myself" (Chandler 1976, 53). The split in the voice is a recurring symptom of the modern detective's profound psychological split. Thus despite his efforts to stop it, Marlowe comically fails. The only way to stop the insanity is to cover over it, and to muffle the voice of a split self that will not be silenced, a voice that remains and returns later with greater intensity. Mosley's Easy Rawlins experiences a similar split in his voice halfway through the novel. His other voice, however, is far from confusing. In fact, it has the opposite effect on Easy. "The voice only comes to me at the worst times, when everything seems so bad that I want to take my car and drive it into a wall. Then this voice comes to me and gives me the best advice I ever get" (Mosley 1990, 97). Easy's other voice is not only soothing; far from suggesting insanity, the voice knows what to do. It is the wise voice of a superego that helps Easy survive. "The voice has no lust. He never told me to rape or steal. He just tells me how it is if I want to survive. Survive like a man. When the voice speaks, I listen" (99). Easy's other voice is disembodied (it has no lust), and yet it tells Easy how to "survive like a man," and Easy refers to it with a third-person masculine pronoun. Much the same as happens in Franklin's film, the survival of the black male detective, the coherence of his identity as a man, depends on the removal, the exclusion of threats to an identity clearly in-process, the suturing and covering over of the rifts in its logic, the violent displacement of ambiguity, fragmentation, and instability, to the periphery of the narrative and onto such figures as the mulatta femme fatale.

The Big Slip

The question remains whether Franklin is successful in his attempt at building a black male subject whose stable voice of authority lies outside time and is grounded in a utopian place. Perhaps the answer to this question lies in the permanence in memory of the two characters that have moved out of Mr. Franklin's neighborhood by the end of the film: Daphne and Mouse (Don Cheadle). Significantly, both characters are temporally marked. If Mouse is a character who belongs to the past, Daphne belongs to the future. Significantly, both Daphne's future and Mouse's past are threatening to the subject built by the film.

Mouse is perhaps the film's most memorable character. He is funny because unlike Easy, Mouse is instinctive, impulsive, and unpredictable. He does not agonize over difficult decisions. He shoots first and asks questions later. He is faithful to Easy and does not betray him. He is a friend at his beck and call. But Mouse is more than Easy's friend. Mouse also has a disturbing effect on Easy and even on the narrative itself. He is linked to one of the few moments in the film's narrative when the voice-over's strict control over the time line falls apart. At the beginning of the film, Easy decides to take Albright up on his shady offer. Right before he meets Albright, however, Easy has a disquieting flashback that is significantly different from the series of flashbacks discussed earlier. On the one hand, this flashback substitutes the present of the film. On the other, it is composed of a set of quick, incoherent images that are doubly disturbing. The images are disturbing because they belong to a past before the events on the screen and take us far outside the safe temporal frame of the film. They are also disturbing because they belong to a past that Easy will deny later on in the film, further destabilizing the narrative and confusing the audience. As the film progresses, we learn that Easy helped Mouse kill his stepfather and possibly his stepbrother back in Houston. The flashback then stands for Easy's guilt in the form of an uncontrollable return of fragmented images from the dark past that he wants to deny.

It comes as no surprise, then, that Mouse turns out to be a loose cannon who even points a gun at Easy when he suggests that Mouse might be drunk. The scene suggests a further destabilizing effect of Mouse on the controlled narrative of the film. It suggests that Mouse may even stand for Easy's violent side, his alter ego, opening up the possibility of a split in the main character, and even more seriously of a split in his voice. Fearing for his life, Easy tricks Mouse into "letting him live" by pretending to be a voice that will tell Easy (himself) to be afraid of Mouse every time Mouse walks into a room. That brief exchange significantly disturbs the stabilizing function of voice-over in the film. In that scene, Easy pretends to be a false voice-over that is very hard to locate. Is the voice pretending to be Mouse's inner voice, telling him to let Easy live? Or is the voice pretending to be Easy's inner voice telling him to be afraid? Or is it perhaps that the voice is neither and both at the same time? Is it a voice that precariously preserves the lives of both sides of one divided black man who stands for a black community of men? What is clear is that the voice is literally over both Mouse and Easy. It is also clear that the voice is a pretense, an artifice, a device, to stay alive. It is also momentary; it serves a specific purpose for a specific time. In film noir fashion, the dialogue in this scene between Mouse and Easy contradicts the timeless authority of the voice-over.

The split nature of that scene has its counterpart in the character of Daphne. In Roman mythology, Daphne is a woman who changes into a laurel tree at the moment that the god Apollo wants to possess her. True to her namesake, the Daphne of the film similarly moves between races, worlds, and identities. Berrettini's point about Daphne's duplicitous nature, foreshadowed by Easy's names for her, complements Daphne's racial and mythical split dimension (Berrettini 1999, 75–76). As a ruse to hide his investigation from his friends Odell (Albert Hall), Coretta James (Lisa Nicole Carson), and Dupree Brouchard (Jarnard Burks), Easy purposefully calls Daphne by the mistaken names of Delilah and Dahlia. In this way, the film associates Daphne with two fatal women: the duplicitous woman from the Old Testament who slays the unsuspecting Samson, and the unfaithful wife of George Marshall's 1946 *The Blue Dahlia*. Both names suggest that Daphne is the femme fatale of film noir. She incorporates the mythical force of both Daphne and Delilah. In film noir fashion, Franklin transforms the fears of a crisis in the process of subject formation into an anxiety over a superior, inhuman, and even mythical force. Daphne stands for the other of the ordered, univocal, male, history-laden voice-over that wants to stand over and outside the film.

Not surprisingly, Franklin controls Daphne with the camera and with the narrative. Not only will Daphne be left out of the utopian community where Easy lives, but Daphne remains in the memory of the viewer as a domesticated or tamed version of the femme fatale. As

Berrettini suggests, Daphne's introduction is loaded with the icono-graphy of this noir character: the Barbara Stanwyck hair, the nails, the cigarette and smoke (1999, 76-77). But there is also something notably artificial and fragile about that scene and its main character. Daphne seems to live in a bubble. The camera pans through the room and stops, leaving Daphne off to the side, unbalanced and unstable. She stands over the furnishings, but she doesn't dominate the scene. Instead she appears as a frail and sad statue or object. Notably, Daphne does not seem to have the same sexual force of her predecessors. Unlike her attempts at seducing Easy in the novel, her attempts in the film fail, and Easy steps back in apparent control of his desires.

The scene where Daphne is introduced tames the femme fatale in yet another way. The scene subtly superimposes on Daphne the figure of the tragic mulatta, a convention of U.S. film and fiction, and the embodiment of transgressive miscegenation (Berrettini 1999, 78–79). Daphne's peripheral position, her mournful expression, and her blue dress combine to produce in the viewer, not just a feeling of sexual attraction, but also a feeling of sadness. Her blue dress is an appropri-ate metaphor for the sadness that will later mark her racially split self, a sadness that we will learn results from the loss of her black identity. It could be argued that the introduction of this figure is a corrective device that makes visible the erasures of the Hayes Production Code (the self-regulatory code of ethics created in 1930 by the Motion Picture Producers and Distributors of America, forbidding the presentation of miscegenation on screen). Daphne's sadness and her tragedy stand as overt criticisms of the racial divide that victimizes her. But it can also be argued that Daphne's sadness and her tragedy tame the power of the noir femme fatale.

Daphne's names refer to a double loss: the loss of an identity and the loss of a body. On the one hand, the name "Daphne" refers to the perversity of the protection of the father in the myth: the tragic dehu-manization of Daphne. In the myth, there is a sense in which Daphne will be killed by her transformation into a tree. On the other hand, the name leads back to another dead body. Not only does it hark back to *The*

Blue Dahlia, but it also recalls the infamous case of Elizabeth Short, a black resident of Los Angeles identified with the film's evil femme fatale and murdered a year after the release of *The Blue Dahlia*.

By calling Daphne "Dahlia," Easy superimposes on her the tragic history of that name. The different meanings of Dahlia, her multicolored (blue, white, black) incarnations, burdens Daphne with a heavy composition. She is a helpless victim rather than a powerful victimizer, who suffers from the racialized forces that overdetermine the terrible fate of Elizabeth Short. By calling her Dahlia, Easy makes us remember the tortured history behind that name: the dead black body of Elizabeth Short and her erased identity. Indeed, by the end of the film, we identify with Easy in our sympathy for Daphne's losses. Her loss of a home, a lover, and a name seem to stem from an initial loss of a black identity erased, vilified, and nullified by the racism of her society.

The Devil in a Maternity Dress

Despite the film's condemnation of the social racism that leads to Daphne's loss of identity, the film's identity-driven logic trades on a similar erasure. The femme fatale is not so much replaced as she is displaced by the tragic mulatta, and this displacement in turn hints at a more familiar (if less visible) source for Daphne's losses. These losses can be traced back to her past, to Lake Charles, Louisiana, to her French roots, and to her Creole mother. Near the end of the film, the voice-over tells us that Daphne explained her racial history "like a sinner who wanted to confess," a characterization that suggests that Daphne feels guilty about her racial hybridity. The film traces this sin back to her mother. That sin could also be traced back to the violation of her mother by a white man. But the film's perverse characterization of the maternal in figures like Matthew Terrel, for example, suggests otherwise.[11] Although the film (like the novel) does not describe the exact nature of the relationship between Daphne's mother and her husband(s), it does raise the specter of perverse maternal desire and leaves open the possibility of Daphne's mother's desire for a white man. Indeed, this desire is also found at the bottom of Daphne's multiple losses. The film suggests that the mother's prohibited desire is the fatal flaw that makes Daphne into a sinner.

If Daphne is represented as responsible for her plight, and if the film suggests that she deserves her punishment, it is because she repeats her mother's sin and thus profoundly identifies with her. Like her mother, Daphne too desires a white man. But more so than her mother, Daphne desires to belong to the world of the white man. Protected by a white and wealthy lover, she surrounds herself with color, with expensive furniture and dresses. Her identification with her mother and the concomitant desire to be a part of the white world reinscribe Daphne in the role of the femme fatale. As such, Daphne is involved in different illicit sexual relations, and she embodies forbidden desire. Indeed, her underlying identity as femme fatale seems to be one strong motivating force behind her alias, Daphne Monet. On the one hand, her chosen French nom de guerre identifies her with her Creole mother and seems to be a rejection of her white father's English name, the simple monosyllabic "Hank." On the other hand, the name "Monet" is pronounced like the French word for coin, *monnaie*, suggesting the sinful desire for material wealth that drives her and perhaps drove her mother as well. According to this reading, the blue dress of the film's title works like the figure of the tragic mulatta. They are both screens covering over the red devil underneath: the mother's dangerous sexuality and desire.

The strength of the threat of the mother's sexuality is perhaps best represented by the differences between Franklin's film and Mosley's novel. It is significant that although the novel's references to the racial ambiguity of Daphne are preserved in the film, the more troublesome ambiguity of her double identity as both daughter and lover to her own father is lost. At the end of the novel, Daphne tells the story of her childhood. In the novel, Daphne tells the story twice. According to both accounts, Daphne has an incestuous relationship with her father, and the encounters produce a split in her identity. In her first account, Daphne describes the transition from little girl to lover. "My daddy and I were holding hands so tight that it hurt me but I didn't say anything about it. And when we got back to the car he kissed me. It was just on the cheek at first but then he kissed me on the lips, like lovers do" (Mosley 1990, 191). This sexual encounter leads to loss, a loss suffered both by both Daphne and her mother: "My daddy never took me anywhere again after that year. He left Momma and me in the spring and I never saw him again" (191).

Daphne's story of incest has a strong effect. Both Easy and Daphne fall silent. "She hadn't had anything else to say after her story about the zoo. I don't know why but I didn't have anything else to say either" (192). But it is Easy who has the strongest and most ambivalent response. He is first disgusted by the confession. Then he wants to run away from Daphne but can't because he's "too deep in trouble" (191). Then he is left feeling that "there [was] something wrong with the whole thing" (192). Paralyzed, Easy decides to cut his losses and tells himself a story hoping that will soothe him. He says to himself, "I'm just in it for the money," and repeats, "Daphne was too deep for me" (192). Finally, Easy ends their relationship and leaves Daphne insofar as they never get back together sexually again. By leaving Daphne, Easy completes Daphne's self-fulfilling prophecy. As she explains to Easy about her own father: "He just loved me so much that day at the zoo and he knew me, the real me, and whenever you know somebody that well you just have to leave" (191).

In Daphne's second account of her past, she describes what is perhaps a more disturbing doubling not only into her double life as Ruby Hanks but also into her own mother. "I'm not Daphne. My given name is Ruby Hanks and I was born in Lake Charles, Louisiana. I'm different than you because I'm two people. I'm her and I'm me. I never went to that zoo, she did. She was there and that's where she lost her father. I had a different father. He came home and fell in my bed about as many times as he fell in my mother's" (204). The second account ends on the more violent note of parricide: "He did that until one night Frank killed him" (204). The killing certainly has Oedipal undertones. The father's parricide by the son suggests his own desire for Daphne, his own mother/sister/lover. Frank's lasting relationship to Daphne in the novel seems to bear the complexity of their relationship. But more importantly, in this second account of the incest story, the father is killed because he gets to "know" the real Daphne. The killing is a ritual punishment with biblical undertones because the father violates what is clearly a taboo.

In her second account, Daphne mysteriously emphasizes that she is not like Easy. Unlike Easy, she stresses, her life has turned her into two people; not only is she herself and Ruby Hanks, but she is also daughter and lover, herself and her mother. Perhaps because of Daphne's insistence, the reader suspects that Easy is also two people. For one thing, he acts just like Daphne's father or at least plays the double role of the lover and the father who leave. But Easy is two people in a more disturbing way. Before Daphne's double confession, Easy has a sexual encounter with Daphne that is described in such a way as to suggest a sexual encounter between mother and infant son.

> Daphne Monet, a woman who I didn't know at all personally, had me laid back in the deep porcelain tub while she carefully washed between my toes and then up my legs. I had an erection lying flat against my stomach and I was breathing slowly, like a small boy poised to catch a butterfly. Every once in a while she'd say, "Shh, honey, it's all right." And for some reason that caused me pain. (180)

Like Daphne, Easy is two people in this passage: he acts as both lover and son. Indeed, he is returned to what seems like a primal moment of infantile sexual contact with a mother figure, and it is this fantasy of return that he finds so erotic. Perhaps more significantly, the scene turns Daphne into both his lover and his mother. She simultaneously cleans him, stimulates him, and most importantly soothes him, relieving him of the responsibility for his own pleasure by telling him that "it's all right." Moreover, as in Daphne's incest story, Easy's love is not without pain and loss, and significantly, Easy relates that pain to his mother's death, "the first time I felt love and loss. I was remembering my mother's death, back when I was only eight, by the time Daphne got to my belly" (180).

The passage then holds the key to Easy's uneasiness with Daphne's confession. Her story of incest, of incestuous and forbidden love, and ritual loss reminds him of his own. On the one hand, her story of incest reminds Easy of the precariousness of his identity and indeed of all identity, of the easy slippage into different roles: son, lover, father, or daughter, lover, mother. On the other hand, and most importantly, Daphne's story of incest reminds him of the loss and pain at the center of all identity. The absence of Daphne's father and his impact on her split identity is twice explained. Significantly, however, the absence of Easy's mother is never deciphered. Indeed, the absence of Easy's mother remains a mystery in the novel because it is "too deep." That absence reminds Easy not only of the violence exacted to preserve identity, as in the case of parricide, but of the primal ritual and unspeakable matricide necessary to create identity itself.

In his film, Franklin forecloses the site of incest and the maternal sexuality related to Daphne in the novel, and his foreclosure suggests his own unease with Daphne's ambiguous identity and forbidden desire. Franklin condenses the novel's two confessions into one where the incestuous element is erased. He eliminates Easy's seduction by a maternal Daphne. Indeed, in his master seminar, Franklin talks about Daphne as if she were a threat to his own stable identity as director. He explains the changes he made to Daphne's character as "an attempt to stay with the point of view of the lead character and see it from the camera ... really from his point of view" (Franklin 1998). To do otherwise, to explain her motivations, Franklin says, "we would have had to have gotten too much into her head and split the focus which was something I didn't want to do" (Franklin 1998). Given the stabilizing effect of Franklin's use of the techniques of noir, it is not surprising that he would worry about Daphne's splitting effect on the film's point of view, on its focus on the lead character, Easy Rawlins. Franklin's emphasis on the film's single point of view is not unlike his subtle protection of a disembodied, transcendental voice-over and his indirect defense of a single racial identity. This impulse toward singularity is also evident in Franklin's comment that identifies the point of view of the lead character with the point of view of the camera, a surprising slip for a film director. In so doing, Franklin identifies his point of view with the point of view of the male protagonist of the film and places himself on Easy's side against the split identity of Daphne and her mother, an identity that he perhaps fears will put his identity as filmmaker in crisis.

There is evidence, however, of Franklin's unconscious reinscription of this split into the film. The threat of maternal desire and sexuality returns in the painting that opens *Devil in a Blue Dress*. As in film noir, by the end of the film, Daphne disappears, even if she survives. Where has she gone? Perhaps into the future, into the intensely colored modernity of unquenchable desires, advertisements, and false dreams or nightmares feared by Franklin. In fact, both Daphne and her mother can be said to return with the unsettling vivid red color of the dress worn by the central figure of a painting that Franklin finds during postproduction.

> You know, I selected that painting in post production (says Franklin).
> We had already discussed what we would do ... what we found, in effect,
> was a painting that ... I thought more so than in color, in spirit, kind of
> married with what we had done with the movie because it had a lot ...
> you know, it's got the primary blue color in the painting and it's a little
> more saturated color. We tried to stay away from that and went more
> muted with our color, more earth-tone. (Franklin 1998)

Franklin suggestively comments that the painting marries what "we had done in the movie." In his words, the muted colors of the world of the film marry the primary and more saturated colors of the painting. In temporal and emotional terms, the nostalgia for the past of the film marries the anxiety over the future of the painting (a world of intense color and consumerism) to produce the present of the film. Franklin's description suggests that if his film, the past, and nostalgia stand for the groom in this marriage, then the painting, the future, and anxiety stand for the bride of this odd couple. At the center of the painting stands a red-dressed white woman, revealing Franklin's conflicted feelings toward Daphne, the femme fatale, and the absent mother behind them.

Both the painting and this figure are metaphors for Daphne in more than one sense. If the white woman at its center is dressed in red, the painting's primary color is blue. Perhaps the painting's red highlights and blue background stand for different aspects of the racially split Daphne: red for her lost identity as Ruby Hanks, blue for the melancholia and sadness caused by that loss. But perhaps those colors and their intensity also represent the return of the repressed mother as femme fatale. Despite or perhaps because of the blue colors that surround the painting's white central figure, what leaps out of the painting is her red dress. The color of her dress stands for Daphne's dangerous, true, unstable identity, her sin, which surfaces despite the blue dress of the title, despite the screen of the tragic mulatta. In this sense, the tension produced by the marriage of colors of the painting hints at a loss of integrity, of identity, of coherence, which Franklin locates in a future of uncontrolled consumerism and desire. The threat of that future motivates the film from outside the story, from the place of the film's credits. *Devil in a Blue Dress* represents Franklin's escape to a timeless place of safety, and to an authoritative voice and a stable subject: the film itself. Insofar as these threats are the unconscious point of departure of the film, it is significant that Franklin should begin his film with a painting that condenses them.

But by eerily fixing Daphne in her role as femme fatale, the painting also reveals that the origin of the film's crisis is its own will to a melancholy type of identity. This identity depends on a logic that imposes a sadness on a figure that resists it, which imposition reveals itself as the true origin of the subject's sadness. In a frustrated effort to overcome a future threat of comprehensive poverty, that logic imposes on Daphne the very social, economic, and even psychological loss of which Franklin is so afraid. The imposition is proleptic; it is a defensive mechanism for a loss that Franklin himself feels and anticipates. That primary loss is the loss of an origin that Franklin symptomatically screens in postproduction with a painting that reveals his profound ambivalence (his attraction, desire, repulsion, and fear) toward Daphne and the unstable ambiguity that she represents.

The film and the novel *Devil in a Blue Dress* prove to be a transformation of film noir and detective fiction in two principal ways. On the one hand, they offer a stable and coherent voice for an African American subject that is either objectified, made invisible, or displaced to the background and techniques of film noir. They are attempts at correcting the racism of film noir. To do so, they smooth over some of the tensions and contradictions of film noir and detective fiction through displacement and condensation. Despite their combined efforts, however, *Devil in a Blue Dress* (the novel and the film) cannot help but repeat the tensions and contradictions that continue to make and unmake the process of subject formation. Perhaps these condensations and displacements can be understood as self-disciplining techniques. Made visible by art, these techniques appear to be aimed at controlling the impetuosity, passion, and desire that put into question the stability of our assumed identities.

CHAPTER 9

Make It Real:
Bound's Way Out

In the Wachowski brothers' 1996 film *Bound*, tense relationships between trust, choice, and freedom, on the one hand, and seeing, knowing, and believing, on the other, play themselves out along the precarious sexual divide left in the wake of the demolition of gender stereotypes that have confounded film noir since its beginnings with its tough women and emasculated men.[1] Violet (Jennifer Tilly) is treated like a classic femme fatale. The camera stares at her fragmented, sexualized body parts: legs, lips, hair. She is presented according to classic femme fatale iconography: highly made-up, long clawlike fingernails, tight revealing clothes, high heels, bad-girl looks, and bad-girl actions, smoking, drinking, and sex. Like her femme fatale predecessors, Violet is in control and wants independence through wealth. Unlike some of her predecessors (Helen Grayle, Madeleine Elster, Elsa Banister), although she wants money and freedom, she doesn't try to class-pass as an aristocrat; she is a mob moll. In the position of the classic noir male hero, however, is Corky (Gina Gershon), a butch lesbian ex-con. Like the classic film noir hero, Corky falls for Violet and helps her steal the money she needs to "get out of the business." Like the classic noir hero, Corky is filmed in submissive positions relative to Violet, especially in the sex scene, where it is Corky's orgasmic body and not Violet's that we see exposed. And the opening scene with Corky bound in the closet leads us to believe that like the classic noir hero, she has been double-crossed by the femme fatale. Unlike the classic noir hero, however, Corky is a woman who learns to see past Violet's looks and knows and appreciates her desire.

Bound opens with a long shot moving from the ceiling through a closet to the floor, where a woman is lying bound and gagged. In voice-over we hear the voices of two women and one man talking about "the business," "choices," and wanting "out." In the next scene, we see two women and a man in an elevator. The women are checking each other out behind the man's back. It turns out that one of the women, Violet, lives with the man, Caesar, in an apartment next door to the one where the other woman, Corky, is working. Violet seduces Corky and convinces her to help her steal two million dollars from Caesar and the Mafia. Although Violet and Corky's plan to steal the money does not go off without some major problems, in the end they ride off together in Corky's shiny new truck with the two million dollars.

Seeing and Being Seen

The questions of seeing or not seeing and knowing or not knowing are central to *Bound*. More specifically, questions of seeing or not seeing and knowing or not knowing the femme fatale determine the outcome of the plot. Like classic film noir, *Bound* investigates female sexuality;[2] but instead of taking the suspicious, bewildered, or vengeful perspective of the male detective, *Bound* presents the cautious but understanding perspective of another woman. In classic noir, the femme fatale's sexual power is a mystery to the men around her; they are taken in by her spell. In *Bound*, all of the Mafia men are smitten by Violet; they are taken in by her appearance. None of them suspect or question Violet because all of them see her only as a sex kitten; they see only what she wants them to see. They see only their own ideal woman or stereotype, which is nothing but their own projection and not really Violet. Until her Mafia boyfriend Caesar (Joe Pantoliano) is forced to suspect Violet, Corky is the only one who questions her. Unlike the male detectives of noir, however, Corky doesn't rough Violet up or chastise her.[3] Rather, Corky trusts Violet and not only understands but also shares her desire for freedom. Unlike the Mafia men, Corky doesn't underestimate Violet; she knows that Violet could be dangerous. But rather than fear her or feel threatened by her power, Corky comes to respect Violet. Violet teaches her to look beyond appearances.

At first Corky is suspicious of Violet, not because she is sexual or powerful but because Violet appears to be a heterosexual woman experimenting with lesbian sex; she appears not to be a "real" lesbian. When Violet shows up in Corky's truck after their first intimate encounter and wants to apologize, Corky snaps back that she hates women who apologize for wanting sex. Violet surprises her by insisting that she is apologizing not for what she did but for what she didn't do—give Corky pleasure. Later, when Corky is upset because she has heard Violet having sex with Shelly (another Mafia man, Barry Kivel) through the thin walls, she tells Violet that what she doesn't like about having sex with women is all the mind reading. Presumably when Corky is criticizing women's relations to sex, she is referring to heterosexual women. What is at stake for Corky, and for the success of their plan, then, is whether Violet is a lesbian.[4] Is Violet a femme fatale for men only? Or is she a femme fatale for men only because they can't believe that she is a lesbian, because they fall into the fatal trap of appearances? The success of their plan to steal from the mob, then, also revolves around whether Corky can escape from the fatal trap of appearances into which all of the men have fallen. Even Caesar, who is forced to suspect that Violet might be involved in stealing the money, won't believe that she is a lesbian; he believes what he sees. But as Violet tells Corky when she wants to seduce her, "You can't believe me because of what you see . . . but believe what you feel."

The disjunction between seeing and believing continues throughout the film as Violet and Corky fool the Mafia because the men believe what they see, which is to say that they see what they already believe. Caesar believes that Johnny stole the money because he believes that Violet is his loyal woman and that Johnny hates him. When Violet feigns doubts about Johnny (Christopher Meloni), Caesar yells, "Violet, open your eyes! Johnny hates me." Caesar doesn't suspect that Corky could be Violet's lover because Corky is a woman and ultrafemme Violet appears to be heterosexual.[5] The connection between believing and seeing is what allows Violet to manipulate the mob and what requires that Violet persuade Corky that she should not believe what she sees. Violet teaches Corky that you don't have to believe what you see; rather, what you see is the product of what you believe. And if you change belief, you also change reality.

After the sex scene in her apartment, Corky says, "I can see again." What she means is that she can believe again, that she can trust, love, and live again. Her proclamation "I can see again" has a religious tone, as if through sex Violet had performed a miracle and the scales had dropped from Corky's eyes. If sex with Violet removes the scales from Corky's eyes, it has the opposite effect on the Mafia men. All of the men are blinded to the ways that Violet uses them because the men believe what they see and because they willfully remain blind to Violet's desire. Violet "proves" her desire for Corky by asking her not to believe what she sees but to believe what she feels. Violet challenges Corky to reinterpret what she sees based on new evidence, the proof available to her hands, but not to her eyes. Blinded by their desire to possess Violet like a trophy, the Mafia men don't care about Violet's desire or the proof of it. Presumably, they don't care "to look."

Like a classic femme fatale, Violet manipulates men with her looks. Unlike a classic noir film, *Bound* reveals that the femme fatale persona is a masquerade, that her looks are made to order by patriarchy. Like many femmes fatales, Violet is not what she seems, and her success in the world of men depends on fooling them into believing her appearance. *Bound* shows us that Violet's power over men is made up. Because Corky sees through the makeup, for her, Violet's femme persona is not fatal. Instructing Violet on the plan to steal the money, Corky tells her, "You'll go back and get ready, take your time, make it real. . . . The more attractive you are, the more believable it will be."[6] While we hear Corky in voice-over say, "Make it real," we see Violet with a table full of makeup, putting on her face. When Violet asks Corky how she will be "clean" if the money is gone, Corky responds that if she makes it "real enough," Caesar will believe her: "You have to make it as real as you can.... If it's real enough, he'll believe it, because deep down he'll want to." This time when we hear Corky in voice-over, we see Violet "making it real" for Caesar. He sees what he already believes without interpreting or questioning. For Caesar and the other Mafia men, reality is a given, but for Corky and Violet, it is made.

Violet can use patriarchal fantasies to manipulate these men because deep down they want to believe in their own fantasies rather than see reality. The use of stereotyped fantasies to manipulate men is typical of other neo-noir films such as *Body Heat* (1981), *Body of Evidence* (1993), *The Last Seduction* (1994), and *Diabolique* (1996). In these films, the femmes fatales use patriarchal stereotypes of women against their victims/victimizers. The men in these films are easily duped by women acting like the men expect them to act. Because they want to believe in their ideal of woman, they cannot see the ways in which these femmes fatales use that ideal to manipulate them. Like Violet in *Bound*, Matty (Kathleen Turner) in *Body Heat* plays the sweet, devoted lover to set up the naive Ned (William Hurt); Rebecca (Madonna) in *Body of Evidence* dupes her lawyer Frank (Willem Dafoe) with her sexy sweet talk; Bridget (Linda Fiorentino) cons country boy Mike (Peter Berg) with her eventual confessions of love in *The Last Seduction*; and sweet, innocent Mia (Isabelle Adjani) surprises her husband Guy (Chazz Palminteri) with her cold-blooded murder attempt in *Diabolique*. Their stereotypical images of women make these men easy targets for women who know how to use those stereotypes to their advantage. The men's acceptance of stereotypical ideals of women proves their downfall in these films, including *Bound*.

In *Bound*, because Violet is these men's fantasy, she can use them without their knowing it. In relation to reality, they are passive; they don't create reality but merely react to it. They think that reality is simply a matter of seeing. For example, even the cops arrive on the scene and tell Violet, "See, we're for real"; after watching them in action, practically stumbling over dead bodies without noticing, we can't help but ask, "Are those guys for real?" They mistake their macho charade for reality. Violet, on the other hand, creates her own reality. For the Mafia men, reality is what is before their eyes. For Violet, reality can't be "seen"; you can't believe what you see. She even tells Corky that her defense against mob violence was believing that she wasn't there and it wasn't real. But this particular fantasy defense proves ineffective, and she realizes that she must "make it real."

Making it Real

In *Bound* we see that the femme fatale is a mask, a persona, created by a patriarchal imagination and used by women to gain power in their relations with men. As long as she makes it real enough, then men will believe her. Both Corky's and Violet's successes play off of patriarchal stereotypes and fantasies and depend on the ability to see through them, and also on the ability to see without being seen. When Violet and Corky are planning the heist, Violet repeatedly asks Corky, "What if Caesar sees you?" Corky tries to reassure her that he won't. But Violet is insistent. She is concerned about Caesar "seeing" Corky, seeing Corky for what she is, Violet's lover. Corky is sure that Caesar won't "see" her because she is confident that Caesar doesn't want to see her; if Caesar sees her for what she is, Violet's lesbian lover, then all of his fantasies of possessing Violet are demolished. He will believe that Corky is not a threat to him because deep down he wants to. When pushed to answer Violet's question "What if he sees you?" Corky takes a gun out from under her mattress and says, "If he does.... then I won't have a choice, will I?"

In *Bound*, choice is tied to masquerade, deception, and passing. Having a choice is having the ability to "make it real" by acting, masquerading, passing, or stealing. Having no choice is the result of being imprisoned within a patriarchal economy and its way of "seeing" within which men relate to each other as competitors and women are their possessions. While we repeatedly hear Violet say, "We make our own choices, we pay our own prices," other characters try to deny their choice. In voice-over in the opening scene, Corky asks, "What choice?" Corky tells Violet that if Caesar sees her, she "won't have a choice." In developing the plan for the heist, Corky tells Violet that Caesar will have "no choice" but to run after he discovers that the money is gone. Of course, Caesar does have a choice, and he doesn't run as Corky had predicted. Caesar insists that he shot Johnny and Gino because he "had no choice." When Violet tries to leave, Caesar tells her that he wants to trust her, to believe her, but he has "no other choice." In the face of this fatalism, the fatalism of classic noir, Violet continually insists on her freedom to choose.

A lover's quarrel over Violet's having sex with men becomes a quarrel over their sameness or difference. Violet tells Corky, "You made certain choices in your life that you paid for. You said you made them because you were good at something and it was easy. Do you think you're the only one that's good at something.... We make our own choices and we pay our own prices. I think we're more alike than you want to admit." Corky insists that Violet doesn't understand because Violet is different from Corky, suggesting that Corky is a "real" lesbian and Violet isn't because she has sex with men. Violet responds that they are more alike than Corky will admit, and she defends having sex with men by explaining that this is her work. By the end of the film, Corky agrees with Violet that she doesn't know the difference between them. Their sameness, as Violet suggests, is that they make choices and that they pay for those choices. Both women have served five-year sentences: Corky in prison and Violet with Caesar. Both of them paid for choices they made, because it was easy and they are were good at it. But now Violet wants to make a different choice. She says that she "wants out." She wants out of her restricted, controlled life with Caesar. She wants "out." Although the film opens with Corky "in the closet," Violet is the one who needs to be liberated from "the closet."

Violet's insistence that we make our own choices and pay our own prices, referring back to Corky's own choice, takes on a deeper meaning in relation to a scene that appears in the screenplay but was cut from the film. In the film, after the sex scene, Corky confesses that she served time for "the redistribution of wealth." Violet reassures her that she didn't need to tell her this, and Corky replies with added intimacy that she "wanted to." Apart from the "redistribution of wealth" that they are about to plan, the redistribution of wealth hardly seems like an intimate or surprising revelation, at least not something that Violet would insist Corky didn't need to reveal. In the screenplay, Violet's insistence and the intimacy of Corky's confession make more sense because Corky not only reveals her crime but also her motives and the childhood desperation that led her to steal:

CORKY: I started stealing when I was little. We were piss-poor, which is not an excuse, just a fact.

It isn't like her to talk about this, especially with someone she just met.

CORKY: The first time I remember so vividly. A bunch of us kids were at Waxman's Drugstore, when Mr. Waxman, who was a mean old prick, always worrying about us robbing him, dropped a roll of quarters.

We can almost hear the coins tinkling on the tile floor.

CORKY: I can still hear that sound, those quarters, because right then something clicked inside of me. Some instinct took over and as everyone, including Waxman, dove down, I reached up and emptied the cash register.

Violet smiles. She likes this woman.

CORKY: I gave most of the money to my mom. I told her I found it at the trainyard. She was so happy she cried, calling me her lucky charm. Fifteen years later, I guess my luck ran out.

She swallows that with beer.

CORKY: Sometimes I tell myself that I didn't have a choice, that stealing was surviving. Usually I can admit that's bullshit. I did it because it was a way out. It was easy and I was good at it, real good.

She glances at Violet.

CORKY: I don't usually talk this much. I guess I have been rehabilitated.

Violet laughs.

VIOLET: You didn't have to tell me if you didn't want to.
CORKY: I guess I wanted to.
VIOLET: I'm glad you did.
CORKY: So am I.[7]

It is striking that in this scene Corky talks about her mother. It is even more striking that this scene was cut from the film. As we have argued in other chapters, the mother is missing from film noir. She is often the purloined presence that motivates both the detective and the criminals. In *Bound,* apparently the mother is left on the cutting-room floor. Father figures, on the other hand, abound. Indeed, Corky becomes a father figure for Violet when Violet compares Corky to her father, who could fix anything with his magic hands. Violet continually asserts her knowledge of Corky by second-guessing her and saying, "Of course," as if she already knew what Corky would answer. The film suggests that Violet's knowledge of Corky is based on her knowledge of her own father. More than any of the men in the film, Corky becomes a father substitute for Violet. Conversely, the Mafia, the quintessential patri- archy, gives us a godfather-type father figure, Gino Marzonni (Richard Sarafian). In relation to this *arche* father, his real son Johnny and Caesar compete for the father's respect. This father expects absolute obedience and wields absolute power. From this perspective, Caesar defies this father and commits patricide when he shoots Gino at point-blank range. Corky and Violet defy the Mafia and thereby subvert this most patri- archal of all families. Corky becomes the creative, productive, potent symbolic father substitute who can fix things, while the Mafia men are reduced to destructive impotent fathers/brothers whose mistrust of each other destroys them. While Corky is a father substitute who subverts the patriarchy by impertinently adding her sexual difference to it, Caesar is an illegitimate son and half brother who unsuccessfully tries to usurp patriarchal power by killing figures of "legitimate" patriarchal authority whom he fears and resents.

In *Bound*, the patriarchal nuclear family is replaced with the patriarchal Mafia family, alternatively referred to in the film as "the business" or "the family." Caesar welcomes Corky to the family when he first meets her. Gino reminds his "sons" that they are part of the same family. This family, however, is dominated by the father and completely devoid of mothers. The only woman with whom any of the Mafia men have relations is Violet. Combining maternal care and sexuality, Violet brings coffee to Corky as an overture to seduction. And when Caesar has been working all night washing, ironing, and counting the money, Violet hands him a drink, calling him a "poor boy" just before he grabs her and kisses her. Later Caesar explains to Micky that he didn't answer the phone because Violet was "helping him relax," giving Violet's sexuality a maternal, caring quality. While unlike traditional femme fatale characters Violet combines sexuality and maternal qualities without paying for it in the end, ultimately in relation to the mob she is more like a helpless little girl than a mother. Micky (John P. Ryan), Caesar's boss, is especially protective of Violet. While it is obvious that like all the other mobsters he desires her, Micky protects her from their violence by telling her to leave the apartment when they are torturing Shelly. And when Caesar discovers that Violet has betrayed him, Violet calls Micky to protect her.

For all of its neo-noir twists and gender bending, *Bound* continues to repress the mother and her power. Even as it liberates the femme fatale from the stereotypes of noir and opens up the possibility of lesbian sexuality and desiring women, the film still represses the power of the mother or her life-giving yet sexual body. In *Bound*, the patriarchal power of the Mafia seems to be founded on some primary matricide that leaves the male hierarchy free from the threat of women. Without any maternal figurehead, the Mafia men are free to compete with each other over the place and power of the father. Without the mother, the father's place of authority is unchallenged in relation to his "sons." The father demands their unqualified loyalty and devotion. The repressed feminine/maternal power returns with a vengeance, however, through Violet and Corky, who manipulate the competition between sons to fuel their desires and usurp the paternal authority by killing the son after he has killed the father. In the end, Violet shoots her "poor boy" Caesar, who falls in disbelief that his sweet and innocent Violet is capable of such cold-blooded murder. The sexy maternal figure kills the prodigal son to free herself from the restrictive economy of patriarchy.

This return of repressed maternal desire and sexuality shows up more explicitly in two other neo-noir films, David Lynch's *Blue Velvet* (1986) and Stephen Frear's *The Grifters* (1990). In *Blue Velvet*, singer Dorothy Vallens (Isabella Rossellini), the mother of a kidnapped boy, is called "mommy" by the sinister Frank Booth (Dennis Hopper) as he inhales ether and forces her to have sex with him. The body of this incestuous mother figure is displayed in all of its abjection when Vallens shows up naked and battered on the front lawn of Jeffrey Beaumont's suburban home. The return of repressed maternal sexuality is made most explicit in Frears's neo-noir con film *The Grifters*. There the sexual tension between Roy Dillon (John Cusack) and his estranged mother, Lilly (Anjelica Houston), is palpable. Throughout the film, various characters display shock and disbelief when they discover that Lilly is Roy's mother because she is the classic femme fatale, dressed in tight, low-cut dresses, with long nails, smoking cigarettes. She is the sexual mother, so much so that in the final scene, she tries to seduce her own son to get him to give her his money. Like the sexual yet maternal Violet in *Bound*, and unlike sexual mothers in classic noir, Lilly escapes death or punishment, but only by killing her son. Lilly is the *mère fatale extraordinaire*, the ultimate castrating and abject mother, both fascinating and horrifying, repressed in classic noir now made explicit in this incestuous neo-noir. Lilly makes conscious the threat of maternal sexuality suggested in classic noir and neo-noir, including *Bound*, where the mother is left on the cutting-room floor but shows up again in the relationship between Violet and Corky.

Returning to the scene that was cut from *Bound*—that is to say, returning to the mother—Corky suggests that she steals for her mother. She wants to be the object of her mother's love and desire; she wants to be the one who provides for her mother. Corky takes the place of the father in relation to her own mother in order to "wear the pants" in the family; she wants to be her mother's "lucky charm." This missing scene also suggests that insofar as Corky now steals the money for Violet, she in turn becomes a type of mother substitute for Corky. This transference of love from her primary relation with her mother to Violet begins as a mother-daughter relationship and therefore makes for a very different result than the effect of the classical psychoanalytic substitution of wife for mother by the male heterosexual. Whereas the classical psychoanalytic Oedipal scenario demands that identity remain opposed to desire—that we desire the opposite sex—Corky's and Violet's struggle over identity and desire ends in their agreement that they are the same.[8] Throughout the film, part of the suspense and tension of the plot revolves around the relationship between Violet's identity (as a woman) and her desire (for a woman). How can she both be and desire a woman? Corky's criticisms of having women as lovers ("This is what I hate about sleeping with women") suggests that within her imaginary, lesbians are not women.[9] In this case, when Violet proves herself true to Corky, which is to say when she proves herself a true lesbian, she is no longer one of those women whom Corky hates. Rather, identity and desire become both the same and different simultaneously. Or to put it another way, identity and desire are separate, but with a difference. Violet both is and loves a woman, which is not to say that she loves herself, or that identity and desire are collapsed, but that the relationship between identity and difference, and between identity and desire, becomes more subtle and complex than it is within traditional psychoanalytic theory.

Bound's Way Out of Noir's Fatalism

In Corky's missing confession scene—the one cut from the film—Corky says that she thought that she had no choice but to steal, but then she realized that she had a choice and chose to steal because it was a "way out." Later Violet asks Corky if she could make the same choice again: "You made a choice once. Do you think you would make that same choice again?" "What choice?" Corky replies. "If those quarters fell to the floor," says Violet, "would you still reach up to that cash register?" Violet is asking Corky if she saw a way out, would she take it, would she choose it. Violet's "we make our own choices, we pay our own prices" advocates making our own opportunities, authoring our own ways out. Making our own choices opens up a way out of the patriarchal economy in which women are dependent on men. By authoring their own choices, Violet and Corky become both economically and sexually independent from men. Violet is liberated from her prison with Caesar, and Corky is liberated from her postprison parole that requires her to do the land-lord's bidding. Whereas classic femmes fatales are punished for their attempts to become independent, Violet and Corky succeed. Not only do they become economically independent of men like their neo-noir femme fatale counterparts, but they become sexually independent of men.[10] They don't need men for money or pleasure. Indeed, their plea-sure exists outside of the patriarchal economy.

Within the patriarchal economy of *Bound*, women are seen as property. The male economy operates according to a logic of exchange within which whoever has the most property dominates the others. Men fight over money and women in a fierce competition to dominate. Their pleasure within this economy is produced in their relationships with each other. They take pleasure in "fucking" each other. Caesar imagines Johnny's pleasure, his laughter, at "fucking" Caesar. Even pleasure in their relations with women is determined by their relationships to each other; they take pleasure in possessing women and taking women away from each other, that is to say, "fucking" each other. This kind of econ-omy is what Luce Irigaray calls a hommo-sexual economy: it is by and for men (1985). Within this economy, women do not exist except as property (or absent or dead mothers), and they are prized only for their exchange value—the way that beautiful women increase the status of men in relation to each other. Women are bought and sold. As Violet tells Caesar, "You rent women just like you rented this apartment." Caesar even tries to buy Corky when he first meets her and offers her money so that he knows that she understands how the patriarchal econ-omy works.

Caesar is the envy of all of the other Mafia men because he possesses Violet. All of them want to take her away from him. Shelly asks her to leave town with him the day before he is found out. In the screenplay, the competition between men over Violet is made more explicit when Violet explains to Corky that Shelly isn't in love with her but wants her because she belongs to Caesar and Shelly wants anything that is Caesar's:

> CORKY: He was in love with you, right?
> VIOLET: That's what he told himself. But it wasn't even about me, it was about Caesar. He wanted what Caesar had. That's how they are. I understand them.
>
> She glances around the room; a man at the bar smiles at her.
>
> VIOLET: For Shelly, taking the money was a way to take from Caesar. He could have run at any time, but he didn't because he didn't want out.

Violet is explicit that Shelly's attention isn't about her; rather, it is about Caesar. Shelly's interest in Violet is part of his competition with Caesar. His pleasure in Violet is the pleasure of "fucking" Caesar, of taking something away from Caesar. The patriarchal economy is one of violent competition, revenge, and suspicion between men. Yet these men remain within this violent economy because it gives them pleasure even as it exacts its price.

To break out of this economy, to "get out of the business," Violet uses the logic of exchange against the patriarchal order. As a matter of survival, she takes up her role as property, as eye candy, to lull the men into a false sense of security. She watches and reads them. As she says, she understands them. In the end, she gets revenge and wields the gun against Caesar. While the Mafia men just stand there with their "peckers" (guns) in their hands, Violet uses hers/Corky's to blow Caesar away. She turns the phallic economy against itself. Caesar tries to intimidate Violet by insisting that she doesn't know him, but he knows her, that he is in the position of power and mastery while she is powerless.

Violet responds that he doesn't "know shit" and empties Corky's gun into him.

Unlike the Mafia men, Violet and Corky don't steal from the men as part of a competition in which their sole pleasure is "fucking" the men. The women don't steal for the fun of it and then wait around for the pleasure of seeing the look on the face of the man that they have just "fucked." Rather, the women steal to break free of the patriarchal economy. They steal to become financially independent of men so that they will no longer be treated as property. They steal their freedom. Although they take pleasure in their success, their pleasure in each other exceeds the patriarchal economy of exchange. Their pleasure in each other, and their ultimate success, is based on trust; it is based on believing what they feel and not what they see; it is based on believing in one another, something that is impossible between the Mafia men. Unlike the men, Violet and Corky work together for their shared future, a future created in the film through a combination of flash-forwards and voice-over.

Rather than the flashback and voice-over combination of traditional noir, *Bound* uses a flash-forward and voice-over combination to a very different effect. In traditional noir, the flashback and voice-over combination usually operates as a kind of confession on the part of the male protagonist, who often regrets his involvement with the femme fatale in voice-over while we see his foolishness in flashback. In *Murder, My Sweet*, for example, the detective Marlowe, under bright light, is confessing his involvement in the murders to the police. In *The Lady from Shanghai*, Michael O'Hara is confessing his stupidity to the audience; the voice-over and flashbacks tell us and show us that O'Hara has been a "real prize fat-head." In traditional noir, the male protagonist confesses to being duped by the femme fatale. The femme fatale has been calling the shots behind the scenes while the male protagonist is either unaware of her schemes because he is taken in by her beauty or unable to keep up with her moves until the end when she is killed or imprisoned.

In the neo-noir *Bound*, however, the voice-over is not a confession, the femme fatale does not scheme behind the back of her lover, and the flash-forwards do not show the protagonist duped by the femme fatale. Rather, in *Bound* the voice-over describes the femme fatale (Violet) and her lover (Corky) working together for their shared future (although at Violet's behest, Corky, and not Violet, is the one who develops the plan for the heist and together they scheme to outsmart the mob). The voice-over is not a confession of past stupidity but a prophecy of future success. Directed toward the future and not the past, *Bound*'s voice-over and flash-forwards open up a future that will not be like the past. Unlike the traditional noir protagonist, the detective whose future seems to be determined by his past, these neo-noir heroines make it real by imagining a different future. As Chris Straayer remarks in her essay "*Femme Fatale* or Lesbian Femme," "the film's flashback structure, which originates from midway through the story, is supplemented by a flash-forward that liberates the narrative's conclusion from film noir destiny" (Straayer 1998, 151) and empowers Corky and Violet to "author a series of flash-forwards that puts a success story in motion" (159).

Violet and Corky *author* a new future rather than confess a past. They create their own future with a voice-over that directs the flash-forward action using the future tense: *I will, you will, we will*. As they say the words, the flash-forward makes it real. Like all good feminists, the protagonists in *Bound* know that overcoming oppression requires imagining the future otherwise; it requires imagining the conditions of possibility for an alternative future by imagining the present injustice as already past. All politics of liberation turn on what Jacques Derrida emphasizes as the future anterior tense: it will have been (e.g., Derrida 1996). When we can imagine oppression and injustice as our own past—it will have been—then we can imagine an alternative future. Violet and Corky make their own alternative future by imagining how it will be and a time when it will have been so that they can create a reality together independent of the men who have oppressed them in the past.

With its flash-forwards and prophetic voice-over, *Bound* uses the conventions of film noir against the fatalism of traditional noir. Certainly *Bound* uses many of the conventions of traditional noir: high contrast between light and shadow, the iconography of the femme fatale, flash-backs, voice-over. Yet rather than seal the fate of the protagonist and femme fatale who cannot escape their destinies, in *Bound* these techniques open up an alternative future that challenges the fatalism of traditional noir. If the anxiety of traditional noir often revolves around a sense that the all-powerful fickle finger of fate can point in anyone's direction at any time, *Bound* returns that anxiety with a vengeance by insisting on responsibility and choice: "We make our own choices, we pay our own prices." The fatalism of noir denies these concrete anxieties by turning them into free-floating existential angst about the power of fate. Noir's fatalism relieves the protagonists from any responsibility for their own anxiety or the concrete conditions that produce it. If there is no escaping your fate, then there is no responsibility or blame.

Unlike traditional noir, *Bound* insists on responsibility. Violet doesn't allow Corky to fall back on some sort of fatalism; she repeatedly insists that we make our own choices and pay our own prices. *Bound* turns patriarchal anxiety back on itself by showing a world in which women can become independent of men not only financially but also sexually, a world in which women work together to escape the patriarchal economy and get ahead. It is not fate that has put the finger on these Mafia men; rather, it is the trust and bond between two women that works like a one-two punch that blindsides the unsuspecting men. In the words of the movie's poster, "In their world, you can't buy freedom. But you can steal it." Violet and Corky steal from fate to make their own freedom. By becoming bound to each other, they break out of their male bondage. They are not bound by fate because they create a binding trust between them.

Throughout the film, Violet and Corky debate their sameness or difference. Corky insists that Violet can't understand her because they are different, while Violet insists that they are more alike than Corky will admit. In her analysis of *Bound*, Chris Straayer concludes:

> *Bound* deconstructs the sexual binary, not just through its queer coupling, but also through its complex rendering of feminist and lesbian discourse.

Sexual difference theory, which many feminists and lesbians uphold, sees women and men as naturally different. As a consequence of this, an essential sameness is posited among women and another sameness among men. *Bound* ends on a statement that would support such an ideology. Butch Corky asks femme Violet, "Do you know what the difference is between you and me?" Violet answers, "No," to which Corky adds, "Me neither." The sameness embraced here celebrates their proven trust in one another. Through its narrative, *Bound* suggests that, in contrast to the heterosexual failings of classic film noir, women can trust one another. Because they are same sexed, lesbians make better partners in crime than heterosexual pairings. (1998, 160)

We agree with Straayer that *Bound* begins to deconstruct the sexual binary both with its queer coupling and by reversing gender roles: Caesar is feminine in that he is constantly seen washing, ironing, cleaning, and even blowing on his nail polish, while Corky is masculine in that she is seen using power tools, drilling, wrenching, and covered in grease. But we disagree with Straayer that *Bound*'s challenge to the heterosexual binary is solidified through an essential sameness between women. First, it doesn't follow that because women are different from men, all women are essentially the same, or all men are essentially the same. Men and women can be essentially different from each other at the same time that they are different from other people of their same sex. Second, and most obviously, Straayer's claim overlooks racial, ethnic, and class differences that are significant in the relations of trust that she invokes.

The moral of the story for Straayer is that homosexual pairings make better partners than heterosexual pairings because the partners' essential sameness allows them to understand and trust each other. Yet within the world of *Bound*, it is difficult to imagine two men trusting each other in the way that Violet and Corky do. Moreover, if Violet and Corky are the same, it is not just because they are women but also because they share a similar class background and oppressed position within patriarchal capitalist culture. They have both been imprisoned for five years—this is what they have in common. They both want out of their patriarchal prisons; they have a common goal, freedom. It is not some biological or psychological essence as women that binds Violet and Corky but rather their status or position within an oppressive system. They are forced to trust each other to work together for their freedom and for the possibility of love, not patriarchal love for women as possessions but love between equals. When in the end Violet and Corky agree that they don't know the difference between each other, they suggest that their relationship with each other, unlike their relationship with men, is not hierarchical. They are the same in terms of social position, which allows them to relate to each other as equals. This means that they also have to respect each other's differences. Deconstructing sexual binaries is achieved not by asserting essential sameness over essential difference but rather by challenging hierarchies.[11]

Derrida describes a double gesture of deconstruction: (1) to overturn the binary, and (2) to open space between by making terms undecidable (Derrida 1981, 41). Deconstruction overturns the binary through deferral of each of two opposites through constant displacement of each other; they substitute for each other and are thereby deferred in space and time (Derrida 1976, 268). In the case of gender, we could say that deconstruction shows how masculine and feminine are dependent on each other for their meaning. In this way, the critic shows how any essential or natural meaning of masculine or feminine is deferred through the play of differences between the terms, which is to say their dependence on each other. The binary is first overturned—the privilege accorded to the masculine is now given to the feminine—and then the terms are rendered undecidable, thereby opening up a space for thinking beyond the binary. Although in some respects Straayer makes good use of the Derridean strategy of deconstruction, her conclusion that women share a common essence runs counter to the project of deconstruction.

In *Bound*, Violet and Corky do not start out the same. Indeed, they are very different: They look different and they act different. What makes them the same by the end of the film are their shared choices.

They make their own choices and pay their own prices, together. Their choices bind them together and make them "the same" in spite of their differences. They share a common goal, stealing their freedom from patriarchal hierarchies that subordinate them to men. They steal their future, believing that they can make it real by performing with and against patriarchy.

Women on Top

The women's triumph in *Bound* is typical of a new genre of neo-feminist noir in which the femme fatale succeeds and is in some ways a sympathetic character—or at least admirable for her power and ruthlessness. Unlike classic noir femmes fatales, in neo-noir films such as *Body Heat, House of Games* (1987), *Basic Instinct* (1992), *The Grifters, The Last Seduction,* and *Diabolique,* strong women not only dominate and kill men but also live to tell about it. As we suggested earlier, the women in many of these films use patriarchal stereotypes against patriarchy to dupe men by manipulating sexist stereotypes. In addition, in many of these films, including *Bound,* there is a sense that these women have been wronged by violent men and that their killing rage is merely revenge for their past victimization (e.g., *House of Games, The Last Seduction, Diabolique*); the men deserve what they get.

In other neo-noir films such as *Basic Instinct, Body of Evidence,* and *Jade* (1995), there is the sense that men's deaths are related to sado-masochistic sexual practices through which the femmes fatales again turn the tables on exploitation and manipulate men through sex. As Kate Stables argues, with neo-noir, the body of the femme fatale itself becomes the murder weapon (this is especially true in *Body of Evidence,* where the murdered man is "fucked" to death by the femme fatale), and the femme fatale becomes a sexual performer rather than a sexual presence (Kaplan 1998, 172–73). The power of the femme fatale becomes how well she can physically sexually manipulate men in addition to how well she can mentally manipulate them, not only with her sex appeal but also with her sexual acts. Presented as at once titillating and perverse, these acts are shown and described in detail in films like *Basic Instinct,*

Body of Evidence, and *Jade*. Indeed, they are shown on camera and video-taped by the men whom these women kill. The camera and desire to watch are presented as further signs of these men's perversity.

Like the photographs taken, stolen, and at stake in classic noir (the photo of Velma in *Murder*, the missing photos of Carmen in *The Big Sleep*, the "incriminating" photo of Susie in *Touch of Evil*), pornographic videotapes provide self-referentiality and self-reflection in neo-noir. The perverse desire to watch, exhibited by the men who are punished with death in these films for their aberrance, puts the audience in the position of pervert in relation to neo-noir erotica. The pornographic look of the camera is on display in the narrative of these films; they show us the hidden camera. And the suspense is both built and resolved through evidence of sadomasochistic activities on videotape. In these films, the camera makes the sex scene pornographic, and the videotape makes it perverse. If the femme fatale becomes a performer, the director becomes a pornographer, and the audience is put in the position of the pervert watching instead of doing. Just as the femme fatale manipulates her mark through her sexual performance, neo-noir erotica manipulates

Caesar (Joe Pantoliano) and Violet (Jennifer Tilly) in *Bound*.

the audience through its pornographic titillation. Now wielding sex toys instead of guns, the femme fatale becomes a dominatrix, and hard-boiled noir becomes soft-core porn.

Unlike *Bound*, in most other neo-noir erotica, lesbianism appears as yet another kinky sexual performance by otherwise heterosexual femmes fatales. Whereas in *Bound*, the open lesbian relationship of Corky and Violet is what allows them to escape patriarchal restrictions and male-dominated desire, in *Basic Instinct* and *Jade*, lesbianism is part of the S/M activities of idealized, oversexed women performing for the sake of men. And while *Diabolique* suggests a lesbian attraction between Mia and Nicole (Sharon Stone), and Nicole's affection for Mia is what saves them, the attraction is never explicit, and in the end the women are pitted against each other. If in *Bound* the lesbian is not a woman, in other neo-noir films lesbianism is presented as a perverse sexual activity that proves that a woman is man's idealized sex partner who will "take it anyway" and do anything like Katrina (Linda Fiorentino) in *Jade*. *Bound* is unique among neo-noir films in that it presents lesbianism as a real alternative to patriarchy while it opens up the possibility of a fluid female/lesbian desire independent of men.

CHAPTER 10

The Space of Noir

In *Noir Anxiety* we argue that film noir is a visual manifestation of a process of identity formation. We claim that film noir shows, reveals, or displays the mechanisms responsible for building and consolidating identity, mechanisms such as displacement, condensation, repression, matricide, and uncanny doubling. We further argue that in film noir, identity is formed, consolidated, or fortified against unconscious threats. In other words, our interpretation of film noir shows how its process of identity formation is a defensive mechanism. Identity is built by protecting it from the threats of ambiguous borders, threats variously represented in film noir as feminine power in men, incomprehensible language in foreigners, uncertain identity, racial mixing, and maternal sexuality. Indeed, we argue that the same process of identity or subject formation is also responsible for the production of the object embodying the threat of film noir: fate, the femme fatale, the racial stereotype, the good and bad mother, the servant and the dummy. Thus we claim that the very process that builds, consolidates, and fortifies identity in film noir also drains identity of meaning, creates holes or vacuums at its center, and produces the anxiety that haunts film noir. This anxiety takes the form of vertigo, phobia, melancholia, abulia, or fatalism.

The process of identity formation in film noir is further exposed by its representation of space. The psychological identity of the subject, the circumstance of his affect, and the state of his morals have an architecture and a geography in film noir. In this chapter, we will study the architecture and the geography of film noir as further signs of its unstable and paradoxical process of identity formation. Like its filming techniques, sound track, and narrative structure, the sets of film noir help to make visible the process of identity formation. The mind of its hero is often represented in film noir as a room with symbolic architectural features. These features in turn mirror the emotional or affective disposition of the subject of noir. Is the subject open or closed to outside influence, is he defensive or vulnerable, fortified or sensitive? Look at his room. Ranging from locked doors to thick walls, the architectural features of noir rooms often make references to the besieged mind of noir subjects. Similarly, the furnishings of these rooms are signs of the subject's state of mind: mirrors for the self-absorbed, beds for the tired, or empty chests of drawers for the drained subjects of noir. Conversely, the hero's search for a moral center, his concern over his origins, his purpose and his end, have symbolic geographic coordinates. The northern mountains, western coast, eastern cities, and southern borders of film noir combine to form a moral topography over which the noir hero travels and against which the subject defines himself. Moreover, film noir's insisting network of geographic landmarks and architectural features is manifest in the titles of many of its films. As Nicholas Christopher has noted, city addresses and telephone numbers are frequently the titles in film noir: *99 River Street, 711 Ocean Drive, Call Northside 777, Southside 1-1000* (Christopher 1997, 44). Classic noir titles also include the names of streets (*Sunset Boulevard, Scarlet Street, Flamingo Road, Pickup on South Street, Thieves, Highway*), landmarks and locales (*The Blue Gardenia, Brighton Rock, Chinatown, Key Largo, Niagara, Station West*), places of origin (*The Lady from Shanghai, The Maltese Falcon*), references to a location (*North by Northwest, House across the Bay, Under Capricorn*), and road signs (*Detour, One Way Street, Danger Signal*).[1]

Paradoxically, film noir's insistence on symbolic architectural features and geographic landmarks, its obsessive repetition of allegorical addresses, numbers, and locations, has as disconcerting an effect on the viewer as on noir's often clueless and directionless protagonists. Their confusion is perhaps most memorably represented by the opening shot of *Murder, My Sweet,* which introduces a blindfolded Philip Marlowe (Dick Powell). Similarly confused by the landscapes of noir, critic Alain Silver writes that "in a very direct and tangible way, [noir's] landscape and cityscape defy the spectator to anticipate them, draw emotional impact but resist systematic interpretation" (Silver 1999, 127). Silver concludes that the landscape of noir cannot be intellectualized. He compares them to the mirror fragments hanging from the walls of a dark corridor in *Vertigo;* he likens the landscapes of noir to the small seams cracking the walls of Madeleine's dream (127). Like Madeleine, Silver finds the loss of meaning, the end of representation, madness itself, at the end of noir's corridor.[2]

The confusion caused by the hyper-demarcated space of noir, the loss of meaning produced by its architectural symbols and geographic allegories, recalls a passage in Freud's *Civilization and Its Discontents.* As is well known, Freud was partial to spatial representations of the mind.

Al (Tom Neal) and Vera (Ann Savage) in *Detour.*

He described the psyche as determined by an "architectural principle" and as susceptible to "topographical dissection."[3] In his study of memory, Freud goes so far as to compare the past of the mind to the past of a city. Freud imagines the mind as "an entity ... in which nothing that has once come into existence will have passed away and all the earlier phases of development continue to exist alongside the latest one" (Freud 1930, 18). He imagined the mind as an impossible eternal city with buildings superimposed on one another. "This would mean that in Rome the palaces of the Caesars and the Septizonium of Septimius Severus would still be rising to their old height on the Palatine and that the castle of S. Angelo would still be carrying on its battlements the beautiful statues which graced it until the siege by the Goths, and so on" (18). Despite the obvious relish with which Freud described this imaginary eternal city (pointing out its palaces, statues, battlements, terra-cotta antefixes, pantheons, churches, temples), he ended the exercise in frustration at the absurdity of the image. The time-thickened walls of his imaginary city also emptied it of meaning and sense. "There is clearly no point in spinning our phantasy any further, for it leads to things that are unimaginable and even absurd" (19). Most importantly, the image became for Freud an apt representation of the failure of representation itself. "It shows us how far we are from mastering the characteristics of mental life by representing them in pictorial terms" (19).

Like the spatial symbols and allegories of noir, the eternal city of Freud gets quickly out of hand. As happens with Silver, Freud's confusion is the result not of a dearth of symbols to interpret, of signs to follow, but of its very opposite. It is the plethora of walls in Freud's eternal city that makes it an absurd, unimaginable, unrepresentable image. There is a direct correlation between the superimposing walls, or the continuous stratification of the psychic apparatus, and loss of meaning. It is as if Freud's imagination were excessive and running wild. It's as if it could not stop itself from producing buildings upon buildings, walls upon walls, layers upon layers for the mind, until there was no room to breathe, until the mind represented by the image was so compressed as to be drained of life.

In *Powers of Horror*, Julia Kristeva diagnoses similar architectural imaginaries as the result of psychotic subjects who surround themselves with the insurmountable walls of their own making. "An encompassment that is stifling (the container compressing the ego) and, at the same time, draining (the want of an other, qua object, produces nullity in the place of the subject).... An empty castle, haunted by unappealing ghosts—'powerless' outside, 'impossible' inside" (Kristeva 1982, 48–49). Recall that for Kristeva, all subjectivity is borderline insofar as all subjectivity emerges from a border state—abjection —anterior to psychosis and neurosis, anterior to the difference between subject and object. For Kristeva, the process of subject formation is a paradoxical process that produces, negotiates, and manages that border and the paradoxical forces that both give rise to it and come to bear on it. The walls of identity are protective walls against the threat of that ambiguous state, but such protective defenses can also become stifling tombstones architecturally represented by paintings like Holbein's *The Body of the Dead Christ in the Tomb* (1521).[4] This place of self-fortification becomes insufficient and suicidal insofar as it dematerializes the enabling affective fantasies and dynamic relations produced in contact with the irreducibly ambiguous state out of which, or against which, identity is formed.

Film noir is another example of this fortified and yet insufficient space. In the dramatic ending of *The Secret beyond the Door*, Celia (Joan Bennett) tells Mark Lamphere (Michael Redgrave), "Search your mind, darling. There's something hidden in your mind so deep, hidden so far back, that you no longer know it is there. You are keeping something locked up in your mind, Mark. For the same reason you are keeping this room locked up. Because you don't want anybody to know what's in it." Celia compares Mark's mind to a room that is locked up. The door to that room is the door of the film's title: it is a door with a lock that keeps Mark's secret from himself even as it contains it. Mark's mind has its material counterpart in mystery room number 7. Like Holbein's *Dead Christ*, the room is the architectural manifestation of a fortified subject. Not only is its door always locked up but even its windows are walled up. Like the empty castle Kristeva describes in *Powers of Horror*, Mark's room is both stifling and draining, as manifested by its emptied-out shelves, nightstands, armoires, and chests of drawers.

Mark's fortified room, its locked door, and the self-constitutive function of both are common tropes of film noir and neo-noir. Similar versions of that architecture of identity appear as Philip Marlowe's room in *The Big Sleep, Murder, My Sweet,* and *The Long Goodbye,* Sam Spade's room in *The Maltese Falcon,* Lund's (the Swede) room in *The Killers,* Davie Gordon's room in *Killer's Kiss,* and Easy Rawlins's house in *Devil in a Blue Dress.* They are all spaces that both mirror and constitute the identity of the haunted subject of noir. Sometimes these films go so far as to post the character's identity on the door. For example, in *The Big Sleep,* we are shown a sign on the door to the protagonist's apartment (not to his office); the sign reads "Philip Marlowe" and in smaller print "private detective." Not surprisingly, in these architectural mirrors of the protagonist's self, we often see their occupants looking at themselves in the mirror. The imaginary safety and cherished intimacy of these spaces is represented by the fact that in them the main character usually appears in a state of near undress (often in a T-shirt, less frequently in his pajamas), relaxation (drinking or smoking), or near sleep. As Easy Rawlins reminds us in *Devil in a Blue Dress,* these rooms are fortified against an outside that always spells trouble: "Step out your door in the morning and you're already in trouble."

But as we argue in *Noir Anxiety,* noir doesn't only represent the fortified subject; it also manifests the processes and mechanisms of identity formation and fortification, which in turn reveal the breaches, ruptures, and gaps in the thick walls of the psyche. So while we are often shown the subject as having control over who goes into his room (and there is usually one scene where he stands at the threshold blocking the entrance to unwanted guests), just as often we see him looking with fear at the door to his room, unable to stop evil from barging in, or entering his own space with the anxiety that someone else is already there waiting for him. In fact, the frequency with which the forces of evil suddenly force the door open and change the direction of the narrative is only surpassed by the times mysterious uninvited guests appear in the middle of the detective's room. "How did you get in here?" is a stock question in noir. Moreover, although we are often shown the bed at the center of this room where the subject is promised rest from the fatigues of the day, never does the noir subject get a good night's sleep. On the rare occasion when the insomniac detective of noir sleeps, he is abruptly awakened by a sound from the outside, usually an impertinent and inopportune telephone call.

Mark Lamphere's room is perhaps the best example of the ambiguous architecture of these noir rooms. Despite the fact that we are shown Mark's room in his house—the room where we see him in the shower, getting dressed, looking out the window, etc.—room number 7 is Mark's secret room. And yet, as Celia tells us, the door has the uncanny ability to keep everybody out of this room, including Mark, who stands both outside and inside of its secrets. In fact, we find out that Mark's mystery room is both his room and not his room at all. In a series of chilling revelations, we find out it is a room that condenses and displaces several rooms, including that of his dead first wife's, Celia's, his mother's, and his own room when he was a child. Like Freud's metaphor for the psyche in *Civilization and Its Discontents*, Mark's fortified room is an unimaginable and even absurd space that violates the three dimensions of mass, length, and time. "The same space cannot have two different contents" (Freud 1930, 18). The rooms both displace one another and are all condensed in the uncanny locked door to all of them: a magic door that opens up to the same and to another time, to the same and to another place, a door that is the space of ambivalence, passage, the unstable space of abjection. That door is locked in an effort to protect against that process. The abject is created and returns through this door.

In *Noir Anxiety*, we have argued that the free-floating existential anxiety of film noir is an anxiety over ambiguous spaces. Its heroes are homeless, directionless, wandering travelers who unsuccessfully try to escape their past and find themselves caught between a rock and a hard place with nowhere to turn and nowhere to go. Like "the Swede" (Burt Lancaster) at the beginning of *The Killers* (1946) or Al Roberts (Tom Neal) at the end of *Detour*, the protagonists of film noir are often weary wanderers who are tired of running and finally let their past catch up with them. Indeed, the past or time itself is often a metaphorical place or space where these characters are trapped and from which they try to run away, to no avail. Disoriented and jaded from their travels or from their attempts to escape their fate, the protagonists of film noir commit a form of suicide by deciding to stop running, to stick it out, to stay put, to face their fate or to find their true north. Thus even though at the beginning of *Out of the Past* Jeff Bailey (Robert Mitchum) tells Ann Miller (Virginia Huston) that he's been to one too many places and wants to "build a house ... marry [her], live in it and never go anywhere else," by the end of the film, he is again caught in a web of intrigue, on the road, and escaping with Kathie Moffett (Jane Greer), the femme fatale; the only way to end, it seems, is to betray her, to call the cops for help. But even this seals his fate, as Kathie realizes what has happened, shoots him, and they crash into the roadblock.

If the protagonists of noir are metaphorically and literally lost, if noir is populated by opening images of characters walking, running, or driving aimlessly on lonely, deserted roads (*Detour, Hitch-Hiker, Kiss Me Deadly*), the same films provide the characters and the viewers with signposts, visual cues, and even maps that permit one to follow the characters' tracks. These maps, signals, and cues are repeated in other noir films, giving the viewer a sense that although noir's protagonists may be lost, their world is nevertheless well demarcated. These signposts are to noir's geography what the walls are to its architecture: they are fortifications in an unstable process of identity formation, but fortifications made with an unstable material. The landmarks of noir's geography have corresponding moral coordinates that become familiar and even natural with repeated viewings. These geographic and moral coordinates have corresponding markers that locate racial and sexual difference in the place of "the unknown," "the other," and "the fearsome."[5] From this mapping, noir's organizing perspective wants to emerge as stable and coherent. But the coordinates of noir's geography are nothing if not fluid, contradictory, and dynamic. Its signposts are insistent to the point of meaninglessness. Indeed, the signs of noir's geography condense and displace the ideas, desires, and fears of a defensive subject who undermines his own identity by obsessively mapping it out. Thus to study the geography of noir is not only to see through the screen of the lost, wandering subject and to trace the coordinates of its route but also to realize that the maps we are left with are not fixed but instead a changing series of peripheral and intersecting lines and markers that destabilize identity even as they attempt to fortify it.

For example, Al Roberts, the protagonist of *Detour*, travels from east to west, and from New York's seedy bars to Hollywood's life of hope and promise with his awaiting sweetheart Sue Harvey (Claudia Drake). As he hitchhikes across the country, the film produces road maps for the viewer that detail Al's progress toward the promise of a better life. When Al reaches the Arizona desert, however, he is picked up by Charles Haskell Jr. (Edmund MacDonald), a shady character who signals the beginning of Al's detour. Haskell is a morally corrupt character, a citizen of noir's underworld, a bookie who hasn't been back home since he was fifteen or sixteen. The son of Haskell Sr., he is both homeless and a lost soul who turns against both his earthly and spiritual father as he tries to swindle Haskell Sr. by pretending to be a Bible salesman. Haskell Jr. mysteriously dies in the night and on the road, forcing Al to assume his identity. This proves to be Al's fatal mistake, and he is trapped within that identity by Vera (Ann Savage), the femme fatale who suspects Al of murdering Haskell. Vera is the catalytic agent who seals Al's transformation into Haskell and turns Al's journey west to a better life into Haskell's directionless escape away from the moral center of many noir films: the father, his law, his intact family, and his home.

The passage from a corrupt East to the hopeful western frontier of the United States in search of a better life is, of course, a common journey of Hollywood films of the forties and fifties, including the Western genre. But in noir this is not so much a journey toward the future as it is a return to something that has been lost. This often unsuccessful return home is an insistent trope of film noir repeated in such films as Stanley Kubrick's *Killer's Kiss* (1955). In that film, we meet the protagonist after he has left his home in a farm near Seattle and has become a prizefighter in New York City. The nostalgia for that simpler life out west is emphasized throughout the film by means of the photographs of an idyllic farmhouse, cows, fields, and family. It is also communicated by the soothing, fatherly, and concerned voice of Uncle George heard in voice-over when Davie Gordon (Jamie Smith) reads his letters in the subway or when he telephones his uncle from his makeshift and solitary apartment after losing his last fight. Davie's life in New York City reflects the noir protagonist's loss of a center, true north, and family values only preserved by noir's small towns in precarious bell jars. Uncle George lives in one of the small towns that dot the noir landscape, towns that we almost never see, and that are often but reminders of the loss of the original family (Davie's absent or dead mother and father). Uncle George is an honest worker (a horse trader), and he offers Davie the alternative of a family life to his solitary existence in a city.[6] Uncle George's family and his marriage to an aptly named Aunt Grace are the antithesis of the solitary existence and loss of spiritual guidance suffered by Davie. A member of the select group of redeemed or miraculously saved protagonists of noir, Davie manages to get on a train headed back home, west to Seattle with his sweetheart Gloria, to the still-distant promise of family and family values.[7] However, as happens with all the other lucky protagonists of noir, we never see Davie get home.

Three other lost protagonists of noir are Emmett Myers (William Talman), Gilbert Bowen (Frank Lovejoy), and Roy Collins (Edmond O'Brien) in Ida Lupino's 1953 *The Hitch-Hiker*. A fascinating reinterpretation of *Detour*, *The Hitch-Hiker* begins with a shot of a solitary road at night, and with the same sense of loss of direction that is gradually substituted by a familiar geography. It begins with a woman's murder by Emmett Myers, referred to in the film as a "Kansas desperado" and as the devil. A character from the country's heartland, who is also a starker version of *Detour*'s Haskell Jr., Myers is displaced by his own family after "they took a look at this puss of mine and they told me to get lost." This rejection from his family and ejection from his home turns him to a life of crime and brings him south to Baja California, from where he plans (like many other noir characters) to escape to mainland Mexico. Also in Baja California, two family men from El Centro, California, make the mistake of leaving their families in a town called "the Center" in Spanish and instead go for a hunting and fishing vacation alone in the Chocolate (read black) Mountains. The decision is made worse by their change of direction in the middle of their journey. They turn away from the mountains and go south to San Felipe in Baja California instead. Their change of direction runs them straight into Emmett Myers, who is the lesson or punishment exacted for turning south, away from the center, away from the true north of family and family values within noir's strict moral geography.[8] As in other noir films, this detour is carefully plotted in maps made visible to the viewers in scenes where a national version of family values is represented by the cooperation of Mexican and United States border officers—Roosevelt's Good Neighbor policy at work.

But as in *Killer's Kiss*, the decision to go south is also the result of a move away from a center that is already lost to these characters. Davie's absent parents are here replaced by Emmett Myers's cruel parents and by the displaced location of Gilbert and Roy's town: a border town ironically named "the Center" in Spanish. Similarly, while the North, or the center, is evoked throughout the film by references to family values such as love, cooperation, and belief in God, the film leaves the characters down south literally and metaphorically. At the end of the film, they are free again, but they are also changed and displaced. Like *Detour*'s Al Roberts, Roy Collins changes identity with the film's evil character (Emmett Myers). By the end of the film, Collins wears Emmett Myers's clothes as a result of Myers's unsuccessful attempt to escape unharmed. The change of clothes is symbolically appropriate. Collins is a character predisposed to vice and solitude. Like *Detour*'s Al Roberts, he is a budding noir protagonist. At the beginning of the film, he suggests to Bowen that they stop at the cabarets and bars of the border town of Mexicali to do some "fishing" and to look for the mythical seductive Florabella at the Alhambra Club. By the end of the film, Collins blooms into a rebellious, violent, and independent character, a proto-Myers. Not surprisingly, we leave him in Baja California, and we never see his return to family, home, or to the mythical center of film noir.

The only classic noir directed by a woman, Lupino's *Hitch-Hiker* is an interesting variation on Ulmer's *Detour* insofar as it does two things: on the one hand, like *Killer's Kiss* and other noir films produced during the fifties, *Hitch-Hiker* exposes the displaced nature of the origin from which the characters emerge, its strictly mythical aura of order and happiness. On the other hand, unlike more traditional noir films, it dispenses with the femme fatale. Thus, in this film, evil is the result either of a primal dislocation by Emmett Myers's originally intact family or of the dislocation that comes from the characters' violent treatment of women. Not only will Emmett be punished for the murder of the woman that begins the film, but Collins and Bowen will also be punished for attempting to escape their parental responsibilities, to get away from wives and kids at a home described as stifling, to go in search of adventure no matter how lethal: "You know [says the older Gilbert Bowen], except for the war, this is the first time I got away from Morty and the kids." If Bowen and Collins's vacation turns into another conflict or into a struggle for survival, if they become the targets of the murderer's games, within the guilt-ridden logic of noir, they have no one to blame but themselves. In this film, however, their fate is sealed not by the mythical noir furies (fate incarnate in the femme fatale) but by their decision to leave their families, to go south, to run for the border. Evil is then displaced away from a mythical dangerous female sexuality (Florabella, who "must be dead by now") and onto the characters' desires, to fears of ugliness, and to the desolate and hostile landscape of Mexico and the South. Despite these displacements, however, the anxious identity logic of noir remains in place. Like the protagonists of *Detour* and *Killer's Kiss*, the characters of *Hitch-Hiker* will be punished for breaching the patriarchal law that binds them to a changing center and to a north increasingly difficult to pinpoint.

An equally complex but somewhat different geography is laid out by Jacques Tourneur's *Out of the Past*. Unlike many noir films where the mythical center is mentioned but remains invisible for the most part, in this film the center of noir takes its clearest shape. The film begins with uncharacteristic shots of uncorrupted natural beauty: snowy peaks, mountain lakes, glaciers, mountain ranges, pine trees. It seems to be Big Sky Country, God's Country. It is, however, the Spanish-named Sierra Nevada. The camera pans to the right to show us a road sign that gives us a clearer sense of position and direction. The road sign includes paradigmatic destinations. The closest is the mountain town of Bridgeport (1 mile away); the farthest is the coastal city of Los Angeles (349 miles away). Like many small towns of noir (Levender Falls in *The Secret beyond the Door*, Banning in *D.O.A.*, Brentwood in *The Killers*, Wheeling in *The Big Clock*, El Centro in *Hitch-Hiker*), Bridgeport is the land closest to noir's heart. It holds the promise of friendship and close community ties. It is the place of neighborliness, family, and innocent, pastoral, and idyllic love. Thus Ann Miller is the longtime and childhood sweetheart

Jeff Bailey (Robert Mitchum) and Ann Miller (Virginia Huston) in *Out of the Past.*

of an aptly named Jack Fisher (Steve Brodie). She is a version of *D.O.A.*'s Paula Gibson, *Key Largo*'s Nora, *The Big Clock*'s Georgette Straud, and *Hitch-Hiker*'s invisible Mrs. Bowen: noir's nurturing woman.[9]

But the heartland of noir, like its nurturing women, is never static, undemanding, and dull. Like *Hitch-Hiker*'s El Centro, Bridgeport is also aptly named. It may be the mythical center of family values, but it is also a bridge and a portal to the periphery of normalcy.[10] As often happens in noir, the arrival of the outsider to the small town puts things out of whack. Jeff Bailey's presence rearranges the emotional landscape of the small town; he upsets the order of things. Against the clear wishes of her family, Ann Miller falls in love with him and rejects Jack Fisher. But Jeff Bailey's presence is not the only reason why there is trouble in the heartland. In fact, against the viewer's expectations, Jeff even tries to assume the role of the cautious father figure with a dissatisfied Ann. After she tells Jeff, "Every time I look at the skies, I think of all the places I've never been," he discourages such thoughts and their implied wanderlust by telling her, "Yes, and every time you look up, they're all the same." Ann's thoughts, as well as her readiness to leave with Jeff for Lake Tahoe and abandon her family at the drop of a hat, suggests that Ann is not the happy camper of noir's chaotic adventure. They suggest that she is not only willing but even eager to get away from her pastoral landscape. Despite Ann's suggestion that there is one kind of woman for every place, like *Murder, My Sweet*'s Ann Grayle (Anne Shirley), and countless other so-called nurturing women of noir, Ann Miller is a proto–femme fatale, displaying the same curiosity, the same desire, and the same willingness to travel to all the exotic places where the noir hero is headed or from where he has returned. All is not well in noir's version of Kansas. Indeed, if Kansas breeds desperadoes in noir, it breeds perversion in previously innocent protagonists in neo-noir (e.g., *Blue Velvet, House of Cards*).

Ann might be a more domestic and tame version of Kathie Moffet, the film's femme fatale, but they are both visually associated with a potentially dangerous nature. Despite the beauty and peaceful appearance of the mountain landscape, it is in the mountains that Joe Stefanos

(Paul Valentine), Whit Sterling's (Kirk Douglas) goon, is killed. Significantly, Joe is killed not by Jeff Bailey, who is doing some harmless fishing, but by his deaf-mute assistant Jim (Richard Webb), who pulls Joe off a high ledge, sending him into the roaring rapids below just as Joe is about to shoot and kill Jeff. Jim is an interesting character. He is Jeff's garage assistant, his young messenger, but he is also a messenger for Kathie Moffet, and he is also very much a part of the landscape of the Sierra Nevada. He was in Bridgeport and its surrounding mountains and lakes before Jeff arrived, and he remains there after he leaves. Indeed, he can be read as the pliant son of Jeff and Ann or of Jeff and Kathie: both natural families. At times he follows the maternal directions of the sexually marked feminine landscape, incorporating and deploying its silent and potentially deadly force to protect Jeff, while at other times he follows the patriarchal law of the protagonist. It is Jim, following Jeff's instructions, who keeps Ann in place at the end of the film. When she asks Jim whether Jeff was leaving with Kathie, Jim lies and nods affirmatively, forcing Ann to return to Jack Fisher, thereby avenging Kathie Moffet by preserving the order of things. As Ann walks away, Jim turns and salutes Jeff Bailey as he confirms his final wish. This order, however, is both the command of a father figure and a trick by a dead outsider, making it extremely precarious.

Like all the other small towns of film noir, Bridgeport is the threshold, the portal, or the bridge to the South, the geographic opposite of noir's true north. If Bridgeport is what remains of the paradisiacal past out of which Jeff Bailey falls, Acapulco is Bridgeport's dark sister town.[11] Like the small towns of noir, the South is often reduced to an imaginary destination: the mythical place of escape in films like *Double Indemnity* and *Dark Passage* (1947). When it does appear on-screen, however, as it does in *Out of the Past* and in its sister film *The Big Steal* (1949), the South displays similar contradictions to the small town.[12] Acapulco is associated with disease early on in *Out of the Past* when Jeff Bailey, in Sherlock Holmes mode, rightly concludes that the offhand remark about Kathie Moffet's vaccination by her African American friend is the clue to Kathie's whereabouts. Indeed, the contradictory description of noir's South, like the description of noir's dislocated true north or center, betrays the anxious and guilt-ridden identity logic driving the movement of noir's subject.

Like noir's description of the mainland, the South is also divided into the coastal city or town and the interior. *Out of the Past*'s passionate, dangerous, and sexually promiscuous Acapulco is the very opposite of *The Big Steal*'s innocent, safe, and romantic interior town of Tehuacán. In *The Big Steal* the interior of Mexico stands for the mythic center of noir's nostalgic gaze, a look back at a primitive time when family values ruled supreme, a time when there was faith in God. In this place and time, a forgotten and different language is spoken. When Bowen, Collins, and Emmett Myers stop at a store in the middle of nowhere, Mexico, Bowen protects a little girl and then sends her off by telling her in Spanish, "Vaya usted con Dios." Emmett Myers fires back, "What did you say to her?" and Collins answers, "You wouldn't understand." The scene is representative of noir's portrayal of Spanish as the primitive language of faith. Similarly, in *The Big Steal*, Duke Halliday (Robert Mitchum) is improving both his manners, his character, and his Spanish as he goes along. Jane Greer now plays Joan Graham (alias Chiquita), a traveling version of *Out of the Past*'s nurturing Ann Miller. Like Ann Miller, Joan Graham feels right at home in Mexico's small town. She speaks their kinder and gentler language, both literally and figuratively.

The ambivalence felt by the noir hero in the face of this forgotten language and its moral lessons is made clear, however, during a shootout scene when Duke finally confesses his love for Joan in Spanish ("Amor mío") but abruptly cuts short the romantic interlude, leaving it for later, to put himself in danger instead. Similarly, at the end of the film, Duke expresses his wish to leave this idyllic portrayal of the South and Mexico by returning to English. "Home, the man said, in two thousand well-chosen words." When Joan tries to convince him to stay ("After a while the boy takes the girl home, chaperoned, of course. Then he stands outside a window and sings"), Duke responds, "Oh, charming custom, but my way is better. You waste an awful lot of time down here."

To which Joan answers, "Oh, I don't know," looking at a long line of Mexican children. This ending leaves the characters at the crossroads between Duke's way (sexual satisfaction) and Joan's way (romantic love and family), between Duke's and Joan's different interpretations of home. For Duke, home means a familiar English-speaking place where time is not wasted and satisfaction is immediate. Home is the place of speed, progress, modernity. For him, home is not slow-paced Spanish-speaking Mexico, perhaps because such a place is also a cipher for small-town family values.[13]

Of course, this is not to say that there are no differences between the mythical small town of noir and the small towns found south of the border and in the interior. Instead, this analysis suggests that noir's South is more than the dangerous, passionate, evil origin of a femme fatale like Kathie Moffet in *Out of the Past*. Noir's South shares with its Center or North a fundamental moral instability, but unlike them, noir's South is also beyond good and evil. The South in noir's moral geography is associated with uncivilized nature, with a lost past before the systematization of patriarchal law. It is a landscape populated with animals that cover the range from the exotic and dangerous alligators and snakes of *The Lady from Shanghai* to *The Big Steal*'s harmless, slow-moving oxen, which are little more than obstacles on the road to progress and, not incidentally, wealth. The primitive vehicles and tools of noir's Mexico are in sharp contrast to the ultramodern technology of noir's big cities (the huge clock, elevators, and intercoms in *The Big Clock*, the fancy cars and extravagant answering machine of *Kiss Me Deadly*, all examples of noir's obsessions with the planes, helicopters, ships, cars, and phone lines crisscrossing its landscape). Similarly, like the local police inspectors in *The Big Steal* or in *Gilda*, south-of-the-border law is underdeveloped and peripheral. Its representatives stand at the margins watching the plot develop without intervening. They are passive witnesses, or merely reactive agents both to the characters' actions and to the effect that the landscape has on them. Equally important is the poverty that marks the South in film noir. Perhaps the result of the primitive state and undeveloped state of its patriarchal law, or perhaps the effect of its only partially restricted rule of feminine nature, the interior and small towns south of the border are always poor. Significantly, the land of noir's South is never cultivated; it is desolate and deserted, unlike the fertile fields of noir's heartland, whose towns are also distinguished by their small businesses and by their modest but sufficient amounts of wealth.

Despite these differences, however, women are always at home in noir. They are noir's natural translators. They are bilingual; they know noir's primitive and civilized languages.[14] As *Out of the Past*'s Ann Miller shrewdly suggests, within Jeff Bailey's skewed logic, women are never the travelers and are always equivalent to a place that is only apparently fixed and that proves to be extremely unstable. When Jeff confesses to having been to "a lot of places," Ann asks him, "Which one did you like the best?" When he answers, "This one right here," Ann knowingly responds, "Bet you say that to all the places," not only suggesting that she can see through Jeff's suddenly developed taste for a stable life but also calling attention to the fact that place and woman are equivalent according to Jeff's stabilizing identity logic. However, Ann's wanderlust in *Out of the Past* and Joan's fluent Spanish in *The Big Steal* are two counterexamples to Jeff's logic. The anxiety and guilt produced by these counterexamples, and by the resulting chaos, explain noir's geographic instability, its simultaneous fascination with, and fear of, the border town setting of a number of its films, the most obvious of which is Welles's *Touch of Evil*. They also explain the strong attraction and repulsion exacted by southern port towns like Acapulco. They further explain the implicit identification of those geographic thresholds with noir's female characters, and conversely the association of their bodies with liquid landscapes marked by water. Noir's women are always in the place of the in-between, whether they are nurturing women like Ann in *Out of the Past*'s Bridgeport (whose sexuality exceeds the boundaries that Jeff wants to impose on her) or women like Gilda (Rita Hayworth), the femme fatale who turns into a redemptive woman in Buenos Aires. Like the changing landscape of noir, they prove to be an overwhelming challenge to the wandering noir heroes, always nostalgic for the lost secure, safe, and fixed coordinates of their own maternal origins. To the surprise and eternal consternation of the noir hero, women refuse to remain trapped in that place, fixed within those stable coordinates. In *Out of the Past*, such consternation turns into evident disapproval as a surprised Jeff Bailey greets the obviously well traveled Kathy Moffet with the words "We meet in all sorts of places."

Noir's north-south axis is mainly concerned with cultural and sexual differences. It demarcates, even as it unsuccessfully attempts to fix, a changing landscape with the coordinates of high and low ground, wealth and poverty, civilization and barbarism, law and Nature, good or maternal, and evil or seductive women. Noir's East Coast–West Coast axis, however, is organized by related, but also somewhat different, concerns and markers. Indeed, the significant reversals and dislocations suffered by noir's unsuccessful attempts to clearly fix its north-south axis are intensified and interiorized in the complementary opposition between coasts (both similarly distant from the healthy landscapes of the heartland's mountainous regions). Perhaps most significantly, the focus on external landscapes, culture, and sexual difference is here complemented by an emphasis on internal landscapes, blood, and racial difference.

As suggested at the beginning of this chapter, many of noir's characters travel from the corruption of eastern cities to the unfulfilled promise of the western mirage. That quest, however, occurs well within noir's dynamic geographic dislocations, where the West becomes a cipher of noir's displaced center: the heartland, or true north. But there are also many noir films that focus on the big coastal cities themselves: New York, Los Angeles, San Francisco. Representative noir films like *The Woman in the Window*, *The Big Clock*, *The Naked City*, *Killer's Kiss*, or *Odds against Tomorrow* all take place in New York City, and the big cities of the West are best represented in *The Maltese Falcon*, *The Big Sleep*, *D.O.A.*, *Kiss Me Deadly*, *The Lady from Shanghai*, and *Murder, My Sweet*. In these films, the alternately lonely and bustling streets of coastal cities, their cabarets and bars, their mansions and slums, are the haunts of noir's protagonist. Of similar interest to these films is the internal configuration of the protagonist's psyche (often represented by nightmares or nightmarish sequences), as well as the effect of the urban landscape on his internal organs.[15] This does not mean, of course, that the concerns defining the north-south axis of noir disappear in the East Coast–West Coast axis. It does mean, however, that there is in noir an attempt (albeit unsuccessful and problematic) to lay out the coordinates of a demarcated territory that will help govern an unruly body politic, not unlike the efforts of fifteenth- or nineteenth-century European travelers and explorers to map the unknown American, African, and Asian territories to better govern and exploit them.

Perhaps Rudolph Maté's *D.O.A.* (1949) is the most blatant example of noir's racial paranoia and strong eugenicist undercurrent inflected by the combined coordinates of sexual difference. Like many noir protagonists, Frank Bigelow (Edmond O'Brien) is a regular Joe, an unsuspecting CPA who travels from the small town of Banning to a big city (first San Francisco and then L.A.) to escape from a serious commitment to his sweetheart and secretary, Paula Gibson (Pamela Britton): "You are just like any other man, only a little more so. You have a feeling of being trapped, hemmed in, and you don't know whether or not you like it," she insightfully tells him. In true noir fashion, the fickle finger of fate seems to point him out for the apparently innocuous fact that he has notarized a bill of sale. However, the film also suggests that behind that fatalism hides the fact that Frank escapes from his responsibilities, from the family values of small-town life. Within the strict moral geography of noir, this unsuccessful attempt to escape the heartland and its promise of family will cost him his life.

Frank's journey into the city, and the curious form in which his murder takes place, however, also signal a change in the direction of noir's concerns pointing to a complementary aspect of noir's logic. Looking for a good time, Frank joins two couples whose women want to "howl" one last time before they go back to being dutiful housewives, and visits a commonplace of city noir: the bar or cabaret. In this bar, the viewer is exposed to the racially marked underbelly of noir's urban landscapes and its effect on the unsuspecting white body. It is a smoky, seedy, and vicious place, frequented by a racially mixed clientele, that showcases a loud and extremely energetic band of African American jazz players. Their individuality is flattened into a dangerous, formless mass by the fact that all of the members are individually and collectively referred to as "the fisherman," which also happens to be the name of the bar. The evil and perverse effect of their music on the white members of the audience is visually represented and commented on by the white bartender, who explains to Frank the language of this musical, lascivious, and disorderly race. In the conversation, the suggested emphasis is on miscegenation, and on the dangerous effect of their influence on the attractive body of a white woman sitting at the bar. When Frank asks about her, the bartender explains that she is "jive crazy." When Frank asks what that means, the bartender replies, "Ah, you ain't hip, pal. Jive crazy means that she goes for the stuff. Just between you and me, I don't get it either. But I gotta listen to it. They're all connoisseurs, music lovers, me, I like Guy Lombardo." True to the fears driving noir, the woman is the connoisseur; she clearly belongs to a high social class, but she nevertheless frequents these seedy bars, she is familiar with their musical language, and she "goes for the stuff" (suggesting that, like the femme fatale, she might be complicit with the bar's disorderly and sexually promiscuous practices).[16]

The film, however, is mostly concerned with Frank Bigelow's innocent body, poisoned at the bar by a mysterious figure of undetermined race. The murderer gives his victim a deadly poison referred to in the film as luminous toxic matter: a poison "for which there is no antidote" that "attacks the vital organs," and whose gradual effect explains the title of the film. When Frank Bigelow arrives at the police station to tell his story, he is already a dead man. Eric Lott has convincingly argued that film noir is a "white face dream work" where specific social threats are not presented outright but subsumed into the "untoward aspects of white selves" (Lott 1997, 90). *D.O.A.* is a prime example of the displacement performed by film noir's dream-text. But not only does the film racialize the interiors of its white heroes, as Lott suggests, fixing and preserving a black-and-white dichotomy that now divides the same body morally into an external white (innocent) appearance and an internal dark (villainized) essence. The anxious and guilt-ridden dream-text of noir will not perform in such a clear-cut way. Instead, it is a geographically tortured text that attempts to fix racial coordinates even as it undermines them. For that reason, the displacements that drive noir films such as *D.O.A.* transform the racially marked poison and the murderer into an intensely white glow-in-the-dark substance served by an Aryan-looking character. It is the extreme intensity of the whiteness of the poison and the murderer, however, that betrays the guilty conscience of the logic that represents both.[17]

D.O.A. is an example of West Coast noir, and its geographic coordinates are not easily tamed.[18] Noir's West is not only the cipher for the center of the promised heartland; it is also a displaced East. The noir films that focus on Los Angeles or San Francisco are also Orientalist, as they tend to emphasize and demonize their Asian collectives and locales.[19] From the hideaway of *D.O.A.*'s Persian Majak (Luther Adler), West Coast noir takes us on an Orientalist tour that includes Geiger's Asian opium den in *The Big Sleep*, the apartment of noir's first homosexual Hong Kong–based and Istanbul-bound family in *The Maltese Falcon*, or to the similarly marked beach house of Jules Amthor in *Murder, My Sweet*, who is looking for his jewels (which happen to be Chinese). In West Coast noir, the West is a threshold to the racialized East, and the sexually perverse Chinatown is often the portal.

The evil that lurks behind noir's Orientalized East is significantly different from the evil that noir fixes south of the border.[20] Unlike the frequently traveled South, the original location of noir's racialized evil (in both its Asian and African varieties) only exists as a synecdoche. Different from the interior landscapes of Mexico, East-West noir shows its viewers its racial evil in parts: as jewels, as cabarets, as musical sounds, as theaters, as neighborhoods, as difference in skin color or lighting. We are never taken to Shanghai, Serbia, Hong Kong, or Istanbul; and Africa doesn't even exist as an invisible series of cities, but rather as an entirely invisible continent. We hear of the evil of these places only by proxy, making them all the more fearsome and attractive for being so far off to the side. Africa and Asia are so displaced as to be outside the visual map of noir. If noir's hero never travels to Africa, and if Africa is only seldom mentioned, its remarkable absence speaks volumes about the limits of the imaginary travels and the borders of the maps of noir's producers and consumers, both of whom are exposed to, and responsible for, noir's racialized and sexualized landscapes. Thus the few times when Africa is even mentioned (halfway through *Gilda*, for example), it is the eastern-most place where evil escapes. It lies even farther away than South America (where the action of *Gilda* takes place) in noir's racialized and sexualized moral geography. Africa is beyond the gambling city of Buenos Aires. It is an invisible but imagined place beyond the pale. It is even beyond a good death. It is identical with suicide, all the more per-verse for being cleverly staged by *Gilda*'s evil German character Ballin Mundson (George Macready). This invisible and remote place, named Africa, the Orient, the South's East, the West's East, is also the place of the noir hero's suicide, the place to which his own actions and his own imagination (not his fate) bring him.

But if this invisible location is the farthest place where the noir hero and the noir viewer travel, it too is a threshold, a portal, which returns the hero and the viewer home. Thus *Gilda*'s Johnny Farrel finds that the remote city of Buenos Aires is just like home. The hero's imaginary return home is a visible symptom of a mental process shared by the viewers of noir who, cued by its insistent but peripheral signs, signposts, and signals, superimpose imaginary and supplementary maps even as they sit through noir's convoluted moral, racialized, and sex-ualized landscapes. This symptomatic return home to a familiar map of racial and sexual stereotypes, even as we accompany the noir hero's anx-iety-ridden travels through exotic landscapes, is a metaphor for the bad faith of noir's logic. The anxiety-driven and paranoid identity logic that drives film noir ultimately believes itself to be located at the very cen-ter of evil and is pathologically determined to kill itself, to push itself off the uncertain map of noir. Taken to its extreme, the logic of noir has the depressive effect best represented by *The Killer*'s Swede. Despite, or because of, all his travels, in spite or because of his exotically Aryan name, he cannot or will not get out of bed to save his own (white) skin.

In *Noir Anxiety* we expose the crumbling walls of the subject's fortified castle; we unmask its indifferent pseudo-objects; we expose the subject effect "fleeting, fragile, but authentic"; we open the interspace that is abjection (Kristeva 1982, 48). In *Noir Anxiety* we study film noir's guises for the fortified subject and list some of the threats to its architecture, such as feminine power in men, incomprehensible language, uncertain identity, and maternal sexuality. The threats are noir's abject, the desirable and repulsive indifferent force that calls into question the borders of identity. Here we describe and study examples of obsessive masking of pseudo-objects like the femme fatale, the racial stereotype, fate and fatalism, the good and the bad mother, the servant and the dummy. We also describe the mechanisms responsible for creating these objects and subjects. These are principally the mechanisms of repression, matricide, uncanny doubling, condensation, and displacement. We diagnose the symptoms these same mechanisms and processes create: the melancholy for an irretrievable lost object, the vertigo from a hole in the ego, the feeling of being haunted. Finally, we also describe noir's ambiguous other, the mechanisms and the logic that compete in noir with the attempt to build a stable subjectivity: mechanisms such as the stereographic voice, polysemia, the radically dislocated bad joke, and the flash-forward, all of which are means to pursue pleasures outside the logic of identity.

We end with a discussion of *Bound*, not because it is the film that ends noir's historical development, but because in a way unlike most of the other films, it opens access to a space between the undecidable, displaced, constantly deferred binary terms of subject and object. In *Bound* we find a space like the uncanny rooms of classic noir. But in opposition to classic noir, there is no evident attempt at fortification in this film. Indeed, this neo-noir transforms the room of noir. Far from the fortified, apparently stable pads of noir's bachelors, Corky's room has no appearance of stability. Her room is a room-in-process. It is temporary, messy. We see her putting a snake down its pipes, painting its walls. She sleeps on a mattress on the floor of a room that is not her own. She is finishing a room for somebody else, for the landlord or for the next tenant.

Most importantly, unlike the insurmountable walls of noir's forti-fied rooms, the walls of Corky's room are not thick. At one moment in the film, Violet says to Corky, "The walls here are so terribly thin. Really, it's like you're in the same room." And indeed, the film visually and acoustically explodes the boundaries of space and time not only through flash-forwards that enable a future for the characters but also through camera work and images that cross over the conventional bound-aries of film into a space that is both outside and inside Corky's room. Just as the water in the plumbing connects two bathrooms, so the cam-era connects the two spaces. It takes the viewer on a submarine journey through the toilet's plumbing from the bathroom, where a character is being tortured, to Corky's bathroom, where we see her listening to the torture. The toilet water stained with blood is doubly abject and works like the conductor of pain and suffering. In two other scenes, the camera similarly breaks down visual boundaries that construct space in film. In one scene, Violet and Corky touch each other through a wall. The cam-era floats above both characters in an impossible third space showing us the inside of the thin wall that unites them. In another scene, the camera again brings Violet and Corky together through another conven-tion used in film to separate space. Corky and Violet are shown on the phone with each other, but instead of showing us Corky, then Violet, then Corky, then Violet, as called for by the typical phone conversation, here the camera follows the conversation between them as if it were their voices itself; the camera is transformed into the energy running through the telephone wires that connect them.

Finally, there is the space of the door. As we have suggested, the door is the uncanny space of the noir room. It stands as evidence directly contradicting Freud's claim that the same space cannot have two different contents. In *Bound*, the uncanny aspect of the door, its ability to transport the subject both outside and inside, to the same and another time and place, is here manipulated, used, and appropriated to carry out the escape from Caesar's room. His room represents obsessive order, cleanliness, stability. It is the room that hides its bloody stains, the bullet holes in its walls. It is the room of noir anxiety. Recall that we hear and see the moment of planning and the execution of the escape plan simultaneously through flash-forward and voice-over. The key to Corky's plan, however, is the door, and it is a fluid space of escape. At the moment that Violet steps out of the apartment to buy a replacement for the bottle of whiskey she has just broken, Corky steps into the apartment to steal the money. The trick entails seeing that a door is a threshold that allows you passage both out of and into the room. The trick is to use the threshold to one's advantage. Occupying analogous in-between spaces can be a means to escape the logic of identity that blinds and kills the subjects of noir. Analysis, interpretation, and creative thinking offer the promise of opening such spaces, of keeping open the door to noir's room. They promise to keep the haunted inhabitants of noir alive.

Notes

Introduction

1. For a good selection of early essays on whether or not film noir is a genre, and whether it is truly American or European, see Silver and Ursini 1996. Some essays in their book also attempt to catalog the essential or universal characteristics of film noir (e.g., see chapters by Borde and Chaumeton, Durgnat, Place and Peterson, and Damico). For a discussion of the defining characteristics of film noir, see also the first book written on film noir, Raymond Borde and Étienne Chaumeton's *Panorama du Film Noir Américain* (1955); see also Silver and Ward 1992; Karimi 1976; and Place 1998. Although our analysis has implications for these debates over the genre and the essential characteristics of film noir, we will not directly engage in those debates. Rather, working from definitions presented in earlier works (especially Place 1998), we turn our focus to how the techniques and classical elements of film noir relate to, and create, representations of race, sex, and origin (maternal and national) in film noir.

2. See especially Krutnik 1991; Maxfield 1996; Naremore 1998; Christopher 1997; and Walsh 1984.

3. With the notable exception of 50,000 Japanese women interned during the war, women in the labor force increased by 57 percent, or 6.5 million, during the war. By 1945 there were nearly 20 million women workers (Baker 1980, 3). The percentage of women in manufacturing rose 140 percent between 1940 and 1944; in metals, chemicals, and rubber, the percentage of women rose 460 percent; and the number of women in agriculture rose to 1.9 million, a 900 percent increase from 1940 (Walsh 1984, 54–55). Once the war ended, many women refused to give up jobs and go back to domestic service. For example,

whereas in 1941, 95 percent of women working expected to quit in peacetime, by 1944, nearly 75 percent of women working wanted to keep their wartime jobs (Walsh 1984, 74).

4. Although African American women, unlike white women, had always worked outside their homes, primarily as domestic workers for white women, along with white women many of them moved into the labor force needed to support the war effort. With significant numbers of women moving into the labor force, the need for domestic workers, traditionally African American women, increased dramatically. In its 19 September 1949 issue, in an article entitled "The Servant Problem," *Newsweek* reported that domestic workers had decreased by 500,000 while female workers had increased by 4.5 million, which resulted in the reappearance of "slave markets" on city streets where white women bid for black domestic help (48). Andrea Walsh points out that "black women experienced rapid wartime occupational mobility. Although black females in the prewar labor force (40 percent) outnumbered whites two to one, they were heavily concentrated in domestic service (70 percent) and farming (16 percent). Although discrimination persisted, the war crisis and the political mobilization of blacks challenged racial as well as sexual barriers in employment. As the ranks of black female domestics and farm laborers dwindled rapidly, the number of black women working in defense more than doubled" (Walsh 1984, 58). Walsh argues that the changing roles of women during the 1940s are reflected in the films of the period.

5. For example, see Borde and Chaumeton 1955 (they also attribute some noir anxieties to historical changes but ultimately opt to talk about an existential anxiety that results from moral ambiguity); Porfirio 1976; and Glenn Erickson's "Expressionist Doom in Night and the City," in Silver and Ursini (1996). See also the 1994 PBS documentary *Film Noir* in the American Cinema series directed by Jeffrey Schon. Without naming it as such, Barbara Deming describes the existential angst in 1940s Hollywood masculinity in *Running Away from Myself* (1969).

6. For example, Janey Place and Lowell Peterson argue that "no pat political or sociological explanations—'postwar disillusionment,' 'fear of the bomb,' 'modern alienation'—can coalesce in a satisfactory way such disparate yet essential film noir.... The characteristic film noir moods of claustrophobia, paranoia, despair, and nihilism constitute a world view that is expressed not through the films' terse, elliptical dialogue, nor through their confusing, often

insoluble plots, but ultimately through their remarkable style." See Place and Peterson, "Some Visual Motifs of Film Noir," in Silver and Ursini 1996, 65.

7. Ibid.

8. See especially the history of early film noir criticism as it is collected in Silver and Ursini 1996. The early debates focus on defining film noir, categorizing films as noir or not noir, and identifying not only the cultural or political origins of noir but also its national origins. Silver's introduction to the collection is especially anxious about insisting that film noir is an American genre. For a discussion of the difficulties of classifying film noir as a genre, see Krutnik 1991, 15–32.

9. This description of condensation is based on the summary given in Laplanche and Pontalis 1973, 82–83.

10. For interesting analyses of the psychic effects of dropping the atomic bomb and our entrance into a nuclear era, see Juliet Flower MacCannell's *The Regime of the Brother*, especially chapter 4 (1991); Dean MacCannell's "Baltimore in the Morning ... After: On the Forms of Post-nuclear Leadership" (1984); Martha Bartter's "Nuclear War as Urban Renewal" (1986); and Peter Schwenger's *Letter Bomb: Nuclear Holocaust and the Exploding Word* (1992).

11. Quoted from Lucia Bozzola's review of *Kiss Me Deadly* on the All Movie Guide Web site.

12. Many of these images were modeled after images found in men's magazines like *Esquire* and *Men Only* and in comic strips like *Terry and the Pirates*, and *Male Call*.

13. See Christopher 1997, 55. Christopher points out that "nuclear angst made itself felt in films of all genres after Hiroshima, with a notable infusion of hysteria after that 1949 Soviet test" (54). He concludes that "such films [as *The Lady from Shanghai* and *Gilda*] were merely mirroring, and focusing, the increasingly bizarre, frantic, and often contradictory statements regarding the American city and the Bomb that were surfacing in the new media, government agencies, universities, and among city planners" (55).

14. See Kelly Oliver's analysis of Freud's fear of birth in *Womanizing Nietzsche* (1995). See also her analysis of the association between the mother and death for Freud in *Family Values* (1997).

15. For feminist criticism of film noir see Kaplan 1998; Molly Haskell's *From Reverence to Rape*, chap. 5, "The Forties" (1974); and Lucy Fischer's *Shot/Countershot*, chap. 2 (for a discussion of *The Lady from Shanghai*) and chap. 6 (for

a discussion of *Dark Mirror)* 1946) (1989). For analysis of the figure of the femme fatale in film in general see Mary Ann Doane's *Femmes Fatales* (1991); chap. 5 is on *Gilda*. For discussions of representations of women in film in general, see Kaplan 1989; Walsh 1984; Gledhill 1987; Eren 1990; Landy 1991; Doane 1987; de Lauretis 1984, 1987; and Staiger 1995.

16. Christine Gledhill argues that "rather than the revelation of socio-economic patterns of political and financial power and corruption which mark the gangster/thriller, film noir probes the secrets of female sexuality and male desire within patterns of submission and dominance" (1998, 28). The crime in film noir is just a pretext, then, for the detective's investigation into the sexuality of the femme fatale. Gledhill concludes that this investigation into female sexuality creates a conflict in the treatment of women in film noir. Women are not seen in traditional family roles as wives, mothers, or dutiful daughters, but they are still seen from a male perspective (1998, 28–29). Within this male perspective, women are divided into good girls and bad girls, both of whom are desirable and dangerous in different ways. The good girl is safe but boring and stifling; the bad girl is sexy and exciting but dangerous, even deadly.

Janey Place describes the two poles of female archetypes within patriarchy as the nurturing woman, who is the pure, virgin mother, and the spider woman, who is the evil seductress (1998, 47). This split between good and bad women is the stereotypical split between Madonna and Whore. Place describes how "the source and the operation of the sexual [spider] woman's power and its danger to the male character is expressed visually both in the iconography of the image and in the visual style. The iconography is explicitly sexual, and often explicitly violent as well: long hair (blond or dark), make-up, and jewelry. Cigarettes with their wispy trails of smoke can become cues of dark and immoral sensuality, and the iconography of violence (primarily guns) is a specific symbol (as is perhaps the cigarette) of her 'unnatural' phallic power.... They control the camera movement, seeming to direct the camera (and the hero's gaze, with our own) irresistibly with them as they move" (1998, 54, 56). The asexual, nurturing good girl, on the other hand, is filmed in fixed poses, often in pastoral settings with open spaces and bright sunlight, with light-colored, modest clothes (Place 1998, 60). She doesn't have the femme fatale's independence or drive, and she isn't overtly sexual. Yet as Gledhill points out, often in film noir we see contradictory combinations of characteristics of both good and bad women in one female character (1998, 31).

17. In *The Desire to Desire: The Woman's Film of the 1940s*, Mary Ann Doane describes the ambivalent or polar representations of good and bad mothers as a reflection of the changing roles of women during World War II in the 1940s. She argues that "coincident with a war-time reorganization of sexual roles and the corresponding introduction of ambivalence about mothering, the maternal becomes a fractured concept in the '40s.... The sheer weight of the symbolic role of motherhood offers a strong resistance to the potentially profound implications of the socioeconomic roles now accessible to women in production" (1987, 78–79). On the one hand, patriotism required that mothers work to support the war effort; on the other hand, family values demanded that mothers stay home to care for their children. Mothers were put in an impossible double bind that is reflected in the fractured and ambivalent concept of maternity in Hollywood films of the 1940s.

With new jobs for women, particularly white women entering the workforce for the first time, the responsibilities of motherhood become more problematic. Even while government institutions encouraged women to take jobs to help the war effort, they continued to expect women to care for children. Public child care was seen as a shameful neglect of maternal responsibility and carried the stigma of taking public charity (Walsh 1984, 62). Less than 10 percent of children in need of day care received it (63). The meager emergency child care facilities put in place during the war were dismantled by 1946, and all state aid to day care was cut by 1948. "By 1947, the *New York World Telegram* red-baited public childcare as a plot against the family concocted by Communist social workers" (76).

Several books published in the 1940s describe the "evils" of mothers and of working women. Lundberg and Farnham's *Modern Woman: The Lost Sex* (1947) describes career women as suffering from "masculine overcompensation" and "penis envy," since they have turned against their biological necessity to care for men and children (Walsh 1984, 77). They conclude that "contemporary women ... are psychologically disordered and ... their disorder is having terrible social and personal effects involving men in all departments" (Fischer 1996, 105). They claim that "rejecting," "oversolicitous," and "domineering" mothers "slaughter the innocents" (105). They argue that these evil mothers "produce delinquents" and "criminals" (105). Philip Wylie's *Generation of Vipers* (1942) describes the mother as a "Hitler" who masters "a new slave population continually go[ing] to work at making more munitions for momism" (Fischer 1996,

104). Wylie criticizes "parasitic mothers" who damage their children with "smother-love" and in particular emasculate their sons (Walsh 1984, 77). In *Their Mothers' Sons* (1946), Edward Strecker claims that "no nation is in greater danger of failing to solve the mother-child dilemma than our own" (Fischer 1996, 104). These books reflect the 1940s anxiety over maternity, an anxiety that we still see today reflected in popular culture and film.

Blame-the-mother films from the 1940s (the heyday of film noir) such as *Now, Voyager* (1942), *Mildred Pierce* (1945), and the gangster film *White Heat* (1949) display this ambivalence about motherhood. In *White Heat*, James Cagney stars as the psychotic criminal and momma's boy Cody Jarrett. His mother, Ma Jarrett (Margaret Wycherly), is herself a criminal mastermind, domineering and demanding even as she babies Cody, who at one point sits on her lap while she massages his temples. In the end of the film, Cody is enraged after he is set up by undercover cop Hank Fallon (Edmond O'Brien) and climbs atop an oil refinery and yells, "Made it Ma! Top of the world!" as he commits suicide by firing into the oil tank, setting off a huge explosion (which reminds the viewer of a nuclear explosion). Lucy Fischer argues that *White Heat*'s blame-the-mother psychology is a reflection of 1940s pop psychology about the evils that mothers thrust onto their sons (1996, 100–108). She describes Cody as a demented mix of violent masculinity and pathological femininity associated with the headaches and seizures he suffers in relation to his mother (1996, 94–95). *White Heat*, then, displays not only the 1940s ambivalence about mothers but also an ambivalence about masculinity.

The bad mother loves too little or loves too much. The mother is blamed for being too concerned with her child or not concerned enough, loving too little or loving too much. The black mother in *Imitation of Life*—Delilah in Stahl's *Imitation of Life* (1934) and Annie in Sirk's *Imitation of Life* (1959)—claims that she is a bad mother because she loves too much. Mildred Pierce loves to the point of obsession. Mothers like Helen Morrison in *The Blue Dahlia* (1946), on the other hand, love too little; the sexually promiscuous good-time girl Helen confesses to her husband, returning veteran Johnny Morrison, that she got drunk and killed their son in a car accident. Bad mother Mrs. Vale in *Now, Voyager* practically admits that Charlotte was an unwanted child. And bad mother Ellen Berent in *Leave Her to Heaven* (1945) throws herself down the stairs in order to cause a miscarriage because she is jealous of her unborn child. The mother is caught between the rock of too much maternal love and the hard place of too little. She either becomes evil and pathological by making her sacrifice known to her child and causing her child guilt (her self-sacrifice should remain a secret as Stella's in *Stella Dallas* or Jody's in *To Each His Own*) or becomes evil and pathological, suffering from "penis envy" or sexual perversions, if she has any interests other than her child, especially work or men.

18. Most critics of film noir stop with this observation and don't go further to analyze the haunting presence of her absence. Even Sylvia Harvey's "Woman's Place: The Absent Family of Film Noir" does not address the missing mother; rather, Harvey focuses on the noir protagonist's inability to settle down and take a wife and the dangers that the lack of family pose for him (1998).

19. For example, Joyce Nelson, "*Mildred Pierce* Reconsidered" (1977); Pam Cook, "Duplicity in *Mildred Pierce*" (1998); Albert J. La Valley, *Mildred Pierce* (1980); Walsh 1984, chap. 3; Janet Walker, "Feminist Critical Practice: Female Discourse in *Mildred Pierce*" (1982); Linda Williams, "Feminist Film Theory: *Mildred Pierce* and the Second World War" (1988); Pamela Robertson, "Structural Irony in *Mildred Pierce*, or How Mildred Lost Her Tongue" (1990); Mary Beth Haralovich, "Too Much Guilt Is Never Enough for Working Mothers" (1992).

20. See the All Movie Guide Web site entry for *Mildred Pierce*.

21. In her analysis of this film, Mary Ann Doane argues that Donnelly falls in love with the maternal aspect of Mrs. Harper, comparing her to his own mother: "My mother wanted to make a priest out of me. I never wanted to do a decent thing until I met you.... Don't make the same mistake my mother did"; he becomes a son and therefore cannot be a lover (1987, 93–94). Doane concludes that in *The Reckless Moment*, "pathos is generated by a situation in which maternal love becomes a sign of the impossibility of female desire" (1987, 94).

22. Freud describes the Oedipus complex as the male infant's desire to kill the father and possess the mother. To become properly socialized, the infant must overcome the Oedipus complex. For Freud, the infant can leave its dyadic dependence on the maternal body only through the agency of the father. The father threatens the child with castration if it does not leave its mother. The male child takes these threats seriously and sublimates his desires for his mother. But he must also give up his identification with his mother; it is this identification that threatens his ability to become social. He is coaxed into identifying with his father with the promise of a future satisfaction of his incestuous desire

for his mother with a mother substitute. He identifies with his father's virility, his ability to satisfy his desire and his woman.

For Freud, the female child must separate from her mother to become autonomous and social, and yet to become feminine, she must continue her identification with her mother. Because she continues her identification with her mother, and because she cannot completely fear the threat of castration from the father, since she is already castrated, the female child does not become fully social. She has an inferior sense of justice, since she doesn't have a fully developed superego because she doesn't fear castration. She gains what autonomy she has by resenting her mother for not having a penis and envying her father for having one. The female child, along with the mother, is stuck in nature because her anatomy prevents her from feeling the father's threats. Whereas castration threats resolve the male Oedipus complex, they merely initiate the female Oedipus complex, which according to Freud is never completely resolved. See Freud 1924, 1925, 1931, 1936.

23. For a more detailed analysis of Kristeva's theory of abjection, see Kelly Oliver's *Reading Kristeva* (1993).

24. Kristeva, like Freud, assumes a male infant and a heterosexual desire in the development of her theory of abjection in *Powers of Horror*. The (male) infant experiences a horror at its dependence on the maternal body that allows the weaning process, but the (male) infant also experiences a fascination with the maternal body that allows an eroticization of the female body. Females do not split the mother but merely try (unsuccessfully) to rid themselves of her. Kristeva diagnoses female sexuality as a melancholy sexuality in *Black Sun*. This is a limitation of her theory that we hope to work beyond.

25. This is why in *Black Sun* Kristeva calls feminine sexuality a melancholy sexuality (1989). (Within heterosexist culture) a woman can neither eroticize the abject maternal body nor leave it behind. Kristeva maintains that instead the maternal body becomes a "Thing" locked in the crypt of her psyche.

26. Kristeva says in *Powers of Horror* that abjection "is an extremely strong feeling which is at once somatic and symbolic, and which is above all a revolt of the person against an external menace from which one wants to keep oneself at a distance, but of which one has the impression that it is not only an external menace but that it may menace us from inside. So it is a desire for separation, for becoming autonomous and also the feeling of an impossibility of doing so" (1982, 135–36).

1. Noir in Black and White

1. See E. Ann Kaplan's "The Dark Continent of Film Noir" (Kaplan 1998, 183–85).

2. For an analysis of the blackness of whites in film noir, see Eric Lott's "The Whiteness of Film Noir" (1997).

3. Compare Wallace's analysis of black female spectatorship to bell hooks's analysis in "The Oppositional Gaze: Black Female Spectators," where she suggests that the two alternatives for black female spectators are either to get pleasure out of a film by identifying with the white female protagonist or to get pain out of a film by adopting an oppositional gaze that criticizes the film's racism (presumably the oppositional gaze provides the spectator with the plea-sure of criticism if not the pleasure of identification) (1996, 201–2).

4. In his analysis of passing in contemporary films, Mark Winokur con-cludes: "Passing as a strategy of racial compatibility in film allows the cultural hegemony simultaneously to perpetuate the notion that by the 1980s America had solved the 'race problem' and to deny the depiction of authentic empower-ment. Instead, films create a black population of individuals who are merely unique; they are created in order to devalorize cultural Otherness. Make the black man white and render his power charismatic, not political. Make the white man black and perpetuate all the stereotypes about stupidity and failure to understand the dominant social codes so that whoever behaves in this fashion deserves disempowerment. Subordinate the dialogue about race relations in an allegory dependent on technology to furnish a racist utopia in which blacks seek their unempowerment and alienation from the dominant culture" (1991, 208–9). Winokur's argument resonates with Lott's argument that by making white characters black, evil and stupidity are associated with darkness.

5. For sustained, if limited, discussions of race in film noir, see Kaplan 1997, 99–132; Naremore 1998; Lott 1997; and Diawara 1993. For discussions of race and ethnicity in cinema in general, see Cripps 1977, 1978; Diawara 1993; Friedman 1991; hooks 1996; Leab 1975; Mapp 1972; Nesteby 1982; Murray 1973; Nell 1975; Pines 1975.

6. For an insightful analysis of ethnicity in *Gentleman's Agreement*, see Friedman 1991.

7. Michele Wallace (1993) discusses the representations of African Americans in *Lost Boundaries, Home of the Brave*, and the 1948 documentary *The Quiet One*.

8. Jacqueline Bobo cites *Home of the Brave* (United Artists), *Lost Boundaries* (Film Classics), and *Pinky* (Twentieth Century Fox) as the top three money-making films for their studios in 1949. She also points out that by 1942 there were 430 black movie theaters in thirty-one states and 200 more white theatres with black sections, and that by 1943 blacks were spending $150 million a year on movies (Bobo 1991, 424).

9. For insightful and provocative discussions of the issue of race in both versions of *Imitation of Life*, see Lucy Fischer, ed. *Imitation of Life*, especially Fischer's introduction and the essay by Sandy Flitterman-Lewis, "Imitation(s) of Life: The Black Woman's Double Determination as Troubling 'Other'" (Fischer 1991); and E. Ann Kaplan's *Motherhood and Representation*, chap. 8 (1992). For a discussion of the connection between race and gender, particularly the connection between race and maternity, see Ginsberg 1996.

10. For original reviews, biographical background of the director and actors, and an excellent introductory essay that puts the film in its historical context, see Fischer 1991. In her introduction, Fischer also examines the question of women and work, the issue of race, and the relationship between the story of the film and Lana Turner's biography.

11. Sandy Flitterman-Lewis analyzes the way in which Sara Jane tries to use sexuality to free herself from racism; Flitterman-Lewis points out that her failure is partially because sexuality is controlled by patriarchy (in Fischer 1991, 325–37).

12. Both Stahl's and Sirk's versions of *Imitation of Life* are prime examples of white women who have careers only because black women take care of their children at home. *Mildred Pierce*, *The Great Lie* (1941), *Since You Went Away* (1944), and *The Reckless Moment* (1949) all have black servants as maternal caregivers. Even the lower-class Stella Dallas has a black servant for some time. Mary Ann Doane describes these black maternal figures who haunt the background of so many women's films of the 1940s as "meta-mothers" because they not only take care of the children but also take care of the adults (1987, 80). She explains that "this representation … [is] fully consistent with psychological theories of the 1940s which held that the black woman symbolized 'the primitive essence of mother-love.' Perceived as closer to the earth and to nature and more fully excluded from the social contract than the white woman, the black woman personifies more explicitly the situation of the mother, and her presence, on the margins of the text" (1987, 80). Doane's "the primitive essence of mother-love" is a quotation from Ehrenreich and English 1979, 220.

2. Poisonous Jewels in *Murder, My Sweet*

1. For a discussion of abjection and ambiguity see the introduction to this volume.

2. Richard Dyer argues that film noir "is characterized by a certain anxiety over the existence and definition of masculinity and normality.... This problematic can be observed in, on the one hand, the films' difficulty in constructing a positive image of masculinity and normality, which would constitute a direct assertion of their existence and definition, and, on the other hand, the films' use of images of that which is not masculine and normal—i.e., that which is feminine and deviant—to mark off the parameters of the categories that they are unable actually to show" (1998, 115).

3. See Gledhill 1998, 20–35, 47–69. In different ways, Geldhill and Place argue that the patriarchal narrative in film noir is undermined by its visual style, which empowers the femme fatale and has a more potent effect on the unconscious of the viewer.

4. Chandler's novel *Farewell, My Lovely*, on which *Murder* was based, was born along with the Manhattan Project and published in 1940. The film *Murder, My Sweet* came out in 1944, three years after Pearl Harbor was attacked and the United States joined the Allied forces, and a year before the United States dropped the atomic bombs on Japan.

3. Stereotype and Voice in *The Lady from Shanghai*

1. Written, directed, and produced by Orson Welles in 1946 but released by Columbia Pictures in 1948, *The Lady from Shanghai* is considered a film noir. It is a noir in the sense that it displays the promising tensions and contradictions highlighted in feminist readings of film noir. Christine Gledhill, for example, has described the plot of the typical film noir as a struggle between different voices for control over the telling of the story (Gledhill 1998, 30). This struggle is also often described as one between the male voice-over or authoritative linear narrative and visual devices like flashback, associated with the femme fatale. Critics point out that it is often the case in film noir that the dangerous woman is destroyed at the end of the film's narrative, while the male voice-over survives. But as Janey Place has argued, it is just as likely that the audience leaves the theater with a mnemonic and psychic imprint of the femme fatale, suggesting that the visual devices like flashback ultimately master the narrative devices like voice-over. Not surprisingly, the story of the triumph of the visual over voice and over linear narrative in film noir is also the story of popular culture itself,

which has exploded the contradictions and possibilities of the visual and has left voice-over very much behind, as is evidenced in the style of filmmaking of directors such as Alfred Hitchcock. See chapter 5 in this volume.

For feminist critics of film noir, the deployment of voice-over and the insistence on the linear aspect of narrative are the filmmakers' efforts to maintain or establish control not only over the story of the film but also more broadly over a cultural narrative and a social identity that filmmaking both produces and represents. Popular culture and film are understood by critics such as Ann Kaplan as arenas where boundaries for identity are drawn and managed, where the battles are fought between unconscious and conscious forces for control of the social psyche. But for these critics, popular culture in general and film noir in particular are also places where knowledges about those identities are produced and made visible. This production in turn leads to the visibility of the process of identity making, which can then lead to its unexpected and promising appropriation by the filmmaker, the critics, and the audience. See Kaplan 1998, 183–201; and Modleski 1988, 87–100.

2. For a psychoanalytic and Lacanian discussion of voice in cinema as an imaginary site of defensive control and coherence of a subject affected by a fundamental lack or castration, and for a critique of the complementary fantasy of a protective maternal voice fundamentally imagined as embodied, see Kaja Silverman's *The Acoustic Mirror*.

3. The legal process of citizen production began in 1943 with the Magnuson Act, which repealed the Chinese exclusion act of 1882, established a quota for Chinese immigrants, and made the Chinese eligible for citizenship, negating the 1790 racial bar (Lowe 1996, 20). Lisa Lowe argues that state-sponsored enfranchisement of Chinese Americans into citizenship helped to classify racialized Asian immigrant identities. Quoting the legal theorist Neil Gotanda, Lowe emphasizes that the sequence of laws "that excluded immigrants from China, Japan, India, and the Philippines, combined with the series of repeal acts overturning these exclusions to construct a common racial categorization for Asians that depended on consistently racializing each national-origin group as 'non-white'" (19). She further argues that the ostensible lifting of legal discrimination in fact rearticulated "the historical racialization of Asian-origin immigrants as non-white 'aliens ineligible to citizenship'" (20). Thus Lowe suggests that this ambivalent drive to produce white American subjects while enfranchising Asian American citizens simultaneously produced contradictory stereotypes for the

Asian immigrant during the 1940s. Lowe suggests that stereotypes of the Asian immigrant as "the invading multitude, the lascivious seductress, the servile yet treacherous domestic, the automaton whose inhuman efficiency will supersede American ingenuity" not only preceded and survived the production of the enfranchised Asian American citizen but were also its concomitant effect.

4. Cheefoo is the original Chinese place name for Yantai. It is located on the China coast of the Yellow Sea, in Shandong province.

5. Born in Brooklyn, Hayworth's father was a famous Spanish-born vaudeville dancer. She was named Margarita Cansino at birth and became first known as her father's dancing partner. The Cansinos were billed as "Spanish Dancers" in their engagements in the United States, but in casinos across the U.S. border, in Tijuana, for example, Margarita Cansino played the part of a Mexican dancer (Leaming 1989, 16). In the thirties Fox Studios wanted to cultivate Rita as a Latin type and abbreviated her name to Rita Cansino. But later in the decade, Harry Cohn (the mogul of Columbia Studios) would suggest that she change her Spanish-sounding last name, and this led to the transformation of Rita Cansino into Rita Hayworth. Significantly, Hayworth was Rita's mother's maiden name. Volga Hayworth was born in Washington, D.C. (Leaming 1989, 6, 28, 36).

6. In a fascinating essay on Hayworth, Adrienne McLean argues that her image was celebrated because it showed a body that successfully suppressed the evidence of its ethnicity while simultaneously insisting on the presence of a national ethnic identity in the same body (McLean 1992–1993, 19; we want to express our gratitude to Katy Vernon for suggesting McLean's work to us). According to McLean, the audience's dislike for *The Lady from Shanghai* was due to the fact that Rita Hayworth's popular nonwhiteness was doubly erased. Not only was she turned into "the whitest of women," but her singing voice was domesticated as well. According to McLean, the audience's negative reaction to *The Lady from Shanghai* proves that Margarita Cansino's ethnicity was well preserved, and remained visible, under Rita Hayworth's alias.

7. The ambivalence over her image is perhaps best illustrated by the fact that after *Gilda* (1946), military servicemen literalized her status as a metaphorical bombshell by painting her image on the atom bomb dropped on Bikini Atoll in the same year. See Leaming 1989, 129–30. This infamous publicity stunt was significantly made over the protestations of Rita Hayworth, who, according to Welles, was "shocked by it."

8. That she would be granted a very public divorce from Orson Welles on the same date that *Life* magazine proclaimed her as "one of our most prevalent national myths—the goddess of love" is a testament to the resilient artificiality of Hayworth's public persona (Leaming 1989, 142).

9. Welles's description of the uses of the "shock effect," and its deployment in the film's sequence inside a Mandarin theater, coincide with the theory of the alienation effect as described by Bertolt Brecht in his essay "Alienation Effects on Chinese Acting." In that essay, Brecht discusses "traditional Chinese acting" as a "primitive form" and its alienation effect as the artistic counterpart of "a primitive technology, and a rudimentary science" (Brecht 1964, 96). He suggests that revolutionary theater must "pry loose" this "transportable piece of technique" from the Chinese theater in its efforts to "further the great social task of mastering life" (95–96).

10. For a discussion of the deconstructive effect of Michael O'Hara's voice-over narration on the "macho male protagonist" and a discussion of the limits of this effect, see chapter 4 of Kaplan's *Women and Film: Both Sides of the Camera* (1989).

11. Tellote insightfully reveals the connection between Welles's story about the sharks and a similar passage in Melville's *Moby Dick* (Tellote 1989, 63–64).

12. See Fischer 1989, 32–62; Tellote 1989, 57–73.

13. Franklin's *Devil in a Blue Dress* attempts to build a similar authoritative voice with similar consequences. See chapter 8 of this volume.

14. In his fascinating piece on *The Lady from Shanghai*, Tellote psychoanalytically naturalizes the tendency of its voice to turn toward self-consumption and annihilation as Welles's discovery of his own death instinct. This essay is an attempt to move away from this naturalization of man's melancholy nature. See Tellote 1989, 69–71.

15. See "Poisonous Jewels in *Murder, My Sweet*," chapter 2 of this volume.

16. Of the extravagant picnic in Acapulco, O'Hara's voice-over says, "It was no more a picnic than Bannister was a man."

17. McLean points out that Bhabha's discussion of the stereotype's power is "masculine," but she does not explain in what way his discussion of fetishism is "masculine" as a simultaneous fascination with, and disavowal of, the difference of the stereotype (McLean 1992–1993, 18, 24 n).

18. The addition of voice to this model of subject formation complicates

matters in a positive way and opens up the closed circuit of discipline and pleasure where Bhabha's analysis fixes what amounts to a stereotype for the mother.
Adrienne McLean has gone some distance in the necessary aural direction that
could constructively challenge Bhabha's visual argument (McLean 1992–1993,
3–16). Seeking to productively complicate the discussion of the representation
of women in film, McLean convincingly argues that musical numbers in film
noir are sites where women have an effect that escapes noir's otherwise masculinist logic. Instead of inscribing women in a voyeuristic economy, these
sites disrupt the scopophilic pleasure and open up a different aural economy.
"Visually, we may sort out the world and fix it into discrete entities, according to
patriarchal psychic economies predicated on sexual difference. Sound, on the
other hand, seems to provide what Burrows calls the 'great alternative' to this
fixity" (McLean 1992–1993, 4). Citing David Burrows, McLean argues that
voice in film noir provides either a "communal" space of identification across
sexual boundaries (and a "sense of community" between performer and listener)
or a space for the expression of the woman's individual pleasure. (David Burrows
is the author of *Sound, Speech, and Music*).

But McLean's reduction of the site of sound in this passage to a "ritual
of solidarity" and to a "communality" is also problematic. It both suggests an
idealized maternal experience and reduces the female body to material and un-
problematized tissue, as when she agrees with Burrows's description of the sound
of the singing voice as "galvanized by the source of the sound into acting as a
vibrant connective tissue" (McLean 1992–1993, 4, 5, 7). Modifying McLean's
argument, one can perhaps argue that voice in *The Lady from Shanghai* simultaneously opens an in-between space for the individual experience and for an
experience that exceeds the individual. McLean argues that Welles successfully
nullifies and disciplines the threat represented by Rita Hayworth's singing voice
in the film. Instead, we argue that the stereophonic voice ambivalently deployed
throughout the film is an alternative to what Bhabha calls the "primordial
Either/Or." These sites of sound go some distance in the interruption of the
identity logic of film noir, which not only splits "woman" into either the narcissistic sexualized and violent femme fatale, or the "good," asexual, and nurturing
woman/vessel, but also condenses mother and other into the same demonized
figure.

19. The acoustic nature of these symptoms is perhaps associated with
the voice of Welles's lost mother, Beatrice Ives. Several biographers of Welles

remark on Beatrice Ives's voice and on her relationship to voice. Not only is she described as performing "original compositions, to which she sang in a 'deep lovely voice'" (Leaming 1985, 12), but she is also described as having "an elegant speaking voice and great sensitivity to the spoken language" (Brady 1989, 2). Both biographers also emphasize the influence of Beatrice Ives's voice on the young Welles. Whereas Leaming emphasizes heredity and calls her voice "a decisive legacy to Orson" (Leaming 1985, 12), Brady emphasizes socialization and describes the linguistic discipline to which Welles was subjected by his mother. "Beatrice frowned upon verbal sloppiness and impressed Orson with the importance of choosing his words with care. And she succeeded: he was speaking in polished sentences, with invisible commas and semicolons where they belonged, all syntactically precise, by the age of two" (Brady 1989, 2).

20. We want to thank Jiahui Li for her translations of the film's Cantonese into English, for her incisive and enlightening commentaries on Chinese opera, and for her subtle commentary on the disposition of the Asian American actors and actresses as they speak Cantonese and as they inflect it with various degrees of self-assurance or doubt.

4. Sleeping Beauty and Her Doubles

1. For a discussion of the ways in which Lang's *The Secret beyond the Door* breaks out of the genre of gothic film and fits into the genre of film noir, see Cowie 1998, esp. 149.

2. For an interesting discussion of the use of psychoanalysis in film noir, see Krutnik 1991, 45–55 and Thomas 1993.

3. Elizabeth Cowie discusses the incestuous relationship between Celia and Rick. She argues that in the course of the film, Celia must give up her incestuous attachment to Rick and find in Mark an acceptable substitute (1998).

4. Cowie (1998) draws a comparison between *The Secret beyond the Door* and the story of Bluebeard's locked door, behind which he keeps the bodies of his murdered wives. Certainly the evocations of Bluebeard give Blaze Creek a haunted quality.

5. See our analysis of *Vertigo* in chapter 5 of this volume.

6. For example, see Reid and Walker 1993; McCannell 1993; Naremore 1998; Berrettini 1999; Davis 1991.

7. James Naremore's *More than Night* is the most sustained analysis of other places in noir, and his commentary points out the ways the places are

stereotyped without presenting any in-depth analysis of why or how these places and stereotypes motivate the central action of film noir.

8. In Perrault's "The Sleeping Beauty in the Wood," after the prince wakes the princess, they celebrate in the great hall of looking glasses (1912).

5. Mad about Noir

1. See the essays by Christine Gledhill and Janie Place in Kaplan 1998.

2. See the discussion of *Murder, My Sweet*, in chapter 2 of this volume.

3. Quoted in the *Limited Edition Booklet: Production Information*, accompanying the 1996 restored video release. To our surprise, most of our undergraduate students find *Vertigo* boring and long.

6. The Borderlands of *Touch of Evil*

1. Writing from a humanist perspective, Bruce Crowther interprets film noir as a fundamentally and intentionally ambiguous genre. "Deceit and duplicity run their crooked courses through these stories" (1989, 7). "In film noir there is no simple conflict between the good guys and the bad. Here there are just the bad guys and the ambiguous ones" (12). Writing from a similar perspective, Paul Schrader considers *Touch of Evil* to be the last and most intense example of classic noir's ambiguous style and protagonist. For Schrader, the film represents both the end of the line for the noir antihero (the morally complex private eye and lone wolf) and the end of an ambiguous style of filmmaking that combines social criticism with aesthetic experimentation (Schrader 1999, 59, 61).

If for Crowther and Schrader, noir's moral ambiguity is intended and self-conscious, for film critics such as William Anthony Nericcio, the ambiguity of a film like *Touch of Evil* may still be fundamentally moral, but it is not intended, and it even has the effect of putting into question the notion of a conscious self in control of the film. Coming from a critical race studies perspective, Nericcio claims that *Touch of Evil* is not so much the end of noir as the beginning of a new type of film: the border film. For him, a film like *Touch of Evil* unwittingly breaks or fractures the apparent stability of the social order by showing the prevalent violence and the "wounds" necessary to keep the pretense of stability. Nericcio claims that the film takes the violent and fragmented experience of the subject living in the border as its point of view, and succeeds in problematizing the desire for a stable and coherent account of a subjectivity that depends on such exclusions (Nericcio 1992). According to this interpretation of the film, *Touch of*

Evil would be the forerunner of such films as *The Border* (1982), Robert Rodriguez's *El Mariachi* (1992), and John Sayles's *Lone Star* (1996). See Naremore 1998, 233, for a similar perspective.

2. Eliot Ness's book gave rise to the highly successful 1959 TV series *The Untouchables* by Phil Carlson, and to the 1987 film by Brian De Palma. They recount the story of the depression-era war between Chicago gangster boss Al Capone and Treasury man Eliot Ness. After being humiliated in an early raid on Capone's stronghold, Ness organizes a group of detectives whom he calls "the Untouchables" because they cannot be bought off by Capone.

3. For an interesting analysis of the fact that Susan is not heard within the acoustic logic of the film, see Silverman 1988, 54–56.

4. For an analysis of the film's acoustic logic, its use of voice-over and voice-off, and the significance of the final scene to that logic, see Silverman 1988, 55.

5. "So if you want to really hurt me, talk badly about my language. Ethnic identity is twin skin to linguistic identity—I am my language. Until I can take pride in my language, I cannot take pride in myself. Until I can accept as legitimate Chicano Texas Spanish, Tex-Mex and all the other languages I speak, I cannot accept the legitimacy of myself. Until I am free to write bilingually and to switch codes without having always to translate, while I still have to speak English or Spanish when I would rather speak Spanglish, and as long as I have to accommodate the English speakers rather than having them accommodate me, my tongue will be illegitimate. I will no longer be made to feel ashamed of existing. I will have my voice: Indian, Spanish, white. I will have my serpent's tongue—my woman's voice, my sexual voice, my poet's voice. I will overcome the tradition of silence" (Anzaldúa 1987, 59).

6. This embarrassment is not so plain to an interviewer like James Delson, who praises Heston for the "feat" of holding his own (in front of Welles) in the interrogation scene by "subduing every gesture and restraining [himself]" (Comito 1998, 214). Milan's powerful performance is also unremarkable to Delson.

7. Jokes in *Chinatown*

1. Informed by psychoanalysis, Wexman argues that Polanski reveals the scopophilia of the viewer, his private-eye fantasy, unmasking and criticizing our desire and the sadistic sexual impulses underlying it (Wexman 1985, 95, 99,

101). We would agree with her convincing argument that the audience is implicated by Polanski in this scopophilic economy. But we would also argue that rather than make the audience occupy the space of the patient to Polanski's doctor (who treats by unmasking and uncovering deep-seated desires), the film sublimates the energy of those fantasies and desires into a third space: the opened space of the film-text. This space is the risky and hopeful space of analysis where the roles of patient and doctor are far from fixed but flow continuously, inviting interpretation and promising transformation.

2. Freud developed these fascinating views on language and thought after he read Karl Abel's *Philological Essays* (1884). Freud reviews and quotes extensively from the philologist's work: "It is clear that everything on this planet is relative and has an independent existence only in so far as it is differentiated in respect of its relations to other things.... Since every concept is in this way the twin of its contrary, how could it be first thought of and how could it be communicated to other people who were trying to conceive it, other than by being measured against its contrary" (Freud 1910, 157).

3. What makes a joke different from the comic is its psychic localization. The joke's contribution to the comic is strictly from the realm of the unconscious (Freud 1905, 208), while the comic seems to shuttle back and forth from that place.

4. Freud insists that humor, displacement, and the comic are unlike dreams insofar as they are located not strictly in the unconscious but in the preconscious and are automatic (Freud 1905, 220). This strikes the reader as odd insofar as Freud also makes displacement into the principal process of humor, talks about humor as a defensive process, and compares it to repression (233), all of which associations should make the operations and contents of humor at least partially unconscious: see Laplanche and Pontalis's (1973) definitions of displacement (121) and repression (390–94).

5. We wish to thank Jiahui Li for her translation of this line from Cantonese into English.

6. According to Freud, such words are the point of intersection of psychic energies that are otherwise displaced along different associative chains (Laplanche and Pontalis 1973, 83), nonsense "inhibited by objections raised by critical reason" (Freud 1905, 171).

7. The joke goes as follows. "So there's this fellah who's tired of screwing his wife and his friend says why not do what the Chinese do? So he says what

do they do? His friend says the Chinese they screw for a while and then they stop and they read a little Confucius and they screw some more and they stop and they smoke some opium and then they go back and screw some more and they stop again and they contemplate the moon or something and it makes it more exciting. So this other guy goes home to screw his wife and after a while he stops and gets up and goes into the other room only he reads *Life* magazine and he goes back and he screws some more and suddenly says excuse me a second and he gets up and smokes a cigarette and he goes back and by this time his wife is getting sore as hell. So he screws some more and then he gets up to look at the moon and his wife says, 'What the hell do you think you're doing?... You're screwing like a Chinaman.'"

The joke and Evelyn Mulwray's interrupting effect have been the object of much critical attention. Virginia Wright Wexman interprets the "clumsy joke" as an example of Gittes's adolescent bigotry against "Orientals" and his smug sexist pride, and as one of the many devices used by Polanski to debunk the privileged perspective of his hard-boiled detective hero (Wexman 1985, 100). John Belton interprets the "off-color" "dirty" joke rather differently as an example of Robert Towne's (the author of the screenplay) and Polanski's suspect abstractions or associations of Chinatown with mystery, inscrutability, and female sexuality. Belton also comments on Evelyn's interrupting effect on the joke but nevertheless associates her with the joke's "sexual otherness" by virtue of her contiguity with it, or her "proximate association" (Belton 1991, 946). James Maxfield interprets it similarly as the detective's "second fall" and rather obliquely remarks on the juxtaposition of Evelyn Mulwray with the Chinaman of the joke (Maxfield 1996, 123). In our reading of the joke, Evelyn Mulwray is partly responsible for the joke's interruption. It is also interrupted by the strength of the unpleasurable and interior affect that Jake Gittes originally suppressed: his guilt over the publication of the compromising photographs. Moreover, Evelyn Mulwray is not so much condensed with the Chinaman or with an abstract Orientalism as much as with the silent object of the Chinaman's desires, which object is wholly unknown and other to us.

8. We wish to thank Bennett Sims for his insight that Polanski is not a director who merely finds the best visual vehicle for a script but a director who changes and transforms the script to give the film his own "signature." This is most evident in the changes Polanski made to the end of the script, discussed later in this chapter.

9. As Wexman insightfully points out, there is a scene where the same technique is used against Evelyn Mulwray. "When Escobar interviews her in the morgue, he stands to her right. To escape his disturbing questions, she tries to turn away, only to be startled by Loach (Dick Bakalyan), who is lurking on the left side of the broad Panavision composition" (Wexman 1985, 96). Wexman's point is that Polanski uses "deep space" to prefigure Evelyn Mulwray's fate and to designate Noah Cross as the evil force behind the mystery. Instead, we suggest that Polanski's deep space has a more playful and perhaps even a therapeutic function.

10. Polanski opens a similar space for the same effect in the scene at the Albacore Club, where Evelyn Mulwray looks outside the picture frame to the invisible menacing supervisor waiting at the wings to jump in and stop Jake Gittes's revealing conversation with the old women.

11. Noah Cross asks the first question regarding Evelyn Mulwray's idea that her husband might have been murdered. When Jake Gittes answers straightforwardly that he is the one who gave her the idea, Noah Cross, taken aback, changes the direction of the conversation with a reference to Jake Gittes's broiled fish: "I hope you don't mind. I believe they should be served with the head." The statement comes clearly after Jake Gittes has been having trouble biting into his meal, apparently because the idea of a fish served with its head disgusts him. He confirms this with a joke: "Fine, as long as you don't serve chicken that way," after which they both laugh. This seems to allow Jake Gittes to overcome his initial disgust, and he begins to eat. After some innocuous questions, Noah Cross gets personal and asks whether Jake Gittes is sleeping with Evelyn Mulwray. This time it is Jake Gittes's turn to change the topic of conversation with a threat and a joke: "If you want an answer to that question, I can always put one of my men on the job. Good afternoon, Mr. Cross." When Noah Cross tries to convince Jake Gittes to stay, he asks, "For what?" This leads Noah Cross to another evasive answer, this time with an elliptical reference to Chinatown: "You may think you know what you're dealing with, but believe me, you don't." The answer strikes Jake Gittes as funny because it reminds him of what the D.A. used to say to him. When Noah Cross asks him whether the D.A. was right, it is Jake Gittes's turn to be evasive, and he shrugs. This is followed by some talk about finding Hollis Mulwray's "girlfriend," which leads Jake Gittes to the all-important question "When was the last time you saw [Hollis Mulwray]?" This is again followed by an evasive answer and by Noah Cross's attempt to change the

topic of conversation by ridiculing a group of Mexican musicians in the background: "Sheriff's gold posse … bunch of damn fools who pay $5,000 apiece to the sheriff's reelection." Jake Gittes persists, however, and asks again, which leads Noah Cross to a gentle poke at himself, in another effort to evade the question: "At my age, you tend to lose track." And so on and so forth.

12. We wish to thank Temma Kaplan for her insightful commentary about this scene and its representation of Noah Cross as someone who is testing Jake Gittes to see whether he is willing to go past the socially acceptable and break social taboos.

13. If the script's broken humor points the viewer and Jake Gittes in the direction of interpretation and analysis, the visual component of the scene works hard to foreclose attempts to gain such a space. Like a successful joker, Polanski manipulates the space of the "third person" in this scene to open a deceptive space for Jake Gittes and the audience, which hides the constricting structure of the visual joke keeping Jake Gittes in his place and in the dark. The joke, however, is also visually undone by the striking and memorable effect of the images used and manipulated to collapse the space necessary for interpretation and analysis, or the efforts to simulate such a space with the intention of keeping it closed.

14. The scene is visually divided into seven takes. It begins with a take in deep focus that includes Noah Cross in front and his servant in the background. We see both figures from the side, and both figures are wearing a white shirt. The camera follows the servant in the background, who walks out of visual range to the right, and the shot produces a balanced triangular composition that finds Noah Cross sitting on the left directly across from Jake Gittes. Out of visual range, we see the servant's hands serving the fish with the head to Jake Gittes. As the servant moves to the background to prepare the next dish, the camera shows us Jake Gittes's surprised reaction to his dish and Noah Cross's evident relish in it as he puts on his glasses to observe the fish more clearly. The camera then cuts to the second take: a close-up of the fish, the only close-up of the five-minute scene. The close-up forces the viewer to see what should not be seen and hints at the broken culinary taboo that stands for a more serious one. The close-up violently collapses into a single plane the triangular composition carefully crafted in the first take. In so doing, it echoes Noah Cross's defensive evasiveness in the script. This is followed by the third take, which again opens the space by means of deep-focus photography and by the inverse shuttling of the servant from the background to the foreground back to the "top" of the composition.

The fourth take is another abrupt flattening of space. It is a close shot of Jake Gittes, who has just been accused of sleeping with his client. Space is again collapsed to parallel the defensive posture taken by Jake Gittes in the script. This is followed by the fifth take, which shows us Noah Cross isolated in his "corner" in a visual representation of the aggressive and pugilistic tone the conversation is taking. The sixth take goes from Jake Gittes's close shot to a composition that puts Noah Cross in the front left of the screen and Jake Gittes in a second plane, off to the right. This arrangement lasts until Jake Gittes asks Noah Cross when he last saw Hollis Mulwray, and the question displaces Noah Cross, who gets up and walks to the back of Jake Gittes, as if to reflect Jake's upper hand. This is followed by the seventh take, which reverses positions and places Noah Cross in the foreground, his servant in the background, and Jake Gittes in the middle surrounded by both and with his back turned to the camera. This arrangement is not significantly changed until Jake Gittes exits and we leave Noah Cross and his servant alone on the screen in a version of the first take.

15. Noah Cross occupies a vulnerable space with his back turned to the camera only once and briefly, as a result of Jake Gittes's pointed question about his meeting with Hollis Mulwray.

16. Released in 1974, *Chinatown* has been described by critics as an example of the "70's Noir revival" (Gledhill 1998, 33; Christopher 1997, 241), which included films like *Klute* (Alan Pakula, 1971), *The Long Goodbye* (Robert Altman, 1973), *Farewell, My Lovely* (Dick Richard, 1975), and *Night Moves* (Arthur Penn, 1975). Some critics describe *Chinatown* as a revision (Shepard 1999), a critique (Wexman 1985, 95), and even a parody of classic film noir (Maxfield 1996, 120); others consider the film to be an "expansion" of film noir (Hirsch 1981, 150). In two of the most interesting critical pieces on the film to date, William Galperin argues that *Chinatown* puts into question and exceeds Western notions of representation while adhering to noir's conventions (Galperin 1987, 1152), and John Belton suggests that *Chinatown* separates noir from its origins in nineteenth-century rationalism and brings it "face to face with the Real" (Belton 1991, 949). Following Fredric Jameson, Belton understands that the Real is "a field of simultaneity," an "interplay of various knowledges" that contains various forms of activity including immanent intrinsic satisfaction. According to Belton, the field and interplay of the Real is best represented by classical dramas like *Oedipus Rex*. There is also a substantial bibliography on the Oedipal aspects of the film. For a suggestive example, see Linderman 1981–82.

17. The stage is extended to Jack Nicholson's and Robert Towne's sequel, *The Two Jakes* (1990).

18. Belton and Galperin have written perhaps the most provocative essays on this film. But they perform a condensation and a displacement in their commentary on *Chinatown* that remains unexamined and deserves closer attention. On the one hand, they play with the double meaning of the film's title and condense Chinatown (the place) with *Chinatown* (the film). On the other hand, they interrupt that play by displacing the radically dislocated (the indeterminate or the irrational) to the mechanism that takes the viewer to that place of irreducible indeterminacy or irrationality, giving in this way material and visible form to the out-of-place.

A critic with a deconstructive background like Galperin will argue that *Chinatown* demystifies the idealized self-conception of the West (its melancholy "will to power," its self-destructive proclivity toward the "positive") by confronting the audience with truth and reality as irresolute and indeterminate. He sees promise in *Chinatown*'s noirish challenge to the idealized conceptions of Western audiences, and he values positively its emphasis on "the alien order that has infiltrated our own" (Galperin 1987, 1157). Conversely, a critic of post-structuralism like Belton sees in *Chinatown*'s proximity to the "essential incomprehensibility of human desire" (Belton 1991, 945), and to the "unnatural" knowledge that exceeds language (942), the ill-fated logical consequences of film noir. He values negatively the paralysis and frozen order symbolized by Gittes's confrontation with an irrational Real: his final "barely articulate mutterings" (948).

Despite their different evaluations of *Chinatown*'s engagement with the indeterminate or with the unintelligible core driving the film's screening processes, both critics agree that this core contains an absence significantly associated with place: "Like other aspects of *Chinatown* in this film, the confluence of East and West remains a signpost to otherness, to the presence or 'background' we would mystify into absence" (Galperin 1987, 1158); "Because *Chinatown* is ... not seen until the last few minutes of the film, its meaning ... floats. The object or place to which the word refers remains unseen, enhancing its status as place of mystery and enabling it to function abstractly" (Belton 1991, 946). Galperin understands that in the most venerable of Judeo-Christian traditions, the West achieves an aura of reality by creating "a second concealed meaning," by displacing a presence into an absence, by pushing the Other (the East or *Chinatown*) into the background. "In 'Odysseus' Scar,' Auerbach observes that, in contrast to Homeric representation, the stories of the Old Testament are fraught with 'background' and mysterious [and contain] a second, concealed meaning." From the standpoint of [Homeric] 'representation' this 'meaning' is necessarily absent, just as with the rise of 'interpretation,' as Auerbach observes, the stories [of the Old Testament] soon lost their [aura of] 'reality'" (1169 n. 21). Galperin suggests that the demystifying effect of *Chinatown* is in part due to the dislocation Polanski brings to the film, as an expatriate and as an outsider to Hollywood. But most importantly, drawing from Walter Benjamin's famous essay "The Work of Art in the Age of Mechanical Reproduction," Galperin argues that this demystification is due to the "democratic" medium of film itself, which displaces the "conventional subject," relocates it in, and returns it to, a "larger," "more expansive, collective" optical unconscious (1169 n. 15). Significantly, for Galperin, film is then both the medium that brings the viewer to this unconscious place and also the place of the optical unconscious. Galperin similarly describes *Chinatown* as both the "mechanism" refuting "Western" reality and the locus of a specific or repeated action in the film (1157).

Belton, on the other hand, suggests that *Chinatown*'s effect is not so much democratic and demystifying as it is disabling and silencing. For him, the medium of film is part of an epistemological regime of "the Symbolic and the Imaginary," to which detective fiction and psychoanalysis also belong. Like other examples of contemporary culture, film in general and *Chinatown* in particular attempt to abstract and reduce the Real to a rational epistemology. Unlike other examples of contemporary culture, however, film puts us in a unique location; it "put us, as subjects, in contact with that which remains, in part, resolutely other" (Belton 1991, 940). That is, a film like *Chinatown*, Belton suggests, puts us in the place of a pathological version of the Real: the place of the irrational. Within the film, Chinatown becomes a metaphor both for this place and for the process of abstraction and reification that takes us to this place. Thus Chinatown represents floating "meaning" itself, "a quality or attribute that attaches itself to certain characters ... or ... ideas" (946). For Belton, Chinatown becomes both a pathological place and the mechanism of contemporary culture's pathological processes of abstraction.

8. Franklin's New Noir

1. Humanist film criticism tells us that fatalism is an essential ingredient of film noir. Bruce Crowther, for example, says that the protagonist of noir

is often foredoomed and is aware of his ultimate fate. Crowther concludes that fatalism is essential to the story and determines the ultimate destruction of its main characters. The doom and fatalism of noir are incorporated into its female protagonists. Its femmes fatales, described by writers like Crowther as animals ("predators") or as invincible natural forces ("maelstroms"), ensnare, enslave, and ultimately destroy the weak-willed male protagonists. Similarly, in his recent documentary *Film Noir* (1994), Jeffrey Schon argues that noir not only poses the humanist question "Why me?" but more significantly goes on to answer, "For no reason at all."

2. Much has been written about the causal connection between the experience of World War II and a racial polarization in the United States. Film noir has been interpreted as reflecting the extension of that social crisis to the issue of race. As Michele Wallace points out, World War II "had a profound impact both on women's roles and on perceptions of the status of race in general, and Blacks in particular" (Wallace 1993, 262). The need to present a united front during the war effort forced North American society and the United States government to attempt to liberalize race relations. Not only were a number of films attacking racism made during the war, and not only did the government encourage the production of liberal films about racial problems, but after intense debates, African Americans were allowed to fight in the front lines, carrying and using weapons against white Europeans (Naremore 1998, 126, 237). Moreover, after the war, African Americans returned as members of a victorious army and veterans of a triumphant war and thus qualified for the benefits guaranteed by the 1947 GI Bill of Rights. These benefits not only included funds for higher education and training but also made purchasing property easier by eliminating transaction requirements such as cash reserves and down payments, by eliminating application fees, and by lowering closing costs and interest rates. These changes in the culture's perception of "race" and in the status and even social class of African American veterans created a crisis for a still-segregated society and a racist social order (it was not until 1954 that *Brown vs. the Board of Education* overturned the "separate but equal" doctrine and made public segregation illegal). The open discussion of racial issues on the screen became "communist propaganda" during the hearings by the House of Representative's Un-American Activities Committee, and the postwar polarization of race went underground in the film industry (Naremore 1998, 126). In film noir, the argument goes, these race matters surfaced in an indirect way, transformed into the angst of the

white antihero fated to live in an underworld of shadows and condemned to a fatal end.

3. In "Noir by Noirs: Toward a New Realism in Black Cinema," Manthia Diawara (1993b) suggests that it is a mistake to trace back both the origins and the effects of noir films by black directors like Carl Franklin's *One False Move* (1992), Bill Duke's *A Rage in Harlem* (1991), Spike Lee's *Malcolm X* (1992), and John Singleton's *Boyz N the Hood* (1991) to film noir. Diawara identifies the most significant origins of black film noir to a tradition of black cultural production that includes (and perhaps privileges) the literary, including texts such as *Native Son* and *Invisible Man*. Diawara argues that this is the tradition of black rage.

Black noir is black rage, according to Diawara. Black rage is the epiphenomenal force behind the new realism of black noir. It leads black directors to appropriate the experimental techniques and the violently racist cinematic language of film noir, and to put these techniques to a realistic end. Black directors deploy the obscuring techniques of noir to make visible the desperate but also the differentiated forms of the black experience. Black noir is a rage in a language that can be understood by the dominating white culture. Black noir is the visual correlative of a scream, the effect of which can be seen by the white-dominated film industry.

A significant effect of black noir and black rage is the deconstruction of the racist principle behind film noir and behind its techniques (e.g., the figure of the femme fatale, the use of extreme lighting, the use of voice-over). By using the racist techniques of noir to make visible the black experience rather than to morally and visually obscure it, black noir/rage unhinges film noir and its principal effect. That is, black noir disturbs film noir's main exclusionary cultural, economic, social, and political practice: its naturalization of the metaphorical relation between black and evil, between white and good. For a sustained criticism of this approach, see chapter 1 of this volume.

4. Diawara writes, "It is clear that formalist criticism of the noir genre runs the risk of reducing films noirs by noirs to a critique of patriarchy or of capitalism, and thus of minimizing on the one hand the deconstruction of racism in the renewed genre, and on the other hand a delineation of a black way of life in America" (Diawara 1993b, 263).

5. Franklin then brings to the surface what Ann Kaplan has called "film noir's repressed unconscious Signifier." If, as Kaplan suggests, terms like "noir" were adopted as a way to prevent viewers from confronting black even as a

category for a set of films, *Devil in a Blue Dress* makes explicit the threat (Kaplan 1998, 183–201). See chapter 1 in this volume.

6. From this perspective, it is perhaps not coincidental that *Devil in a Blue Dress* was made in 1995, the same year as the Million Man March. That march (organized by the Nation of Islam and the NAACP) echoed many of the comments by Carl Franklin in his master seminar. The march was a call to black youth for personal responsibility, leadership, and self-determination, for a commitment to family and self-improvement. The Million Man March was also an attempt to combat the stereotypical images of young black males. As Jesse Jackson points out, black men "are projected as less intelligent than we are, less hardworking than we work, less universal than we are, less patriotic than we are, more violent than we are. Indeed, the courteous and celebratory mood of the crowd was a direct rebuke to the white Washingtonians who stayed away from their workday routines in fear" (Quoted in Oliver 1998, 18). The making of Easy (of his film presence and of his almost heroic stature in the film) can be interpreted as a similar rebuke, but more importantly, Easy's presence and stature are also a new possibility in film in general and in film noir in particular: the affirmation on the screen of a black man who is responsible for his own destiny, and the beginning of a new noir. The emergence of an image so long denied in American history perhaps represents the birth of a new hope (Oliver 1998).

7. Examples of these tensions are those between the visual style (composition and lighting) and the narrative devices (voice-over and dialogue) of film noir, remarked on by Christine Gledhill and Janey Place.

8. This is in striking contrast to the categorical use of the label "film noir," which aims to distinguish these morally ambiguous films from others. In other words, there is a way in which the lighting of film noir exceeds the use of noir as a stable and homogenizing category for what are very different films.

9. "The voice-over technique is usually an authoritative mode, either invoking the authority of the nineteenth-century, omniscient story-teller . . . or pronouncing with a documentary 'voice-of-God.' . . . However, within an investigative narrative with a flashback—and sometimes multiple flashback—structure, the voice-over loses some of its control over events which are locked in the past and which the investigative or confessional voice-over seeks to unravel" (Gledhill 1998, 29).

10. In his study of African American detective fiction, Stephen Soitos gives a convincing structuralist account of the differences between the hard-boiled

version of the detective novel and its black counterparts. His study is mostly of early African American detective fiction, and so it does not really offer a detailed study of Mosley's work. Soitos does mention, however, the odd fact that unlike other black detective fiction writers, Mosley returns to the first-person narrative, one of the defining structural characters of the hard-boiled style. Given Soitos's claim that black detective fiction is detective fiction with a difference that subverts the genre, it is strange but understandable that Mosley's unexpected return to this tenet of hard-boiled fiction remains a mystery within his account. Like Diawara's, Soitos's analysis is also based on the primacy of a lived black African American experience that is reflected in their changes to the genre. It is this empirical premise that makes invisible Mosley's unconscious attraction to Chandler's first-person racist narrative style.

11. The film associates both French decadence and maternity with Matthew Terrel, a feminized, perversely maternal figure who listens to an Edith Piaf–like chanteuse while he sexually fondles a little boy.

9. Make It Real

1. In her article *"Femme Fatale* or Lesbian Femme" Chris Straayer argues that the history of film noir is a history of gender turbulence that leaves us with masculine women, feminine men, and a spectrum of combinations of gender characteristics that make the gender bending in *Bound* possible.

2. In "Klute 1: A Contemporary Film Noir and Feminist Criticism," Christine Gledhill persuasively argues that "rather than the revelation of socioeconomic patterns of political and financial power and corruption which mark the gangster/thriller, film noir probes the secrets of female sexuality and male desire within patterns of submission and dominance" (Kaplan 1998, 28).

3. Straayer says that "swaggering with a difference, Corky is a masculine partner worth romantic coupling." She points out that Corky (unlike other film noir protagonists) shares the femme fatale's desire for money and doesn't get moralistic about crime or murder. Straayer says that in contrast to male protagonists who are sucked in by female sexuality, Corky knows Violet's desire. Corky finally admits that she and Violet are alike, something Violet has been telling her all along (1998, 158).

4. Cf. Straayer 1998.

5. For a discussion of the difference between "femme," lesbian femme, and femme fatale, see Straayer 1998.

6. The second line—"The more attractive you are, the more believable it will be"—is in the screenplay but didn't make it into the film.

7. *Bound*, screenplay by Larry Wachowski and Andy Wachowski, *Scenario: The Magazine of Screenwriting Art*, fall 1996.

8. In various texts, Freud describes the often convoluted operations through which one's gender identity as male or female remains opposed to one's sexual desire for a partner of the opposite sex. Heterosexuality is dependent on identity remaining opposed to desire—we desire what we are not. If we identify as women, then we must desire men and if we identify as men, then we must desire women. This is the essence of what Freud describes as "normal" heterosexual development (see, for example, Freud 1924, 1925, 1931).

9. Throughout her work, Monique Wittig insists that a lesbian is not a woman because "woman" is defined always and only in relation to men within patriarchy. Lesbians break out of this patriarchal economy and thereby begin to break out of the stereotype of "woman." See Wittig 1992.

10. Chris Straayer argues that classic femmes fatales wanted economic independence and not sexual pleasure, but contemporary neo-noir femmes fatales want economic independence *and* sexual pleasure. Straayer gives *Basic Instinct* and *The Last Seduction* as providing examples of contemporary femmes fatales who take both money and sexual pleasure from men.

11. Deconstruction is a method or strategy of interpretation introduced by Jacques Derrida. It is a form of critical reading that attempts to open the text to what is beyond it (Derrida 1976, 158). It shows how the text always says more than it intends; that is, it shows how the text always also says the very thing that it intends to prohibit. In this way, the deconstructive strategy analyzes the effects produced by, and in spite of, the text.

10. The Space of Noir

1. Perhaps the best example of a title that captures noir's simultaneous sense of accuracy and disorientation is John Cromwell's 1947 *Dead Reckoning*.

2. In the scene to which Silver refers, Scottie Ferguson describes back to Madeleine the dark corridor of her dreams, at the end of which is madness, death, and meaninglessness: "There is so little that I know. It's as though I'm walking down a long corridor that once was mirrored. The fragments of that mirror still hang there, and when I come to the end of the corridor there is nothing but darkness. And I knew that when I walked into the darkness that I'll die."

Holding onto meaning, Scottie refers Madeleine back to the fragments. "You didn't know what happened till you found yourself with me. You didn't know where you were. The small seams, the fragments of a mirror. You remember those."

The madness and meaninglessness at the end of noir's corridor is confirmed by the title of several of its films, many of which allude to an unintelligible undiscovered country *(The Asphalt Jungle, Behind Locked Doors, The Big Sleep, Lady in the Dark, Dark Passage, Private Hell, The Secret beyond the Door, Sleep, My Love, So Dark the Night, Somewhere in the Night, They Won't Believe Me, The Unseen,* and *The Unsuspected),* and other titles that refer to its dynamic, unstable, changing, and sometimes even liquid nature *(Dark Waters, Criss Cross, Lady in the Lake, Niagara, Pitfall, On Dangerous Ground, The Spiral Staircase, Strange Illusion, Undercurrent, Vertigo,* and *Whirlpool).*

3. See Freud 1901, 147; Freud 1930, 36.

4. "The unadorned representation of human death, the well-nigh anatomical stripping of the corpse convey to viewers an unbearable anguish before the death of God, here blended with our own, since there is not the slightest suggestion of transcendency. What is more, Hans Holbein has given up all architectural or compositional fancy. The tomb-stone weighs down on the upper portion of the painting, which is merely twelve inches high, and intensifies the feeling of permanent death; this corpse shall never rise again. The very pall, limited to a minimum of folds, emphasizes, through that economy of motion, the feeling of stiffness and stone-felt cold" (Kristeva 1989, 111).

5. Eric Lott argues that "what such films appear to dread is the infiltration into the white home or self of unsanctioned behaviors reminiscent of the dark figures exemplified in the 1940's and early 1950's imaginary by zoot-suiters, pachucos, and Asian conspirators. What the films apparently cannot do is completely remove these figures from the picture, though noir may stave off their most fearsome shapes or place them safely elsewhere" (Lott 1997, 95). In a fascinating attempt to focus on the combined coordinates of racial and sexual markers, Ann Kaplan writes that "the idea of the dark continent moves from literal travelling to lands dubbed by the west 'dark' because unknown and mysterious to the West, into the dark continent of the psyche, and especially the female psyche. The interest of certain Hollywood films in psychoanalysis reflects studio directors' unconscious knowledge of its psychic appeal" (Kaplan 1998, 125).

6. Georgette Straud (Maureen O'Sullivan) raises a similar complaint

with her husband, George Straud (Ray Milland), in *The Big Clock* (1948). She laments the loss of their family life since they've moved to New York City: "We're like two strangers sharing an apartment." Nostalgic for a simpler life, noir's patriotic first family of George, Georgette, and little George (B. G. Norman) pine for a vacation in Wheeling, West Virginia, where they will live in a log cabin, and where the men do the hunting and gathering while the women stay home and cook dinner.

7. The list includes *The Big Steal*'s (1949) Duke Halliday (Robert Mitchum), *The Big Clock*'s George Straud, *The Woman in the Window*'s (1944) Richard Wanley (Edward G. Robinson), and *Gilda*'s Johnny Farrel (Glenn Ford), who at the end of the film is asked by Gilda to take her back home.

8. Other examples of noir as morality play are *D.O.A.*, *Scarlet Street*, *The Woman in the Window*, and *The Big Clock*.

9. As Janey Place has pointed out, Ann is noir's nurturing woman, or the woman as redeemer; and like other such noir women, she is part of a community or a family and belongs to the pastoral environment of noir's heartland: small town, U.S.A. (Place 1998, 61).

10. Neo-noir films like *Blue Velvet* will extend the portal to suburbia.

11. Janey Place is right to associate Jane Greer's Kathie Moffet to Aca-pulco's "misty haze of late afternoon" and to "its tumultuous sea, sudden rain-storm, and the dark, rich textures created by low-key lighting" (Place 1998, 61). But the facile opposition between Bridgeport's healthy whiteness and Acapulco's diseased darkness is misleading and covers over the fact that water, nature, and female sexuality are the determining landmarks of both towns.

12. Don Siegel's *The Big Steal* could very well have been titled *Back to the Past*. Not only does it serve as another vehicle for the Mitchum-Greer pair, but the film's happy ending and idyllic depiction of Mexico as the land of natural pro-creation seem meant as the very obverse of Tourneur's earlier and pessimistic film. A closer analysis of Siegel's film, however, reveals a more complicated picture.

13. For further development of noir's linguistic logic, see chapter 6 in this volume. In that chapter, we argue that language in noir, no matter whether it is English or Spanish, is driven by the same identity logic at the service of a stable subject with a single mother tongue.

14. For a more sustained analysis of noir's linguistic logic and its rela-tionship to ambiguity both sexual and racial, see chapter 3 in this volume.

15. Although recent film critics have studied film noir as dream-text or

dream-work (Naremore 1998, 238; Kaplan 1998, 120; Lott 1997, 90), no one has explored the connection between film noir's specific urban landscape and the psyche as comprehensively as Nicholas Christopher in *Somewhere in the Night*. However, not only does Christopher err in reducing noir to this landscape, but like Silver (and unlike Kaplan or Lott), he dilutes the implications of this connection into the tame humanist epiphany of a universal condition: "The broad cycle of noir that burst forth on the heels of the Second World War can be seen to comprise the complex mosaic of a single, thirteen-year urban dreamscape—often nightmarish, often fantastic and beautiful, always symbol-laden, and sometimes so starkly black and white (literally and figuratively) in its depiction of city life, and of the innermost conflicts and struggles of the human spirit in the city, that it shocks us into moments of recognition and epiphany" (Cristopher 1997, 44).

16. Another example of a parallel intersection of sexual and racial difference can be found in *Killer's Kiss*. In that film, Gloria Price (Irene Kane) is the sister of a famous ballerina who nevertheless finds herself dancing in a Manhattan dance club near Times Square, a club owned by the racially marked and evil Frank Silvera (Vincent Rapallo), who is always introduced by the feverish rhythm of Latin jazz.

17. For a sustained analysis and critique of the logic behind noir's blackened white subject, see chapter 1 in this volume.

18. Falling prey to noir's racialized and sexualized eugenicist rhetoric, Mike Davis calls noir both "a *robust* fiction" and one of the most acute critiques of "the culture of late capitalism, and, particularly, of the tendential *degeneration* of its middle strata," as well as "an ideologically ambiguous *aesthetic*" (Davis 1991, 18, 36, 41; our italics). Davis describes Los Angeles as the product of a facile ongoing struggle between the fiction of sunshine and the realism of noir, fixing in this way the city and noir into clearly demarcated elements of a Hegelian master-slave dialectic.

19. As James Naremore has suggested, the neo-noir *Chinatown* is an extreme example of the way in which these films both construct and deconstruct a map of intersecting racial and sexual coordinates, and it is by no means the only one (Naremore 1998, 229).

20. This significant difference is contrary to the leveled image of otherness suggested by Eric Lott in his critical commentary on noir.

Works Cited

Anzaldúa, Gloria. 1987. *Borderlands / La Frontera*. San Francisco: Spinsters/Aunt Lute.

Baker, Melva Rose. 1980. *Images of Women in Film: The War Years, 1941–1945*. Ann Arbor: University of Michigan Research Press.

Bartter, Martha. 1986. "Nuclear War as Urban Renewal." *Science Fiction Studies* 13, no. 2 (July): 148–58.

Belton, John. 1991. "Language, Oedipus, and *Chinatown*." *MLN* 106: 933–50.

Berrettini, Mark. 1999. "Private Knowledge, Public Space: Investigation and Navigation in *Devil in a Blue Dress*." *Cinema Journal* 39 (1): 74–89.

Bhabha, Homi K. 1994. *The Location of Culture*. New York: Routledge.

Biskind, Peter. 1994. "The Low Road to *Chinatown*." *Movie Magazine* 7 (10): 68–78.

Bobo, Jacqueline. 1991. "'The Subject Is Money': Reconsidering the Black Film Audience as a Theoretical Paradigm." *Black American Literature Forum* 25, no. 2, (summer): 424.

Borde, Raymond, and Étienne Chaumeton. 1955. *Panorama du Film Noir Américain*. Paris: Éditions de Minuit.

Brady, Frank. 1989. *Citizen Welles: A Biography of Orson Welles*. New York: Charles Scribner's Sons.

Brecht, Bertolt. 1964. *Brecht on Theatre: The Development of an Aesthetic*. Trans. John Willet. New York: Hill and Wang.

Chandler, Raymond. 1976. *Farewell, My Lovely*. New York: Vintage Books.

Christopher, Nicholas. 1997. *Somewhere in the Night: Film Noir and the American City*. New York: Free Press.

Cochran, David. 2000. *American Noir*. Washington, D.C.: Smithsonian Institution Press.

Comito, Terry, ed. 1998. *Touch of Evil: Orson Welles, Director*. New Brunswick: Rutgers University Press.

Cook, Pam. 1998. "Duplicity in *Mildred Pierce*." In *Women in Film Noir*, ed. E. Ann Kaplan. London: British Film Institute.

Cowie, Elizabeth. 1998. "Film Noir and Women." In *Shades of Noir*, ed. Joan Copjec. New York: Verso.

Cripps, Thomas. 1977. *Slow Fade to Black*. Oxford: Oxford University Press.

———. 1978. *Black Film as Genre*. Bloomington: Indiana University Press.

Crowther, Bruce. 1989. "What Is Film Noir?" In *Film Noir: Reflections in a Dark Mirror*. New York: Continuum.

Davis, Mike. 1991. *City of Quartz: Excavating the Future in Los Angeles*. New York: Vintage.

de Lauretis, Teresa. 1984. *Alice Doesn't: Feminism, Semiotics, Cinema*. Bloomington: Indiana University Press.

———. 1987. *Technologies of Gender*. Bloomington: Indiana University Press.

Deming, Barbara. 1969. *Running Away from Myself: A Dream Portrait of America Drawn from the Films of the Forties*. New York: Grossman Publishers.

Derrida, Jacques. 1976. *Of Grammatology*. Trans. Gayatri Spivak. Baltimore: John Hopkins University Press.

———. 1981. *Positions*. Trans. Alan Bass. Chicago: University of Chicago Press.

———. 1996. *Archive Fever*. Trans. Eric Prenowitz. Chicago: University of Chicago Press.

Diawara, Manthia. 1993a. *Black American Cinema*. New York: Routledge.

———. 1993b. "Noir by Noirs: Toward a New Realism in Black Cinema." In *Shades of Noir*, ed. Joan Copjec. New York: Verso.

Doane, Mary Ann. 1987. *The Desire to Desire: The Woman's Film of the 1940s*. Bloomington: Indiana University Press.

———. 1991. *Femmes Fatales: Feminism, Film Theory, Psychoanalysis*. New York: Routledge.

Douglas, Mary. 1969. *Purity and Danger*. London: Routledge.

Dyer, Richard. 1998. "Resistance through Charisma: Rita Hayworth and Gilda." In *Women in Film Noir*, ed. E. Ann Kaplan. London: British Film Institute.

Ehrenreich, Barbara, and Deirdre English. 1979. *For Her Own Good*. Garden City: Anchor Books.

Eren, Patricia, ed. 1990. *Issues in Feminist Film Criticism.* Bloomington: Indiana University Press.

Fischer, Lucy. 1989. *Shot/Countershot: Film Tradition and Women's Cinema.* Princeton: Princeton University Press.

———. 1991. *Imitation of Life.* New Brunswick, N.J.: Rutgers University Press.

———. 1996. *Cinematernity: Film, Motherhood, Genre.* Princeton: Princeton University Press.

Frank, Nino. 1946. *Écran Français,* no. 61 (28 August).

Franklin, Carl. 1998. *Harold Lloyd Master Seminar.* Audiotapes of lectures by Carl Franklin, presented at American Film Institute, Los Angeles, 28 October.

Freud, Sigmund. 1895. "Project for a Scientific Psychology." In *The Origins of Psycho-analysis.* In *The Complete Works of Sigmund Freud,* Standard Edition, ed. James Strachey, in collaboration with Anna Freud, 1953–1973, vol. 1. London: Hogarth.

———. 1900. *The Interpretation of Dreams.* In *The Complete Works of Sigmund Freud,* Standard Edition, ed. James Strachey, in collaboration with Anna Freud, 1953–1973, vols. 4–5. London: Hogarth.

———. 1901. "Forgetting of Impressions and Resolutions." In *The Psychopathology of Everyday Life.* In *The Complete Works of Sigmund Freud,* Standard Edition, ed. James Strachey, in collaboration with Anna Freud, 1953–1973, vol. 6. London: Hogarth.

———. 1905. *Jokes and Their Relation to the Unconscious.* Trans. James Strachey. New York: W. W. Norton.

———. 1910. "The Antithetical Meaning of Primal Words." In *The Complete Works of Sigmund Freud,* Standard Edition, ed. James Strachey, in collaboration with Anna Freud, 1953–1973, vol. 11. London: Hogarth.

———. 1913a. "The Theme of the Three Caskets." In *The Freud Reader,* ed. Peter Gay. New York: Norton.

———. 1913b. "Totem and Taboo." In *The Complete Works of Sigmund Freud,* Standard Edition, ed. James Strachey, in collaboration with Anna Freud, 1953–1973, vol. 13. London: Hogarth.

———. 1914. "Remembering, Repeating, and Working-Through." In *The Complete Works of Sigmund Freud,* Standard Edition, ed. James Strachey, in collaboration with Anna Freud, 1953–1973, vol. 12. London: Hogarth.

———. 1916–17. *Introductory Lectures on Psychoanalysis.* Trans. James Strachey. New York: Norton.

———. 1917. "Mourning and Melancholy." In *The Standard Edition of the Complete Psychological Works of Sigmund Freud*, ed. and trans. James Strachey, in collaboration with Anna Freud, 1953–1973, vol. 14. London: Hogarth.

———. 1919. "The Uncanny." In *The Complete Works of Sigmund Freud*, Standard Edition, ed. James Strachey, in collaboration with Anna Freud, 1953–1973, 17. London: Hogarth.

———. 1922. "Medusa's Head." In *Sexuality and the Psychology of Love*, ed. Philip Rieff. New York: Macmillan.

———. 1924. "The Dissolution of the Oedipus Complex." In *The Standard Edition of the Complete Psychological Works of Sigmund Freud*, ed. and trans. James Strachey, in collaboration with Anna Freud, 1953–1973, vol. 19. London: Hogarth.

———. 1925. "Some Psychical Consequences of the Anatomical Distinction between the Sexes." In *The Standard Edition of the Complete Psychological Works of Sigmund Freud*, ed. and trans. James Strachey, in collaboration with Anna Freud, 1953–1973, vol. 19. London: Hogarth.

———. 1927. "Fetishism." In *The Standard Edition of the Complete Psychological Works of Sigmund Freud*, ed. and trans. James Strachey, in collaboration with Anna Freud, 1953–1973, vol. 21. London: Hogarth.

———. 1930. *Civilization and Its Discontents*. Trans. James Strachey. New York: W. W. Norton.

———. 1931. "Female Sexuality." In *The Standard Edition of the Complete Psychological Works of Sigmund Freud*, ed. and trans. James Strachey, in collaboration with Anna Freud, 1953–1973, vol. 21. London: Hogarth.

———. 1936. "Inhibitions, Symptoms, and Anxiety." In *The Standard Edition of the Complete Psychological Works of Sigmund Freud*, ed. and trans. James Strachey, in collaboration with Anna Freud, 1953–1973, vol. 20. London: Hogarth.

———. 1939. *Moses and Monotheism*. In *The Complete Works of Sigmund Freud*, Standard Edition, ed. James Strachey, in collaboration with Anna Freud, 1953–1973, vol. 23. London: Hogarth.

———. 1940. *An Outline of Psychoanalysis*. Trans and ed. James Strachey. New York: W. W. Norton.

———. 1989. *The Freud Reader*. Ed. Peter Gay. New York: Norton.

Friedman, Lester. 1991. "Celluloid Palimpsests: An Overview of Ethnicity and the American Film." In *Unspeakable Images: Ethnicity and the American Cinema*, ed. Lester Friedman. Urbana: University of Illinois Press.

Galperin, William. 1987. "'Bad for the Glass': Representation and Filmic Deconstruction in *Chinatown* and *Chan Is Missing*." *MLN* 102 (5): 1151–70.

Ginsberg, Elaine, ed. 1996. *Passing and the Fictions of Identity*. Durham, N.C.: Duke University Press.

Gledhill, Christine.1998. "Klute 1: A Contemporary Film Noir and Feminist Criticism." In *Women in Film Noir*, ed. E. Ann Kaplan. London: British Film Institute.

———, ed. 1987. *Home Is Where the Heart Is: Studies in Melodrama and the Woman's Film*. London: British Film Institute.

Gledhill, Christine, and Gillian Swanson, eds. 1996. *Nationalising Femininity: Culture, Sexuality, and British Cinema in the Second World War*. Manchester: Manchester University Press.

Haralovich, Mary Beth. 1992. "Too Much Guilt Is Never Enough for Working Mothers." *Velvet Light Trap*, no. 29 (spring): 43–52.

Harvey, Sylvia. 1998. "Woman's Place: The Absent Family of Film Noir." In *Women in Film Noir*, ed. E. Ann Kaplan. London: British Film Institute.

Haskell, Molly. 1974. *From Reverence to Rape: The Treatment of Women in the Movies*. Chicago: University of Chicago Press.

Higham, Charles. 1985. *Orson Welles: The Rise and Fall of an American Genius*. New York: St. Martin's Press.

Hirsch, Foster. 1981. *Film Noir: The Dark Side of the Screen*. New York: A. S. Barnes.

———. 1999. *Detours and Lost Highways: A Map of Neo-Noir*. New York: Limelight Edition.

hooks, bell. 1996. "The Oppositional Gaze: Black Female Spectators." In *Reel to Real: Race, Sex, and Class at the Movies*. New York: Routledge.

Irigaray, Luce. 1985. *This Sex Which Is Not One*. Trans. Catherine Porter. Ithaca: Cornell University Press.

Jameson, Fredric. 1970. "On Raymond Chandler." *Southern Review* 6, no. 3 (summer): 624–50.

———. 1979. *Fables of Aggression: Wyndham Lewis, the Modernist as Fascist*. Berkeley: University of California Press.

———. 1993. "The Synoptic Chandler." In *Shades of Noir*, ed. Joan Copjec. London: Verso.

Kaplan, E. Ann. 1989. *Women and Film*. New York: Methuen.

———. 1992. *Motherhood and Representation*. New York: Routledge.

———. 1997. *Looking for the Other: Feminism, Film, and the Imperial Gaze*. New York: Routledge.

———. ed. 1990. *Psychoanalysis and Cinema*. New York: Routledge.

———, ed. 1998. *Women in Film Noir*. London: British Film Institute.

Karimi, Amir Massoud. 1976. *Towards a Definition of the American Film Noir (1941–1949)*. New York: Arno Press.

Katz, Ephraim. 1994. *Film Encyclopedia*. New York: Harper Perennial.

Kellner, Douglas, and Michael Ryan. 1990. *Camera Politica: The Politics and Ideology of Contemporary Hollywood Film*. Bloomington: Indiana University Press.

Klein, Melanie. 1952. "Some Theoretical Conclusions regarding the Emotional Life of the Infant." In *Developments in Psychoanalysis*. London: Hogarth.

———. 1973. "Ambivalence" In *The Language of Psychoanalysis*, trans. Donald Nicholson-Smith, ed. Jean Laplanche and Jean Bertrand Ponatalis. London: Norton.

Kristeva, Julia. 1982. *Powers of Horror*. Trans. Leon Roudiez. New York: Columbia University Press.

———. 1989. *Black Sun*. Trans. Leon Roudiez. New York: Columbia University Press.

———. 1996. *New Maladies of the Soul*. Trans. Ross Guberman. New York: Columbia University Press.

———. 1998. "Powers of Horror." In *The Portable Kristeva*, ed. Kelly Oliver. New York: Columbia.

———. 2000. *The Crisis of the European Subject*. Trans. S. Fairfield. New York: Other Press.

Krutnik, Frank. 1991. *In a Lonely Street: Film Noir, Genre, Masculinity*. New York: Routledge.

Lacan, Jacques. 1977a. "The Mirror Stage." In *Écrits*, trans. Alan Sheridan. New York: Norton.

———. 1977b. "The Signification of the Phallus." In *Écrits*, trans. Alan Sheridan. New York: Norton.

Landy, Marcia. 1991. *Imitation of Life: A Reader on Film and Television Melodrama*. Detroit: Wayne State University.

Laplanche, Jean, and Jean Bertrand Pontalis. 1973. *The Language of Psychoanalysis*. Trans. Donald Nicholson-Smith. London: Norton.

La Valley, Albert J. 1980. *Mildred Pierce*. Madison: University of Wisconsin Press.

Leab, Daniel. 1975. *From Sambo to Superspade: The Black Experience in Motion Pictures*. Boston: Houghton Mifflin.

Leaming, Barbara. 1981. *Polanski: A Biography: The Filmmaker as Voyeur*. New York: Simon and Schuster.

———. 1985. *Orson Welles: A Biography*. New York: Viking Penguin.

———. 1989. *If This Was Happiness: A Biography of Rita Hayworth*. New York: Viking Penguin.

Linderman, Deborah. 1981–82. "Oedipus in Chinatown." *Enclitic* 5–6: 190–203.

Lott, Eric. 1997. "The Whiteness of Film Noir." In *Whiteness: A Critical Reader*, ed. Mike Hill. New York: New York University Press.

Lowe, Lisa. 1996. *Immigrant Acts: On Asian American Cultural Politics*. Durham: Duke University Press.

Lundberg, Ferdinand, and Marynia Farnham. 1947. *Modern Woman: The Lost Sex*. New York: Harper.

Lyotard, Jean-François. 1973. *Des dispositifs pulsionnels*. Paris: 10/18.

———. 1974. *Economie libidinale*. Paris: Éditions de Minuit.

MacCannell, Dean. 1984. "Baltimore in the Morning.... After: On the Forms of Post-nuclear Leadership." *Diacritics* 14 (summer 1984): 33–46.

———. 1993. "Democracy's Turn: On Homeless Noir." In *Shades of Noir*, ed. Joan Copjec. New York: Verso.

MacCannell, Juliet Flower. 1991. *The Regime of the Brother: After the Patriarchy*. New York: Routledge.

———. 1999. *The Hysteric's Guide to the Future Female Subject*. Minneapolis: University of Minnesota Press.

Man, Glenn. 1994. "Marginality and Centrality: The Myth of Asia in 1970's Hollywood." *East-West Journal* 8 (1): 52–67.

Mapp, Edward. 1972. *Blacks in American Films: Today and Yesterday*. Metuchen: Scarecrow Press.

Maxfield, James. 1996. *The Fatal Woman: Sources of Male Anxiety in American Film Noir, 1941–1991*. Teaneck, N.J.: Fairleigh Dickinson University Press.

McLean, Adrienne. 1992–1993. "'I'm a Cansino': Transformation, Ethnicity, and Authenticity in the Construction of Rita Hayworth, American Love Goddess." *Journal of Film and Video* 44 (3–4): 8–26.

———. 1993. "'It's Only That I Do What I Love and Love What I Do': Film Noir and the Musical Woman." *Cinema Journal*. 33 (1): 3–16.

Modleski, Tania. 1988. *The Women Who Knew Too Much: Hitchcock and Feminist Theory*. New York: Routledge.

Mosley, Walter. 1990. *Devil in a Blue Dress*. New York: Simon and Schuster.

Mulvey, Laura. 1975. "Visual Pleasure and Narrative Cinema." *Screen* 16 (3): 6–18.

Murray, James. 1973. *To Find an Image: Blacks in Films from Uncle Tom to Superfly*. Indianapolis: Bobbs-Merrill.

Naremore, James. 1998. *More than Night: Film Noir in Its Contexts*. Berkeley: University of California Press.

Nell, Gary. 1975. *Black Hollywood*. Secaucus: Citadel Press.

Nelson, Joyce. 1977. "*Mildred Pierce* Reconsidered." *Film Reader* 2: 65–70.

Nericcio, William. 1992. "Of Mestizos and Half-Breeds." In *Chicanos and Film: Representation and Resistance*. Minneapolis: University of Minnesota Press.

Nesteby, James. 1982. *Black Images in American Films*, 1896–1954. New York: Lanham.

Oliver, Kelly. 1993. *Reading Kristeva: Unraveling the Doublebind*. Bloomington: Indiana University Press.

———. 1995. *Womanizing Nietzsche: Philosophy's Relation to the "Feminine."* New York: Routledge.

———. 1997. *Family Values: Subjects between Nature and Culture*. New York: Routledge.

———. 1998. *Subjectivity without Subjects: From Abject Fathers to Desiring Mothers*. Lanham, N.J.: Rowman and Littlefield.

Pines, Jim. 1975. *Blacks in Film*. London: British Film Institute.

Place, Janey. 1998. "Women in Film Noir." In *Women in Film Noir*, ed. E. Ann Kaplan. London: British Film Institute.

Place, Janey, and Lowell Peterson. 1996. "Some Visual Motifs of Film Noir." In *Film Noir Reader*, ed. Alain Silver and James Ursini. New York: Limelight Editions.

Perrault, Charles. 1912. "The Sleeping Beauty in the Woods." In *Perrault's Fairy Tales*, trans. S. R. Littlewood. London: Herbert and Daniel.

Porfirio, Robert. 1976. "Now Way Out: Existential Motifs in the Film Noir." *Sight and Sound* 45 (autumn): 5.

Reid, David, and Jayne Walker. 1993. "Strange Pursuit: Cornell Woolrich and the Abandoned City of the Forties." In *Shades of Noir*, ed. Joan Copjec. New York: Verso.

Rich, B. Ruby. 1995. "Dumb Lugs and Femmes Fatales." *Sight and Sound* 5, no. 11 (November): 8–10.

Robertson, Pamela. 1990. "Structural Irony in *Mildred Pierce*, or How Mildred Lost Her Tongue." *Cinema Journal* 30, no. 1 (fall): 42–54.

Schrader, Paul. 1999. "Notes on Film Noir." In *Film Noir Reader*, ed. Alain Silver and James Ursini. New York: Limelight Editions.

Schwenger, Peter. 1992. *Letter Bomb: Nuclear Holocaust and the Exploding Word*. Baltimore: Johns Hopkins University Press.

Shepard, Jim. 1999. "Jolting Noir with a Shot of Nihilism." *New York Times*, 7 February, 24.

Shetley, Vernon. 1999. "Incest and Capital in *Chinatown*." *MLN* 114 (4): 1092–1109.

Silver, Alain. 1999. "Fragments of the Mirror: Hitchcock's Noir Landscape." In *Film Noir Reader 2*, ed. Alain Silver and James Ursini. New York: Limelight Editions.

Silver, Alain and James Ursini. 1996. *Film Noir Reader*. New York: Limelight.

Silver, Alain, and Elizabeth Ward. 1992. *Film Noir: An Encyclopedic Reference to the American Style*. New York: Overlook Press.

Silverman, Kaja. 1988. *The Acoustic Mirror: The Female Voice in Psychoanalysis and Cinema*. Bloomington: Indiana University Press.

———. 1990. "Historical Trauma and Male Subjectivity." In *Psychoanalysis and Cinema*, ed. E. Ann Kaplan. New York: Routledge.

Soitos, Stephen F. 1996. *The Blues Detective: A Study of African American Detective Fiction*. Amherst: University of Massachusetts Press.

Staiger, Janet, Kristin Thompson, and David Bordwell. 1985. *The Classical Hollywood Cinema: Film Style and Mode of Production to 1960*. New York: Columbia University Press.

———. 1995. *Bad Women: Regulating Sexuality in Early American Cinema*. Minneapolis: University of Minnesota Press.

Straayer, Chris. 1998. "*Femme Fatale* or Lesbian Femme: Bound in Sexual *Différance*." In *Women in Film Noir*, ed. E. Ann Kaplan. London: British Film Institute.

Strecker, Edward. 1946. *Their Mothers' Sons: The Psychiatrist Examines an American Problem*. New York: J. B. Lippincott.

Telotte, J. P. 1989. *Voices in the Dark: The Narrative Patterns of Film Noir*. Urbana and Champaign: University of Illinois Press.

Thomas, Deborah. 1993. "Psychoanalysis and Film Noir." In *The Book of Film Noir*, ed. Ian Cameron. New York: Continuum.

Trigo, Benigno. 2000. *Subjects of Crisis: Race and Gender as Disease in Latin America*. Hanover, N.H.: Wesleyan University Press.

Wachowski, Larry, and Andy Wachowski. *"Bound* Screenplay." *Scenario: The Magazine of Screenwriting Art*, fall 1996.

Wald, Gayle. 2000. *Crossing the Line: Racial Passing in the Twentieth Century*. U.S. Literature and Culture. Durham, N.C.: Duke University Press.

Walker, Janet. 1982. "Feminist Critical Practice: Female Discourse in *Mildred Pierce*." *Film Reader* 5: 164–72.

Wallace, Michele. 1993. "Race, Gender, and Psychoanalysis in the Forties Films." In *Black American Cinema*, ed. Manthia Diawara. New York: Routledge.

Walsh, Andrea. 1984. *Women's Film and Female Experience, 1940–1950*. New York: Praeger.

Wexman, Virginia Wright. 1985. *Roman Polanski*. Boston: Twayne Publishers.

Williams, Linda. 1988. "Feminist Film Theory: *Mildred Pierce* and the Second World War." In *Female Spectators: Looking at Film and Television*, ed. E. Deidre Pribram. London:Verso.

Winokur, Mark. 1991. "Black Is White/White Is Black: 'Passing' as a Strategy of Racial Compatibility in Contemporary Hollywood Comedy." In *Unspeakable Images: Ethnicity and the American Cinema*, ed. Lester Friedman. Urbana: University of Illinois Press.

Wittig, Monique. *The Straight Mind and Other Essays*. Boston: Beacon Press, 1992.

Wollen, Peter. 1996. "Foreign Relations: Welles and *Touch of Evil*." *Sight and Sound* 6 (10): 9–10.

Wylie, Philip. 1942. *Generation of Vipers*. New York: Rinehart.

Filmography

Film Noir

The Accused. William Dieterle, 1948.

The Asphalt Jungle. John Huston, 1950.

Behind Locked Doors. Budd Boetticher, 1948.

Berlin Express. Jacques Tourneur, 1948.

Beware, My Lovely. Harry Horner, 1952.

Beyond a Reasonable Doubt. Fritz Lang, 1956.

Beyond the Forest. King Vidor, 1949.

The Big Clock. John Farrow, 1948.

The Big Combo. Joseph H. Lewis, 1955.

The Big Heat. Fritz Lang, 1953.

The Big Sleep. Howard Hawks, 1946.

The Big Steal. Don Siegel, 1949.

Black Angel. Roy William Neill, 1946.

The Blue Dahlia. George Marshall, 1946.

The Blue Gardenia. Fritz Lang, 1953.

Born to Kill. Robert Wise, 1946.

The Brasher Doubloon. John Brahm, 1946.

The Bribe. Robert Z. Leonard, 1949.

Brighton Rock. John Boulting, 1947.

Caged. John Cromwell, 1950.

Cat People. Jacques Tourneur, 1942.

Cause for Alarm. Tay Garnett, 1948.

The Chase. Arthur Ripley, 1946.

Chicago Deadline. Lewis Allen, 1949.

Christmas Holiday. Robert Siodmak, 1944.

Clash by Night. Fritz Lang, 1952.

Cornered. Edward Dmytryk, 1945.

Crime of Passion. Gerd Oswald, 1957.

The Crimson Kimono. Samuel Fuller, 1959.

Criss Cross. Robert Siodmak, 1949.

Crossfire. Edward Dmytryk, 1947.

Cry Danger. Robert Parrish, 1951.

Cry of the City. Robert Siodmak, 1948.

The Damned Don't Cry. Vincent Sherman, 1950.

Danger Signal. Robert Florey, 1945.

Dark City. William Dieterle, 1950.

Dark Corner. Henry Hathaway, 1946.

The Dark Mirror. Robert Siodmak, 1946.

Dark Passage. Delmer Daves, 1947.

Dark Waters. André de Toth, 1944.

Dead Reckoning. John Cromwell, 1947.

Deadline at Dawn. Harold Clurman, 1946.

Decoy. Jack Bernhard, 1946.

Desire Me. George Cukor, 1947.

Desperate. Anthony Mann, 1947.

Destination Murder. Edward L. Cahn, 1950.

Detour. Edgar G. Ulmer, 1946.

The Devil Thumbs a Ride. Felix E. Feist, 1947.

D.O.A. Rudolph Maté, 1949.

Double Indemnity. Billy Wilder, 1944.

A Double Life. George Cukor, 1948.

Dragonwyck. Joseph L. Mankiewicz, 1946.

Elevator to the Gallows. Louis Malle, 1957.

The Falcon Takes Over. Irving Reis, 1942.

Fallen Angel. Otto Preminger, 1946.

Fear in the Night. Maxwell Shane, 1947.

The File on Thelma Jordan. Robert Siodmak, 1949.

Flamingo Road. Michael Curtiz, 1949.

Follow Me Quietly. Richard Fleischer, 1949.

Force of Evil. Abraham Polonsky, 1948.

Gaslight. George Cukor, 1944.

A Gentleman after Dark. Edwin L. Marin, 1942.

Gilda. Charles Vidor, 1946.

The Guilty. John Reinhardt, 1947.

Gun Crazy. Joseph H. Lewis, 1950.

His Kind of Woman. John Farrow, 1951.

The Hitch-Hiker. Ida Lupino, 1953.

Hollow Triumph. See *The Scar*.

The House across the Bay. Archie Mayo, 1940.

Human Desire. Fritz Lang, 1954.

In a Lonely Place. Nicholas Ray, 1950.

Ivy. Sam Wood, 1947.

Key Largo. John Huston, 1948.

Killer Bait (Too Late for Tears). Byron Haskin, 1949.

The Killer That Stalked New York. Earl McEvoy, 1950.

Killer's Kiss. Stanley Kubrick, 1955.

The Killers. Robert Siodmak, 1946.

The Killing. Stanley Kubrick, 1956.

Kiss Me Deadly. Robert Aldrich, 1955.

Kiss the Blood off My Hands. Norman Foster, 1948.

The Lady from Shanghai. Orson Welles, 1948.

Lady in the Dark. Mitchell Leisen, 1944.

Lady in the Lake. Robert Montgomery, 1946.

Lady on a Train. Charles David, 1945.

A Lady without a Passport. Joseph H. Lewis, 1950.

Laura. Otto Preminger, 1944.

The Letter. William Wyler, 1940.

The Locket. John Brahm, 1946.

The Lodger. John Brahm, 1944.

The Lost Weekend. Billy Wilder, 1945.

Love Letters. William Dieterle, 1945.

M. Joseph Losey, 1951.

The Maltese Falcon. John Huston, 1941.

The Man Who Cheated Himself. Felix E. Feist, 1950.

Manhandled. Lewis R. Foster, 1949.

The Mask of Dimitrios. Jean Negulesco, 1944.

Mildred Pierce. Michael Curtiz, 1945.

Murder, My Sweet. Edward Dmytryk, 1944.

My Name Is Julia Ross. Joseph H. Lewis, 1945.

The Naked City. Jules Dassin, 1948.

Niagara. Henry Hathaway, 1953.

The Night of the Hunter. Charles Laughton, 1955.

99 River Street. Phil Karlson, 1953.

No Man of Her Own. Mitchell Leisen, 1949.

Nora Prentiss. Vincent Sherman, 1947.

North by Northwest. Alfred Hitchcock, 1959.

Odds against Tomorrow. Robert Wise, 1959.

On Dangerous Ground. Nicholas Ray, 1951.

One Way Street. Hugh Fregonese, 1950.

Out of the Past. Jacques Tourneur, 1947.

The Paradine Case. Alfred Hitchcock, 1948.

Perilous Holiday. Edward H. Griffith, 1946.

Phantom Lady. Robert Siodmak, 1944.

Pickup on South Street. Samuel Fuller, 1953.

Pitfall. André de Toth, 1948.

The Postman Always Rings Twice. Tay Garnett, 1946.

The Pretender. W. Lee Wilder, 1947.

Private Hell 36. Don Siegel, 1954.

Pursued. Raoul Walsh, 1947.

Railroad. Anthony Mann, 1947.

Raw Deal. Anthony Mann, 1948.

The Reckless Moment. Max Ophuls, 1949.

Ride the Pink Horse. Robert Montgomery, 1947.

Road House. Jean Negulesco, 1948.

Saboteur. Alfred Hitchcock, 1942.

The Scar (Hollow Triumph). Steve Sekely, 1948.

Scarlet Street. Fritz Lang, 1945.

Second Woman. James V. Kern, 1951.

The Secret beyond the Door. Fritz Lang, 1948.

711 Ocean Drive. Joseph M. Newman, 1950.

Shadow of a Doubt. Alfred Hitchcock, 1943.

Sleep, My Love. Douglas Sirk, 1948.

The Sleeping Tiger. Joseph Losey, 1954.

The Sniper. Edward Dmytryk, 1952.

So Dark the Night. Joseph H. Lewis, 1946.

Somewhere in the Night. Joseph L. Mankiewicz, 1946.

Sorry, Wrong Number. Anatole Litvak, 1948.

Spellbound. Alfred Hitchcock, 1945.

The Spiral Staircase. Robert Siodmak, 1946.

Station West. Sidney Lanfield, 1948.

The Strange Affair of Uncle Harry. Robert Siodmak, 1945.

Strange Illusion. Edgar G. Ulmer, 1945.

Strange Impersonation. Anthony Mann, 1946.

The Strange Love of Martha Ivers. Lewis Milestone, 1946.

The Stranger. Orson Welles, 1946.

Strangers on a Train. Alfred Hitchcock, 1951.

Sudden Fear. David Miller, 1952.

Sunset Boulevard. Billy Wilder, 1950.

Suspense. Frank Tuttle, 1946.

Suspicion. Alfred Hitchcock, 1941.

They Live by Night. Nicholas Ray, 1949.

They Won't Believe Me. Irving Pichel, 1947.

The Thief. Russell Rouse, 1952.

Thieves' Highway. Jules Dassin, 1949.

The Thirteenth Letter. Otto Preminger, 1951.

This Gun for Hire. Frank Tuttle, 1942.

Time without Pity. Joseph Losey, 1957.

T-Men. Anthony Mann, 1947.

Touch of Evil. Orson Welles, 1958.

Under Capricorn. Alfred Hitchcock, 1949.

Undercurrent. Vincente Minnelli, 1946.

The Unseen. Lewis Allen, 1945.

The Unsuspected. Michael Curtiz, 1947.

Vertigo. Alfred Hitchcock, 1958.

Vicki. Harry Horner, 1953.

Where Danger Lives. John Farrow, 1950.

Whirlpool. Otto Preminger, 1949.

White Heat. Raoul Walsh, 1949.

The Window. Ted Tatzlaff, 1949.

Witness to Murder. Roy Rowland, 1954.

The Woman in the Window. Fritz Lang, 1944.

The Woman on the Beach. Jean Renoir, 1947.

Woman on the Run. Norman Foster, 1950.

The Wrong Man. Alfred Hitchcock, 1956.

You Only Live Once. Fritz Lang, 1937.

Neo-Noir

Basic Instinct. Paul Verhoeven, 1992.

Blue Velvet. David Lynch, 1986.

Body Heat. Lawrence Kasdan, 1981.

Body of Evidence. Uli Edel, 1993.

Bound. Andy Wachowski, 1996.

Chinatown. Roman Polanski, 1974.

Devil in a Blue Dress. Carl Franklin, 1995.

Diabolique. Jeremiah Chechik, 1996.

Farewell, My Lovely. Dick Richards, 1975.

The Grifters. Stephen Frears, 1990.

House of Games. David Mamet, 1987.

Jade. William Friedkin, 1995.

The Last Seduction. John Dahl, 1994.

Red Rock West. John Dahl, 1993.

The Two Jakes. Jack Nicholson, 1990.

Other Films

All That Heaven Allows. Douglas Sirk, 1955.

The Best Years of Our Lives. William Wyler, 1946.

Christopher Strong. Dorothy Arzner, 1933.

Craig's Wife. Dorothy Arzner, 1936.

The Defiant Ones. Stanley Kramer, 1958.

The Grapes of Wrath. John Ford, 1940.

The Great Lie. Edmund Goulding, 1941.

Home of the Brave. Mark Robson, 1949.

I Remember Mama. George Stevens, 1948.

Imitation of Life. John M. Stahl, 1936.

Imitation of Life. Douglas Sirk, 1959.

Intruder in the Dust. Clarence Brown, 1949.

Leave Her to Heaven. John M. Stahl, 1945.

Little Women. Mervyn LeRoy, 1949.

Lost Boundaries. Alfred L. Werker, 1949.

Mourning Becomes Electra. Dudley Nichols, 1947.

Mrs. Miniver. William Wyler, 1942.

Now, Voyager. Irving Rapper, 1942.

Pinky. Elia Kazan, 1949.

The Razor's Edge. Edmund Goulding, 1946.

Since You Went Away. John Cromwell, 1944.

Stella Dallas. King Vidor, 1937.

To Each His Own. Mitchell Leisen, 1946.

A Tree Grows in Brooklyn. Elia Kazan, 1945.

Watch on the Rhine. Herman Shumlin, 1943.

Index

Kelly Oliver is professor of philosophy and women's studies at Stony Brook University (SUNY). She is the author of *Witnessing: Beyond Recognition* (Minnesota, 2001), *Subjectivity without Subjects: From Abject Fathers to Desiring Mothers, Family Values: Subjects between Nature and Culture, Womanizing Nietzsche: Philosophy's Relation to "the Feminine,"* and *Reading Kristeva: Unraveling the Double-Bind.* She has also edited several anthologies, including *The Portable Kristeva* and *French Feminism Reader.*

Benigno Trigo is associate professor of Hispanic languages and literatures at Stony Brook University (SUNY). He is the author of *Subjects of Crisis: Race and Gender as Disease in Latin America* and the editor of *Foucault and Latin America.*